Behaviorism

BY JOHN B. WATSON

The Norton Library
W·W·NORTON & COMPANY·INC·
NEW YORK

First published in the Norton Library 1970

W. W. Norton & Company, Inc. is also the publisher of
the works of Erik H. Erikson, Otto Fenichel, Karen Horney and
Harry Stack Sullivan, and the principal works of Sigmund Freud.

SBN 393 00524 0

PRINTED IN THE UNITED STATES OF AMERICA

1 2 3 4 5 6 7 8 9 0

To

STANLEY RESOR

Whose unfailing interest in both industry and science has given me the opportunity to write this book

Contents

List of Illustrations

Introduction

LOOKING back over the history of the behavioristic movement since it began in overt form in 1912, it seems hard at first sight to understand why behaviorism has had to weather such a continuous storm.

Behaviorism, as I tried to develop it in my lectures at Columbia in 1912 and in my earliest writings, was an attempt to do one thing —to apply to the experimental study of man the same kind of procedure and the same language of description that many research men had found useful for so many years in the study of animals lower than man. We believed then, as we do now, that man is an animal different from other animals only in the types of behavior he displays.

I think the forcing of this conviction caused most of the storm. It brought out the same type of resistance that appeared when Darwin's "Origin of Species" was first published. Human beings do not want to class themselves with other animals. They are willing to admit that they are animals but "something else in addition." It is this "something else" that causes the trouble. In this "something else" is bound up everything that is classed as religion, the life hereafter, morals, love of children, parents, country, and the like. The raw fact that you, as a psychologist, if you are to remain scientific, must describe the behavior of man in no other terms than those you would use in describing the behavior of the ox you slaughter, drove and still drives many timid souls away from behaviorism.

The resistance is not due, as some of my colleagues claim, to the way in which the behaviorists presented their findings and convictions. We have been accused of being propagandists, of heralding our conclusions in the public press rather than in the more dignified scientific journals, of writing as though no one else had ever contributed to the field of psychology, of being bolshevists. All of these are emotional criticisms indicative of the fact that behaviorism is treading on the hoof of somebody's sacred cow—it is threatening the established order of things. To accept it means giving up old established mores—giving up that comfortable introspective psychology, which either squares with people's mores or else, when it does not, employs a language so obscure that the reader does not have to react to it.

What has been the result of the storm? First certainly a new literature—a literature of criticism. Some of this has been personal, even vituperative. I have never replied to a criticism. Only rarely has any one taken up the cudgels for behaviorism. Each behaviorist has been too busy in presenting his experimental results or his generalizations to concern himself with answering criticisms. As I look back over this critical literature, I am inclined to think that our science would have been clarified had we taken the trouble to answer criticisms, because some of the most childish misunderstandings and misstatements of our position have crept into psychological literature.

It was only natural that such criticisms should appear. Many of the older psychologists had well-established laboratories—with many introspective publications behind them. Behaviorism called for new laboratories and even new words in which to couch lectures. Even the economic life of the professor was apparently threatened. Again, youngsters trained under some of the older leaders of the introspective school of psychology felt duty-bound to take up a vigorous lance for their teachers. Roback in his "Behaviorism and Psychology" gives us a classical illustration of the latter type. In it, incidentally, he comes perilously close to breaking all the rules of chivalry.

But through it all, without behaviorism being overtly accepted, its influence has been profound during the 18 years of its existence. To be convinced of this, one needs only to compare the contents of our journals title by title for 15 years before the advent of behaviorism and during the past 15 to 18 years. One needs only to compare the books written before and after. Not only have the subjects studied become behavioristic but the *words of the presentations have become behavioristic.* Today no university can escape the teaching of behaviorism. In some its methods and hypotheses are accepted, in others it is taught ostensibly for the purpose of criticism. The truth is that the younger generation of students demands at least some orientation in behaviorism. For such this book is frankly written.

In the rewriting of this edition I have spent considerable time and effort. Neither I nor my publisher was satisfied with the form or the style of the first edition. The first edition was published hurriedly as a series of lectures in print. In this new edition I have first of all tried to improve the style of the book by taking out all tricks of trade by means of which a lecturer tries to keep his audience awake. I have tried to take out most of the overstatements and exaggerations common to all lectures. I have added roughly 100 pages of entirely new material—consisting of new results from recent literature or changes in my theoretical point of view. I have deleted 25 to 30 pages of outgrown material. In general, though, the point of view has not been fundamentally altered.

I have been profoundly interested in Jennings' new book, "The Biological Basis of Human Nature." I wish especially to thank him for the long quotation from his excellent discussion of the genes. Once again I wish to extend my thanks to Prof. K. S. Lashley, to Dr. H. M. Johnson, and to my business associate Miss Anne Juenker for all the help they have given me on both the first and second editions.

JOHN B. WATSON.

August, 1930

I. What is Behaviorism?

THE OLD AND NEW PSYCHOLOGY CONTRASTED

Two opposed points of view are still dominant in American psychological thinking—introspective or subjective psychology, and behaviorism or objective psychology.[1] Until the advent of behaviorism in 1912, introspective psychology completely dominated American university psychological life.

The conspicuous leaders of introspective psychology in the first decade of the twentieth century were E. B. Titchener of Cornell and William James of Harvard. The death of James in 1910 and the death of Titchener in 1927 left introspective psychology without emotional leadership. Although Titchener's psychology differed in many points from that of William James, their fundamental assumptions were the same. In the first place, both were of German

---

[1] In the last few decades there have been two other more or less prominent but temporary points of view—the so-called functional psychology of Dewey, Angell and Judd and the Gestalt Psychologie of Wertheimer, Koffka and Köhler. In my opinion both of these points of view are, as it were, illegitimate children of introspective psychology. Functional psychology, which one rarely hears of now, owed its vogue to considerable patter about the physiologically adaptive functions of the mind. The mind with them is a kind of adjusting "guardian angel." The philosophy behind it smacks very much of the good old Christian philosophy of Berkeley (interaction or control of the body by the deity).

Gestalt psychology makes its patter about "configurational response (really inborn!)." As a psychological theory it cannot gain very much headway. It is as obscure as Kant's treatment of imagination, which it resembles quite a little. The kernel of truth behind it has been very much better and more clearly expressed by William James in his *Principles* in the chapters on Sensation and Perception. Those chapters could be read with profit by the sponsors of Gestalt. Gestalt is still a part of introspective psychology. Incidentally a bit of collateral reading for any student who works on Gestalt is Hobhouse's *Mind in Evolution*.

origin. In the second place, and of more importance, both claimed that *consciousness is the subject matter of psychology.*

Behaviorism, on the contrary, holds that the subject matter of human psychology *is the behavior of the human being.* Behaviorism claims that consciousness is neither a definite nor a usable concept. The behaviorist, who has been trained always as an experimentalist, holds, further, that belief in the existence of consciousness goes back to the ancient days of superstition and magic.

The great mass of the people even today has not yet progressed very far away from savagery—it wants to believe in magic. The savage believes that incantations can bring rain, good crops, good hunting, that an unfriendly voodoo doctor can bring disaster to a person or to a whole tribe; that an enemy who has obtained a nail paring or a lock of your hair can cast a harmful spell over you and control your actions. There is always interest and news in magic. Almost every era has its new magic, black or white, and its new magician. Moses had his magic: he smote the rock and water gushed out. Christ had his magic: he turned water into wine and raised the dead to life. Coué had his magic word formula. Mrs. Eddy had a similar one.

Magic lives forever. As time goes on, all of these critically undigested, innumerably told tales get woven into the folk lore of the people. Folk lore in turn gets organized into religions. Religions get caught up into the political and economic network of the country. Then they are used as tools. The public is forced to accept all of the old wives' tales, and it passes them on as gospel to its children's children.

The extent to which most of us are shot through with a savage background is almost unbelievable. Few of us escape it. Not even a college education seems to correct it. If anything, it seems to strengthen it, since the colleges themselves are filled with instructors who have the same background. Some of our greatest biologists, physicists, and chemists, when outside of their laboratories, fall back upon folk lore which has become crystallized into religious concepts. These concepts—these heritages of a timid savage past—have made the emergence and growth of scientific psychology extremely difficult.

One example of such a religious concept is that every individual has a *soul* which is separate and distinct from the *body*. This soul is really a part of a supreme being. This ancient view led to the philosophical platform called "dualism." This dogma has been present in human psychology from earliest antiquity. No one has ever touched a soul, or seen one in a test tube, or has in any way come into relationship with it as he has with the other objects of his daily experience. Nevertheless, to doubt its existence is to become a heretic and once might possibly even have led to the loss of one's head. Even today the man holding a public position dare not question it.

With the development of the physical sciences which came with the renaissance, a certain release from this stifling soul cloud was obtained. A man could think of astronomy, of the celestial bodies and their motions, of gravitation and the like, without involving soul. Although the early scientists were as a rule devout Christians, nevertheless they began to leave soul out of their test tubes.

Psychology and philosophy, however, in dealing as they thought with non-material objects, found it difficult to escape the language of the church, and hence the concept of mind or soul as distinct from the body came down almost unchanged in essence to the latter part of the nineteenth century.

Wundt, the real father of experimental psychology, unquestionably wanted in 1879 a scientific psychology. He grew up in the midst of a dualistic philosophy of the most pronounced type. He could not see his way clear to a solution of the mind-body problem. His psychology, which has reigned supreme to the present day, is necessarily a compromise. He substituted the term *con-*

sciousness for the term soul. Consciousness is not quite so unobservable as soul. We observe it by peeking in suddenly and catching it unawares as it were (*introspection*).

Wundt had an immense following. Just as now it is fashionable to go to Vienna to study psycho-analysis under Freud, just so was it fashionable some 40 years ago to study at Leipzig with Wundt. The men who returned founded the laboratories at Johns Hopkins University, the University of Pennsylvania, Columbia, Clark and Cornell. All were equipped to do battle with the elusive (almost soul-like) thing called consciousness.

To show how unscientific is the main concept behind this great German-American school of psychology, look for a moment at William James' definition of psychology. "Psychology is the description and explanation of states of consciousness as such." Starting with a definition which *assumes* what he starts out to prove, he escapes his difficulty by an *argumentum ad hominem*. Consciousness— Oh, yes, everybody must know what this "consciousness" is. When we have a sensation of red, a perception, a thought, when we *will* to do something, or when we *purpose* to do something, or when we desire to do something, we are being *conscious*.

All other introspectionists are equally illogical. In other words, they do not tell us what consciousness is, but merely begin to put things into it by assumption; and then when they come to analyze consciousness, naturally they find in it just what they put into it. Consequently, in the analyses of consciousness made by certain of the psychologists you find such elements as *sensations* and their ghosts, the *images*. With others you find not only sensations, but so-called *affective elements;* in still others you find such elements as *will*—the so-called *conative element* in consciousness. With some psychologists you find many hundreds of sensations of a certain type; others maintain that only a few of that type exist. And so it goes. Literally hundreds of thousands of printed pages have been published on the minute analysis of this intangible something called "consciousness." And how do we begin work upon it? Not by analyzing it as we would a chemical compound, or the way a plant grows. No, those things are material things. This thing we call consciousness can be analyzed only by *introspection*—a looking in on what takes place inside of us.

As a result of this major assumption that there is such a thing as consciousness and that we can analyze it by introspection, we find as many analyses as there are individual psychologists. There is no way of experimentally attacking and solving psychological problems and standardizing methods.

THE ADVENT OF THE BEHAVIORISTS

In 1912 the objective psychologists or behaviorists reached the conclusion that they could no longer be content to work with Wundt's formulations. They felt that the 30 odd barren years since the establishment of Wundt's laboratory had proved conclusively that the so-called introspective psychology of Germany was founded upon wrong hypotheses—that no psychology which included the religious mind-body problem could ever arrive at verifiable conclusions. They decided either to give up psychology or else to make it a natural science. They saw their brother-scientists making progress in medicine, in chemistry, in physics. Every new discovery in those fields was of prime importance; every new element isolated in one laboratory could be isolated in some other laboratory; each new element was immediately taken up in the warp and woof of science as a whole. One need only mention wireless, radium, insulin, thyroxin, to verify this. Elements so isolated and methods so formulated immediately began to function in human achievement.

In his first efforts to get uniformity in subject matter and in methods the behaviorist began his own formulation of the problem of psychology by sweeping aside all mediaeval conceptions. He dropped from his scientific vocabulary all subjective terms such as sensation, perception, image, desire, purpose, and even thinking and emotion as they were subjectively defined.

The behaviorist asks: Why don't we make what we can *observe* the real field of psychology? Let us limit ourselves to things that can be observed, and formulate laws concerning only those things. Now what can we observe? We can observe *behavior—what the organism does or says.* And let us point out at once: that *saying* is doing—that is, *behaving.* Speaking overtly or to ourselves (thinking) is just as objective a type of behavior as baseball.

The rule, or measuring rod, which the behaviorist puts in front of him always is: Can I describe this bit of behavior I see in terms of "stimulus and response"? By stimulus we mean any object in the general environment or any change in the tissues themselves due to the physiological condition of the animal, such as the change we get when we keep an animal from sex activity, when we keep it from feeding, when we keep it from building a nest. By response we mean anything the animal does—such as turning toward or away from a light, jumping at a sound, and more highly organized activities such as building a skyscraper, drawing plans, having babies, writing books, and the like.

SOME SPECIFIC PROBLEMS OF THE BEHAVIORISTS

You will find, then, the behaviorist working like any other scientist. His sole object is to gather facts about behavior—verify his data—subject them both to logic and to mathematics (the tools of every scientist). He brings the new-born individual *into his experimental nursery* and begins to set problems: What is the baby doing now? What is the stimulus that makes him behave this way? He finds that the stimulus of tickling the cheek brings the response of turning the mouth to the side stimulated. The stimulus of the nipple brings out the sucking response. The stimulus of a rod placed on the palm of the hand brings closure of the hand and the suspension of the whole body by that hand and arm if the rod is raised. Stimulating the infant with a rapidly moving shadow across the eye will not produce blinking until the individual is sixty-five days of age. Stimulating the infant with an apple or stick of candy or any other object will not call out attempts at reaching until the baby is around 120 days of age. Stimulating a properly brought up infant at any age with snakes, fish, darkness, burning paper, birds, cats, dogs, monkeys, will not bring out that type of response which we call "fear" (which to be objective we might call reaction "X") which is a catching of the breath, a stiffening of the whole body, a turning away of the body from the source of stimulation, a running or crawling away from it. (See page 152.)

On the other hand, there are just two things which will call out a fear response, namely, a loud sound, and loss of support.

Now the behaviorist finds from observing children brought up *outside of his nursery* that hundreds of these objects will call out fear responses. Consequently, the scientific question arises: If at birth only two stimuli will call out fear, how do all these other things ever finally come to call it out? Please note that the question is not a speculative one. It can be answered by experiments, and the experiments can be reproduced and the same findings can be had in every other laboratory if the original observation is sound. Convince yourself of this by making a simple test.

If you will take a snake, mouse or dog and show it to a baby who has never seen these objects or been frightened in other ways, he begins to manipulate it, poking at this, that or the other part. Do this for ten days until you are logically certain that the child will always go toward the dog and never run away from it (positive reaction) and that it does not call out a fear response at any time. In contrast to this, pick up a steel bar and strike upon it loudly behind the infant's head. Immediately the fear response is called

forth. Now try this: At the instant you show him the animal and
just as he begins to reach for it, strike the steel bar behind his head.
Repeat the experiment three or four times. A new and important
change is apparent. The animal now calls out the same response as
the steel bar, namely a fear response. We call this, in behavioristic
psychology, the *conditioned emotional response*—a form of *conditioned reflex.*

Our studies of conditioned reflexes make it easy for us to account
for the child's fear of the dog on a thoroughly natural science basis
without lugging in consciousness or any other so-called mental
process. A dog comes toward the child rapidly, jumps upon him,
pushes him down and at the same time barks loudly. Oftentimes
one such combined stimulation is all that is necessary to make the
baby run away from the dog the moment it comes within his
range of vision.

There are many other types of conditioned emotional responses,
such as those connected with *love,* where the mother by petting the
child, rocking it, stimulating its sex organs in bathing, and the like,
calls out the embrace, gurgling and crowing as an unlearned original response. Soon this response becomes conditioned. The mere
sight of the mother calls out the same kind of response as actual
bodily contacts. In *rage* we get a similar set of facts. The stimulus
of holding the infant's moving members brings out the original
unlearned response we call rage. Soon the mere sight of a nurse
who handles a child badly throws the child into a fit. Thus we see
how relatively simple our emotional responses are in the beginning and how terribly complicated home life soon makes them.

The behaviorist has his problems with the adult as well. What
methods shall we use systematically to condition the adult? For example, to teach him business habits, scientific habits? Both manual
habits (technique and skill) and laryngeal habits (habits of speech
and thought) must be formed and tied together before the task
of learning is complete. After these work habits are formed,
what system of changing stimuli shall we surround him with in

order to keep his level of efficiency high and constantly rising? In addition to vocational habits, there comes the problem of his emotional life. How much of it is carried over from childhood? What part of it interferes with his present adjustment? How can we make him lose this part of it; that is, uncondition him where unconditioning is necessary, and condition him where conditioning is necessary? Indeed we know all too little about the amount and kind of emotional or, better, visceral habits (by this term we mean that our stomach, intestines, breathing, and circulation become conditioned—form habits) that should be formed. We do know that they are formed in large numbers and that they are important.

Probably more adults in this universe of ours suffer vicissitudes in family life and in business activities because of poor and insufficient visceral habits than through the lack of technique and skill in manual and verbal accomplishments. One of the large problems in big organizations today is that of personality adjustments. The young men and young women entering business organizations have plenty of skill to do their work but they fail because they do not know how to get along with other people.

DOES THIS BEHAVIORISTIC APPROACH LEAVE ANYTHING OUT OF PSYCHOLOGY?

After so brief a survey of the behavioristic approach to the problems of psychology, one is inclined to say: "Why, yes, it is worth while to study human behavior in this way, but the study of behavior is not the whole of psychology. It leaves out too much. Don't I have sensations, perceptions, conceptions? Do I not forget things and remember things, imagine things, have visual images and auditory images of things I once have seen and heard? Can I not see and hear things that I have never seen or heard in nature? Can I not be attentive or inattentive? Can I not will to do a thing or will not to do it, as the case may be? Do not certain things arouse pleasure in me, and others displeasure? Behaviorism is trying to rob us of everything we have believed in since earliest childhood."

Having been brought up on introspective psychology, as most of us have, you naturally ask these questions and you will find it hard to put away the old terminology and begin to formulate your psychological life in terms of behaviorism. Behaviorism is new wine and it will not go into old bottles. It is advisable for the time being to allay your natural antagonism and accept the behavioristic platform at least until you get more deeply into it. Later you will find that you have progressed so far with behaviorism that the questions you now raise will answer themselves in a perfectly satisfactory natural science way. Let me hasten to add that if the behaviorist were to ask you what you mean by the subjective terms you have been in the habit of using he could soon make you tongue-tied with contradictions. He could even convince you that you do not know what you mean by them. You have been using them uncritically as a part of your social and literary tradition.

TO UNDERSTAND BEHAVIORISM BEGIN TO OBSERVE PEOPLE

This is the fundamental starting point of behaviorism. You will soon find that instead of self-observation being the easiest and most natural way of studying psychology, it is an impossible one; you can observe in yourselves only the most elementary forms of response. You will find, on the other hand, that when you begin to study what your neighbor is doing, you will rapidly become proficient in giving a reason for his behavior and in setting situations (presenting stimuli) that will make him behave in a predictable manner.

DEFINITION OF BEHAVIORISM

Definitions are not as popular today as they once were. The definition of any one science, physics, for example, would necessarily include the definition of all other sciences. And the same is true of behaviorism. About all that we can do in the way of defining a science at the present time is to mark a ring around that part of the whole of natural science that we claim particularly as our own.

Behaviorism, as you have already grasped from our preliminary discussion, is, then, a natural science that takes the whole field of human adjustments as its own. Its closest scientific companion is physiology. Indeed you may wonder, as we proceed, whether behaviorism can be differentiated from that science. It is different from physiology only in the grouping of its problems, not in fundamentals or in central viewpoint. Physiology is particularly interested in the functioning of parts of the animal—for example, its digestive system, the circulatory system, the nervous system, the excretory systems, the mechanics of neural and muscular response. Behaviorism, on the other hand, while it is intensely interested in all of the functioning of these parts, is intrinsically interested in what the whole animal will do from morning to night and from night to morning.

The interest of the behaviorist in man's doings is more than the interest of the spectator—he wants to control man's reactions as physical scientists want to control and manipulate other natural phenomena. It is the business of behavioristic psychology to be able to predict and to control human activity. To do this it must gather scientific data by experimental methods. Only then can the trained behaviorist predict, given the stimulus, what reaction will take place; or, given the reaction, state what the situation or stimulus is that has caused the reaction.

Let us look for a moment more closely at the two terms—stimulus and response.

WHAT IS A STIMULUS?

If I suddenly flash a strong light in your eye, your pupil will contract rapidly. If I were suddenly to shut off all light in the room in which you are sitting, the pupil would begin to widen. If a pistol shot were suddenly fired behind you you would jump and possibly turn your head around. If hydrogen sulphide were suddenly released in your sitting room you would begin to hold your nose and possibly even seek to leave the room. If I suddenly made the room very warm, you would begin to unbutton your coat and perspire. If I suddenly made it cold, another response would take place.

Again, on the inside of us we have an equally large realm in which stimuli can exert their effect. For example, just before dinner the muscles of your stomach begin to contract and expand rhythmically because of the absence of food. As soon as food is eaten those contractions cease. By swallowing a small balloon and attaching it to a recording instrument we can easily register the response of the stomach to lack of food and note the lack of response when food is present. In the male, at any rate, the pressure of certain fluids (semen) may lead to sex activity. In the case of the female possibly the presence of certain chemical bodies can lead in a similar way to overt sex behavior. The muscles of our arms and legs and trunk are not only subject to stimuli coming from the blood; they are also stimulated by their own responses—that is, the muscle is under constant tension; any increase in that tension, as when a movement is made, gives rise to a stimulus which leads to another response in that same muscle or in one in some distant part of the body; any decrease in that tension, as when the muscle is relaxed, similarly gives rise to a stimulus.

So we see that the organism is constantly assailed by stimuli—which come through the eye, the ear, the nose and the mouth—the so-called objects of our environment; at the same time the inside of our body is likewise assailed at every movement by stimuli arising from changes in the tissues themselves. Don't get the idea, please, that the inside of your body is different from or any more mysterious than the outside of your body.

Through the process of evolution human beings have put on sense organs—specialized areas where special types of stimuli are most effective—such as the eye, the ear, the nose, the tongue, the skin and semi-circular canals.[1] To these must be added the whole muscular system, both the striped muscles (for example, the large red muscles of arms, legs and trunks) and the unstriped muscles (those, for example, which make up the hollow tube-like structures of the stomach and intestines and blood vessels). The muscles are thus not only organs of response—they are sense organs as well. You will see as we proceed that the last two systems play a tremendous rôle in the behavior of the human being. Many of our most intimate and personal reactions are due to stimuli set up by tissue changes in our striped muscles and in our viscera.

HOW TRAINING ENLARGES THE RANGE OF STIMULI

One of the problems of behaviorism is what might be called the ever-increasing range of stimuli to which an individual responds. Indeed so marked is this that you might be tempted at first sight to doubt the formulation we gave above, namely, that response can be predicted. If you will watch the growth and development of behavior in the human being, you will find that while a great many stimuli will produce a response in the new-born, many other stimuli will not. At any rate they do not call out the same response they later call out. For example, you don't get very far by showing a new-born infant a crayon, a piece of paper, or the printed score of a Beethoven symphony. In other words, habit formation has to come in before certain stimuli can become effective. Later we shall take up the procedure by means of which we can get stimuli which do not ordinarily call out responses to call them out. The general term we use to describe this is "conditioning." Conditioned responses will be more fully gone into in chapter II.

It is conditioning from earliest childhood on that makes the problem of the behaviorist in predicting what a given response will

---

[1] In chapter III we shall see how sense organs are made up and what their general relation is to the rest of the body.

be so difficult. The sight of a horse does not ordinarily produce the fear response, and yet among almost every group of thirty to forty people there is one person who will walk a block to avoid coming near a horse. While the study of behaviorism will never enable its students to look at you and predict that such a state of affairs exists, nevertheless if the behaviorist sees that reaction taking place, it is very easy for him to state approximately what the situation was in the early experience of such a one that brought about this unusual type of adult response. In spite of the difficulty of predicting responses in detail we live in general upon the theory that we can predict what our neighbor will do. There is no other basis upon which we can live with our fellow men.

WHAT THE BEHAVIORIST MEANS BY RESPONSE

We have already brought out the fact that from birth to death the organism is being assailed by stimuli on the outside of the body and by stimuli arising in the body itself. Now the organism does something when it is assailed by stimuli. It responds. It moves. The response may be so slight that it can be observed only by the use of instruments. The response may confine itself merely to a change in respiration, or to an increase or decrease in blood pressure. It may call out merely a movement of the eye. The more commonly observed responses, however, are movements of the whole body, movements of the arm, leg, trunk, or combinations of all the moving parts.

Usually the response that the organism makes to a stimulus brings about an adjustment, though not always. By an adjustment we mean merely that the organism by moving so alters its physiological state that the stimulus no longer arouses reaction. This may sound a bit complicated, but examples will clear it up. If I am hungry, stomach contractions begin to drive me ceaselessly to and fro. If, in these restless seeking movements, I spy apples on a tree, I immediately climb the tree and pluck the apples and begin to eat. When surfeited, the stomach contractions cease. Although there are apples still hanging round about me, I no longer pluck and eat them. Again, the cold air stimulates me. I move around about until I am out of the wind. In the open I may even dig a hole. Having escaped the wind, it no longer stimulates me to further action. Under sex excitement the male may go to any length to capture a willing female. Once sex activity has been completed the restless seeking movements disappear. The female no longer stimulates the male to sex activity.

The behaviorist has often been criticized for this emphasis upon response. Some psychologists seem to have the notion that the behaviorist is interested only in the recording of minute muscular responses. Nothing could be further from the truth. Let me emphasize again that the behaviorist is primarily interested in the behavior of the whole man. From morning to night he watches him perform his daily round of duties. If it is brick-laying, he would like to measure the number of bricks he can lay under different conditions, how long he can go without dropping from fatigue, how long it takes him to learn his trade, whether we can improve his efficiency or get him to do the same amount of work in a less period of time. In other words, the response the behaviorist is interested in is the commonsense answer to the question "what is he doing and why is he doing it?" Surely with this as a general statement, no one can distort the behaviorist's platform to such an extent that it can be claimed that the behaviorist is merely a muscle physiologist.

The behaviorist claims that there is a response to every effective stimulus and that the response is immediate. By effective stimulus we mean that it must be strong enough to overcome the normal resistance to the passage of the sensory impulse from sense organs to muscles. Don't get confused at this point by what the psychologist and the psycho-analyst sometimes tell you. If you read their statements, you are likely to believe that the stimulus can be applied today and produce its effect maybe the next day, maybe within the next few months, or years. The behaviorist doesn't believe in any such mythological conception. It is true that I can give the verbal stimulus to you "Meet me at the Ritz tomorrow for lunch at one o'clock." Your immediate response is "All right, I'll be there." Now what happens after that? We will not cross this difficult bridge now, but may I point out that we have in our verbal habits a mechanism by means of which the stimulus is reapplied from moment to moment until the final reaction occurs, namely going to the Ritz at one o'clock the next day.

GENERAL CLASSIFICATION OF RESPONSE

The two commonsense classifications of response are "external" and "internal"—or possibly the terms "overt" (explicit) and "implicit" are better. By external or overt responses we mean the ordinary doings of the human being: he stoops to pick up a tennis ball, he writes a letter, he enters an automobile and starts driving, he digs a hole in the ground, he sits down to write a lecture, or dances, or flirts with a woman, or makes love to his wife. We do not need instruments to make these observations. On the other hand, responses may be wholly confined to the muscular and glandular systems inside the body. A child or hungry adult may be standing stock still in front of a window filled with pastry. Your first exclamation may be "He isn't doing anything" or "He is just looking at the pastry." An instrument would show that his salivary glands are pouring out secretions, that his stomach is rhythmically contracting and expanding, and that marked changes in blood pressure are taking place—that the endocrine glands are pouring substances into the blood. The internal or implicit responses are difficult to observe, not because they are inherently different from the external or overt responses, but merely because they are hidden from the eye.

Another general classification is that of *learned* and *unlearned* responses. I brought out the fact above that the range of stimuli to which we react is ever increasing. The behaviorist has found by his study that most of the things we see the adult doing are really learned. We used to think that a lot of them were instinctive, that is, "unlearned." But we are now almost at the point of throwing away the word "instinct." Still there are a lot of things we do that we do not have to learn—to perspire, to breathe, to have our heart beat, to have digestion take place, to have our eyes turn toward a source of light, to have our pupils contract, to show a fear response when a loud sound is given. Let us keep as our second classification then "learned responses," and make it include all of our complicated habits and all of our conditioned responses; and "unlearned" responses, and mean by that all of the things that we do in earliest infancy before the processes of conditioning and habit formation get the upper hand.

Another purely logical way to classify responses is to designate them by the sense organ which initiates them. We could thus have a *visual unlearned response*—for example, the turning of the eye of the youngster at birth toward a source of light. Contrast this with a *visual learned response,* the response, for example, to a printed score of music or a word. Again, we could have a *kinaesthetic* [1] *unlearned response* when the infant reacts by crying to a long-sustained twisted position of the arm. We could have a *kinaesthetic learned response* when we manipulate a delicate object in the dark or, for example, tread a tortuous maze. Again, we can have a *visceral unlearned response* as, for example, when stomach contractions due to the absence of food in the 3 day old infant will produce crying. Contrast this with the learned or visceral *conditioned* response where the sight of pastry in a baker's window will cause the mouth of the hungry schoolboy to water.

This discussion of stimulus and response shows what material we have to work with in behavioristic psychology and why be-

[1] By kinaesthetic we mean the muscle sense. Our muscles are supplied with sensory nerve endings. When we move the muscles these sensory nerve endings are stimulated. Thus, the stimulus to the kinaesthetic or muscle sense is a *movement of the muscle itself.*

havioristic psychology has as its goal *to be able, given the stimulus, to predict the response*—or, *seeing the reaction take place to state what the stimulus is that has called out the reaction.*

IS BEHAVIORISM MERELY A METHODOLOGICAL APPROACH TO THE STUDY OF PSYCHOLOGICAL PROBLEMS, OR IS IT AN ACTUAL SYSTEM OF PSYCHOLOGY?

If psychology can do without the terms "mind" and "consciousness," indeed if it can find no objective evidence for their existence, what is going to become of philosophy and the so-called social sciences which today are built around the concept of mind and consciousness? Almost every day the behaviorist is asked this question, sometimes in a friendly inquiring way, and sometimes not so kindly. While behaviorism was fighting for its existence it was afraid to answer this question. Its contentions were too new; its field too unworked for it to allow itself even to think that some day it might be able to stand up and to tell philosophy and the social sciences that they, too, must scrutinize anew their own premises. Hence the behaviorist's one answer when approached in this way was to say, "I can't let myself worry about such questions now. Behaviorism is at present a satisfactory way of going at the solution of psychological problems—it is really a methodological approach to psychological problems." Today behaviorism is strongly entrenched. It finds its way of going at the study of psychological problems and its formulation of its results growing more and more adequate.

It may never make a pretense of being a *system*. Indeed systems in every scientific field are out of date. We collect our facts from observation. Now and then we select a group of facts and draw certain general conclusions about them. In a few years as new experimental data are gathered by better methods, even these tentative general conclusions have to be modified. Every scientific field, zoölogy, physiology, chemistry and physics, is more or less in a state of flux. Experimental technique, the accumulation of facts by that technique, occasional tentative consolidation of these facts into a theory or an hypothesis describe our procedure in science. Judged upon this basis, behaviorism is a true natural science.

II. How to Study Human Behavior

ANALYZING PSYCHOLOGICAL PROBLEMS

W HY do people behave as they do—how can I, as a behaviorist, working in the interests of science, get individuals to behave differently today from the way they acted yesterday? How far can we modify behavior by training (conditioning)? These are some of the major problems of behavioristic psychology. To gain these scientific objectives the behaviorist, like any other scientist, has to make *observations.*

There are several different levels of psychological observation. Every day we make casual observations of bits of behavior. Often we do not bring in experimentation to refine observation—there is no need for controlled technique with the use of instruments in the observations we make about the daily life of our neighbors. Our observations of their doings remain always more or less at the casual level.

For example, take a simple uncontrolled observation: the mother of a child is sleeping in a chair. I speak to her but my voice does not call out a response. I make my dog bark gently out in the yard; that likewise fails to call out a response. Then I go to the sleeping room of her child and cause it to cry. Immediately the mother springs from the chair and runs to the child's room.

Another similar example. My Airedale dog lies asleep at my feet. What will happen if I rustle the paper? Only a change in respiration. If I throw down a small note-book? It causes a change in respiration—a quickened pulse and a slight movement of the tail and foot. I get up without touching him—immediately the dog springs up ready to play, fight or eat.

In both of these examples I began to manipulate stimuli—*objects* in the environment of my subjects to find out how I could make them *behave* in a certain way.

The human race has been in existence for many hundreds of thousands of years; during that time we have succeeded in gathering a large amount of data on the effect various stimuli have upon human behavior. Much of this material has been gathered—uncritically to be sure—by observations of the same event many times repeated. We gather these up and draw certain conclusions. Most of the data we have upon how human beings live together have been obtained in this way. Experimental control has been lacking. These data, sound or unsound, are all we have about society. They guide us in "controlling" the behavior of others.

We increase our employees' salaries. We offer a bonus—we offer them homes at nominal rental so they can get married. We put in baths, playgrounds. We are constantly manipulating stimuli, dangling this, that and the other combination in front of the human being in order to determine the reactions they will bring forth—hoping that the reaction will be "in line with progress," "desirable," "good." (And society really means by "desirable," "good," "in line with progress," reactions that will not disturb its recognized and established traditional order of things.)

Sometimes, on the other hand, the commonsense observer works the other way round. The individual is doing something—reacting—behaving. The observer, to make his methods socially effective, to be able to reproduce this reaction at another time (and possibly in other individuals as well) attempts to determine what the situation is that causes this particular reaction.

OBSERVATION UNDER EXPERIMENTAL CONTROL

In the observations so far chosen no question of experimentation or technique has entered in. The observations and conclusions have been lacking in scientific accuracy. Let us take a more complicated bit of behavior—one that can be understood only after experimental control has been introduced. Watch any group of men and women yawning and fighting sleep in a crowded lecture room. Why do they grow sleepy—is it because the lecture is stupid? Or is the ventilation poor? The old theory used to be stated something like this: "You see, in a crowded room the oxygen is used up rapidly—this causes an excess of carbon dioxide in the air we breathe; carbon dioxide is bad for you—it makes you yawny and sleepy and if the tension gets very high it may even kill you." But suppose I am not satisfied with this explanation and begin to experiment? I put my subjects into a closed room until the CO_2 tension is considerably higher than in a crowded theatre, my subjects grow sleepy. Next I pump fresh oxygen into the room; still they grow sleepy. When I merely turn on a fan and stir and cool the air, sleepiness disappears. We conclude: you yawn and grow sleepy because of the increasing heat around your body—especially in the unstirred air spaces between your skin and clothing—the slightly increased CO_2 tension while it is a fact, has nothing to do with the reaction. Scientific method has enabled us not only to find the stimulus causing the reaction but also how effectively to control the reaction by removing or modifying the stimulus.

GENERAL NATURE OF PSYCHOLOGICAL PROBLEMS AND SOLUTIONS

We can throw all of our psychological problems and their solutions into terms of stimulus and response. Let us use the abbreviations S for *stimulus* (or the more complex *situation*) and R for *response*. We may schematise our psychological problems as follows:

S..................................R
Given   ?(to be determined)

S..................................R
?(to be determined)   given

Your problem reaches its explanation always when:

S. . . . . .R
has been determined   has been determined

SUBSTITUTION OF STIMULI OR CONDITIONING OF STIMULI

So far our method has been stated very simply. I have led you
to believe that the stimulus necessary to call out the reaction exists
somewhere as a kind of entity only waiting to be found and presented to your subject. I have talked, too, as though the reaction
were a fixed kind of thing or entity ready to be called out the moment the organism is stimulated appropriately. A little observation
shows that our formulation is inexact and in need of modification.
I pointed out in chapter I, page 12, that some stimuli when first
applied seem to exert no marked effect and certainly not the effect
they come later to exert. Let us illustrate this by going back to our
formula. Suppose for example we take an already established (unlearned) reaction with both stimulus and response known, such as:

S. . . . . .R
Electric shock   Withdrawal of hand

Now the mere visual stimulus of a patch of red light will not cause
the withdrawal of the hand. The patch of red light may produce
no marked reaction whatsoever (what reaction does appear will
depend upon previous conditioning). But if I show the red light
and then immediately or shortly thereafter stimulate my subject's
hand with the electric current and repeat this routine often enough,
the red light will cause the immediate withdrawal of the hand. The
red light now becomes a substitute stimulus—it will call out the
R whenever it stimulates the subject in that setting. Something
has happened to bring about this change. This change, as we have
pointed out, is called conditioning—the reaction remains the same
but we have increased the number of stimuli that will call it out.
To express the new state of affairs we (rather inaccurately) de-

scribe the change by speaking of the *stimulus* as being *"conditioned."* Please remember, though, that when we speak both of conditioned stimuli and of conditioned responses, we mean that what is conditioned is the whole organism.

Contrasted with a conditioned stimulus we have the *unconditioned*. Certain stimuli from birth will call out definite responses. A few examples of unconditioned stimuli are as follows:

S..................................R	
Light	Closing pupil, turning eyes
Tapping tendon below knee	Kickup of leg (Patellar reflex)
Acid in the mouth	Salivary secretion
Pricking, burning and cutting skin	Withdrawal of body, crying, screaming.

Observations on infants show quickly that while there are thousands of *unconditioned* stimuli, they are relatively few when contrasted with the *conditioned*. *Conditioned stimuli* are legion in number. Every one of the printed and written 15,000 words that a well educated individual can respond to in an organized way must be looked upon as an example of a conditioned stimulus. Each tool that we work with, each person that we respond to are equally good examples. The total number of conditioned and unconditioned stimuli to which we can respond has never been determined.

The importance of stimulus substitution or stimulus conditioning cannot be overrated. It enormously widens the range of things that will bring out responses. So far as we know now (actual experimental evidence is lacking) we can take any stimulus calling out a standard reaction and substitute another stimulus for it.

Let us go back to our general formula for a moment:

S..................................R

It is obvious that when we determine S we must now tell whether it is a U (unconditioned) stimulus or a C (conditioned) stimulus. Experiment teaches us as is shown in the above example that a drop of acid in the mouth will from birth produce a flow of saliva. This is an example of a native or unconditioned stimulus. The sight of the smoking hot cherry pie that causes the salivary glands to flow so freely is an example of a conditioned visual stimulus. The sound of the gentle footsteps of the mother that stops the crying of her child is an example of a conditioned auditory stimulus.

SUBSTITUTION OF RESPONSE

Can we substitute or condition responses? Experiment teaches us that the process of response substitution or conditioning does take place in all animals throughout life. Yesterday his puppy called out from a two-year-old child—fondling, pet words, play and laughter:

S.................................R
Sight of dog   Manipulation, laughter.

Today the same dog calls out:

S.................................R
Sight of dog   Screaming,
                            withdrawal of body.

Something happened. Late yesterday the dog bit him too hard in play—broke the skin and caused bleeding. We know that

S.................................R
Cutting, burning of skin   withdrawal of body,
                            screaming.

In other words while the visual stimulus *dog* has remained substantially the same, the reaction belonging to another unconditioned stimulus (cutting, pricking skin) has made its appearance.[1]

The conditioning of responses is just as important as the condi-

---

[1] From a laboratory standpoint there is ultimately no fundamental difference between a conditioned stimulus and a conditioned response.

tioning of stimuli. It possibly has even greater social bearing. Many of us are surrounded by fixed unchangeable situations such as the kind of home we live in, parents who must be petted and handled gently, wives "who do not understand," sex hungers from which there is no escaping (for example, marriage to an invalid or insane husband or wife), malformations of the body (permanent inferiorities), and the like. The reactions that we now make to the permanent stimuli are often abortive, inadequate for adjustment; they wreck our constitutions and may make us psychopathic. The fact that different reactions can be conditioned—Adolph Meyer calls them "substitutive" reactions—gives us a real hope for future generations if not for our own. This process is sometimes called "sublimation." Whether conditioned, substituted or sublimated activity is just as adequate for permanent adjustment as the unconditioned has not yet been completely physiologically grounded. Judging from the lack of permanence of many of the "cures" of the psycho-analyst, one is inclined to think that substitutive reactions, in the realm of sex at any rate, will not remain adequate for the organism.

CAN WE MAKE OR BUILD IN TOTALLY NEW RESPONSES?

Certainly no structurally new pathways are found in the brain after infancy. Neural connections are largely laid down at birth. Yet the number of unconditioned, unlearned responses is too small to care for the adult. May I call your attention, though, to the fact that there are thousands of simple unlearned and unconditioned responses, such as finger and arm movements, eye movements, toe and leg movements, that escape the notice of all but trained observers? These are the elements out of which our organized, *learned,* responses must be formed and apparently by the process of conditioning. These simple, unconditioned, embryological responses, by the presentation of appropriate stimuli (society does this for us), can be grouped and tied together into complex *conditioned responses,* or habits, such as tennis, fencing, shoe-making, mother reactions, religious reactions, and the like. These complex responses are thus *integrations.* The organism starts out life with more unit responses than it needs. Relatively few of its vast resources, numerous as its organized complicated acts seem to be, are ever utilized.

For examples of unconditioned but diffuse and widespread groups of responses to a stimulus changing over into a circumscribed group of conditioned responses (or habits) let us go to the white rat. It has been without food for 24 hours. I put food in a wire problem box opened by raising an old-fashioned wooden latch. The rat has never been in this situation before. By hypothesis we will assume that all of its first reactions are native and unlearned (which is of course not the case). What does it do? It runs round and round, bites at the wire, pokes its nose between meshes, pulls cake toward it, sticks claws into moving door, raises head and smells about the cage. Notice that every part-reaction necessary to the solution of the problem has been many times displayed. These part-reactions are present in its repertoire of unconditioned or unlearned acts. They are (1) walking or running to the door, (2) raising the head (which if done at a given point will result in knocking the latch up), (3) pulling at the moving door with the claws, (4) climbing over the sill to the food. Out of the rat's vast display of unconditioned responses only 4 are needed—if given time it will always accidentally stumble upon the solution. But to solve the problem efficiently these 4 part-reactions must be spaced and timed—patterned or integrated. When integration, patterning or conditioning is complete, all other responses except 1-2-3-4 disappear. We would correctly speak of this 1-2-3-4 response as being a new and conditioned response. We usually call this process the formation of a habit.

Most of us have studied habit formation and at least think we should know a great deal about it. But even if we knew all of the existing data about it we could hardly construct a tenable theory of how habits are formed. Both introspectionists and behaviorists have worked *en masse,* so to speak, in this field in order to settle various questions of fact—such as the factors making for rapidity of habit formation, accuracy of habits, permanence of habits, effects of age on habit formation; the effect of forming two or more habits simultaneously; the transfer of habits and the like. No experimenter, however, has yet set his experimental problems in such a way as to construct from his data a guiding theory of habit formation.

Even today the relationship between what is generally called *habit formation* and the conditioning of stimuli and of responses has not been worked out. Personally I think there is little new in habit formation, but I may be over-simplifying it. When we are teaching the animal or human to go to a red light and not to a green, or to stay on the true pathway and out of the culs-de-sac, or to open the problem box above described, I think we are merely establishing a conditioned response—the stimulus remains constant. We work to get a "new" or conditioned reaction. When, however, there is social or experimental need to keep the reaction constant but to change the stimulus, as happens when an individual for long periods makes love reactions to a certain female who will have none of him (thereby possibly endangering his whole life structure) there is need for stimulus substitution ("transfer," the psycho-analysts call it). If the substitution takes place we have an example of a conditioned stimulus.

While our studies on the formation of habits in both the human and animal realms have lacked theoretical guidance, nevertheless much information valuable for psychology has been obtained from them. Indeed the prosecution of work on "habit formation" can be said to have been the chief business of the psychologist until the very recent introduction of conditioned reflex methods. This is causing a re-envisagement of the whole problem and the rearrangement of our whole experimental program.

We shall postpone further discussion of "habit formation" proper until a later chapter and continue here with experimental work done on "conditioned reflexes." You will notice that most of the experimental work concerns itself really with stimulus substitutions and not with reaction substitutions. There has been relatively little experimental work done upon reaction substitutions. Much of the practical work of the psychiatrists and of the analysts has been of this character. Inhibition of response (by conditioning) is another problem of equal importance but there are relatively few experimental data upon it that have been gathered from human subjects.

CONDITIONED REFLEX METHODS
STIMULUS SUBSTITUTION IN GLANDULAR REACTIONS

Laboratory studies on stimulus substitution have progressed further in the animal field than in the human field. It may be worth while to review some of the work on the dog. Conditioned reflex work began upon the dog and the experimental exactness of the method can there best be demonstrated. The Russian physiologist, Pavlov, and his students have been chiefly responsible for this work.[1]

Please recall for a moment that there are two different sets of tissue with which we can respond: 1, our glands; and 2, our muscles (and there are really two kinds of muscles, striped and visceral. See page 13).

The gland usually selected for experimentation is the salivary gland. According to Dr. G. V. Anrep, a former pupil of Pavlov, the salivary gland is a simple organ, not a composite one like the muscular system of the body. It is far more independent too of the body than is the muscular system, and the activity of the gland can be graduated with greater ease than can muscular action.

The fundamental or unconditioned stimulus, as we have stated before, calling out a salivary response is some food or acid substance introduced into the mouth:

---

[1] The recent book by Pavlov, *"Lectures on Conditioned Reflexes,"* gives a full presentation of the work which has come out of Pavlov's laboratory.

S. . . . . .R
Food, acid   Salivary flow

The problem now is to take some other stimulus that does not call out a salivary flow—indeed it may not call out any marked general response from the dog—and get it to call out the salivary response. Experiment shows that visual stimuli, such as colored discs, geometrical forms, simple noises, pure tones, bodily contacts, will not call out the salivary response. Any one of them can, however, be made to. A simple operation is first performed on the dog by making a permanent fistula of the parotid duct—that is, a small opening is made to lead from the gland to the external surface of the cheek and a small tube is cemented to this outlet. The drops of saliva coming from the gland now pass out through an external tube instead of into the mouth. This tube is made to connect with an apparatus which records automatically the number of drops that flow from the gland. The animal is isolated from the experimenter and from any auditory, olfactory, visual or other stimuli not controlled by the investigator. The application of both the unconditioned and the conditioned stimuli is performed automatically from outside the animal room. The animal is viewed by means of a periscope.

It is found that we may substitute for food or acid any stimulus at will and get the salivary response, provided we apply this stimulus (C) simultaneously with the food or acid stimulus (U); indeed we may even apply the C stimulus before the U stimulus. Apparently, however, if the U stimulus is given first, the conditioning does not take place. For example, Krestovnikov worked for a year giving the U stimulus first and applying the C stimulus only a few seconds later without ever establishing the reaction. When the C stimulus precedes the U stimulus the conditioning takes place after about 20 to 30 combined applications. The time interval between the application of C before the beginning of U may be varied from a few seconds up to five or more minutes.

Suppose in a given case we wish to make a tactual stimulation call out a salivary response. We stimulate the animal tactually for 4 seconds on one spot on the left thigh and then apply after a pause of 4 or 5 seconds the unconditioned stimulus, powdered meat and dog biscuit (U). We continue this routine for approximately two months, giving from four to ten stimulations a day with a pause from 7 to 45 minutes after each. By this time the stimulus substitution will be complete and the tactual stimulus (C) will yield the same number of drops of saliva as the powdered meat and dog biscuit (U).

By this simple procedure we have widened the range of stimuli to which the dog can react in a definite way. Instead of our formula above, it now should read:

S. . . . . R

Powdered meat and dog biscuit	For example, 60 drops
or	of saliva in 30 seconds
Tactual stimulus on the left thigh	each equal to 0.01 c.c.

We have here an example of a complete stimulus substitution. The magnitude of the reaction following upon the conditioned stimulus is the same as that called out by the unconditioned—within the limits of experimental error.

By this simple procedure we can test out the whole range of stimuli to which an animal can respond. For example, suppose we have so conditioned an animal that light of any wave length brings out the salivary response. After conditioning it we next try to find out whether it is sensitive to wave lengths shorter than those that affect the human eye. We start in with green light from the spectrum and gradually increase the wave length of the stimulus light until the reaction fails. This gives the animal's range in the longer wave lengths. Again we build up the reaction to the green light, then gradually shorten the wave length until the reaction breaks down. This gives us its range in the shorter wave lengths. We can work in the same way on the auditory side. It has been found by certain investigators that the dog will react to tones far higher in pitch frequency of vibration than can the human being. Man and the dog have never been tested under identical conditions, however.

With a slightly different procedure we can establish so-called *differential responses*. Suppose, for example, we have conditioned the dog to a given tone A, until tone A calls out the salivary response just as does the powdered meat. Almost any other tone B will at first call out the salivary response (irradiation). Can we so change and build up the dog's reaction system that he will not react to B but only to A? Yes, within the limits of the dog's ability to respond to differences in pitch (which is somewhat in doubt). Anrep claims differential response to very slight difference in pitch. Johnson, working by another method, finds no differential response to pitch differences. When working with differential reactions to tonal stimuli, for example, we proceed to "fix" or circumscribe the stimulus A more narrowly by feeding each time A is sounded but never feeding when B is sounded. Very soon A will call forth the full secretion of saliva whereas B will not call out any secretion at all.

This method is equally applicable in every sense field. We can return answers to the questions: How accurately can the dog react to noises, to differences in wave length, to odors?

Some of the general facts summarized by Anrep, coming from the study of the salivary reflexes in dogs, may be enumerated as follows:

1. The conditioned responses, like all other habits, are more or less temporary and unstable. After periods of no practice they cease to work; they break down. They can, however, be quickly reëstablished. In one observed case in the salivary reflex of the dog a test was made after two years. The condi-

tioned reflex was present but not invariable. After one reinforcement it was completely renewed.

2. The substituted stimulus can be fixed and made specific. No
other stimulus of its class will then call out the reflex. If you
condition the dog to a metronome no other noise will call
out the response.

3. The magnitude of the response is dependent upon the strength
of the stimulus. Increase the stimulus and there is an increase
in the response. Again, if a continuous stimulus—say a noise
or a tone—is interrupted, it has the same effect as strengthening the stimulus—an increased magnitude of response will
appear.

4. There is a marked summation effect. If a dog is conditioned
separately to sound and to color, there is a marked increase in
the number of drops if the stimuli are given simultaneously.

5. Conditioned responses can be "extinguished (Pavlor claims
that they are never permanently extinguished)." Lack of practice extinguishes them. They can be extinguished by very
rapid repetition of the stimulus. "Fatigue" is not the cause
of their being extinguished: in the case of a dog conditioned
separately to sound and to color, if the visual stimulus is extinguished the auditory stimulus will call out the response in
full force.

STIMULUS SUBSTITUTION IN HUMAN SALIVARY REACTIONS

I pointed out on page 30 that to work on salivary responses in
dogs a simple operation has to be performed. This is, of course,
not possible in human beings (except in cases of accident). Dr.
K. S. Lashley, however, has perfected a small instrument which
serves the same purpose. It consists of a small silver disc about the
diameter of a 5-cent piece and about $\frac{1}{8}''$ thick, grooved on one
surface so as to form two non-communicating chambers. Each
chamber has a tiny silver tube leading out from it. The central

chamber is placed over the tiny opening where the gland comes to the inner surface of the cheek. The tube leading from this chamber conducts the saliva outside the mouth to a recording apparatus. The tube from the other chamber leads over to a little aspirator that creates a partial vacuum in this chamber. This serves to make the whole disc cling tightly to the inner surface of the cheek. The whole apparatus, called a *sialometer,* is more comfortable than my description would seem to warrant. One can eat and sleep with it in place.

As in the dog, food substances or acids (U) will call out a salivary response in man:

S...................................R

Food, acid   Secretion of salivary fluid

In humans as well as in dogs stimulus substitutions can be made. The visual stimulus of a medicine dropper will not at first call out a salivary flow—but if the subject watches you dip the pipette into a solution of acid and then apply this acid to his tongue, the sight of the pipette soon comes to call out the salivary flow. Now we have:

S..............................R
Food, acid
    or   Salivary flow
Sight of pipette

We have thus conditioned our subject. Here too, we have in the human widened the range of stimuli that will call out a salivary response.

Conditioning of the human salivary gland takes place apparently on a considerable scale throughout life—the watering of the mouth of the child or the adult at the sight of savory viands is a good example. Until experimental tests are made these conditioned responses cannot be observed. There is no question of "association of ideas"—the subject cannot "introspect about them"; he cannot even tell you whether they are present or not. May I call your attention to the fact that this gland is not under so-called "voluntary" control—that is, that you can't "will" to make it secrete or "will" to make it stop secreting?

CAN OTHER GLANDS BE CONDITIONED?

We certainly know from the work of Pavlov and his students that the glands of the stomach and other visceral glands can be conditioned just as are the salivary glands. Others have shown that such glands can also be conditioned in the human being. We have no experimental work on stimulus substitution in other duct glands. We have reason to believe that urination and the orgasm in the male can be conditioned, but here we are probably dealing with muscular conditions which are discussed on page 36.

The one other duct gland easily accessible to experimentation (but so far as I know yet unexperimented upon) is the tear gland. Probably many of the tears of the infant, of the hardened theatre fan, of the criminal, and the malingering invalid are true examples of conditioning. The glands of the skin may also offer interesting experimental possibilities.

Whether the ductless glands such as the thyroid, adrenal, pineal and others can be conditioned is unknown. But emotional reactions can be conditioned—and here the whole body is involved. If this is the case, apparently the ductless glands have to follow suit and play their own rôle. We have fair evidence that this is the case. In conditioned emotional reactions both adrenals and thyroids apparently do change their rhythm of functioning.

STIMULUS SUBSTITUTION IN STRIPED AND UNSTRIPED MOTOR REACTIONS

IN STRIPED MUSCLE REACTIONS

Bechterew, another Russian physiologist, and his students have taught us that stimuli calling out striped muscular responses of arms, legs, trunk, fingers, similarly can be substituted for. One of the simplest ways to bring about an unconditioned response by an unconditioned stimulus is to use a cutting, bruising stimulus. The electric shock is a convenient one. Our formula would read originally:

S....................................R
Cutting, bruising, burning,   Withdrawal of arm,
    electric shock   leg, finger

If the foot rests upon an electric grill the foot will be jerked up each time the current is turned on. We can record on a smoked drum this jump of the leg or foot. We can likewise record each time the electric shock is given.

As has been pointed out, ordinary visual and auditory objects do not call out this sudden reflex withdrawal of the foot. The noise of an ordinary electric buzzer, for example, will not. But stimulate the subject jointly with the buzzer and electro-tactually 24–30 times (more in some subjects) and the buzzer alone will call out the withdrawal of the foot. Here again we have widened the range of situations that will call out this response. Our formula now reads:

S....................................R
Electric Shock
     or   Withdrawal of foot
Buzzer

H. Cason has shown that stimulus substitution takes place with winking. The unlearned or unconditioned formula is as follows:

S....................................R
(1) Bright light   Rapid wink
(2) Rapid approach of objects (One of the fastest of human re-
    toward eye   flexes)
(3) Irritation of cornea or con-
    junctiva of eye
(4) Injury to lid itself (cutting,
    electric shock)

The noise of a telegraph sounder, or the slight click of a relay will not cause the wink reflex, but if the eyelid is electrically shocked just as the telegraph sounder or relay is sounded the substitution takes place rapidly. It is interesting to note that the substituted stimulus calls out a more rapid wink than the unconditioned stimulus.

It is easy to see how serviceable this method is in teaching us to understand the makeup of a human being.[1] Here too, we can as in the glandular field so "fix" a *given* stimulus, say a tone, noise, sight, or smell, that only that particular stimulus will call out the response. A thousand noises go on around the dozing mother as we showed before, without calling out the response of running to the child, but let the child itself stir or even murmur and up she springs. An auditory stimulus can be so strongly fixed, for example, middle C (*256 d. v.*) that another tone a fraction higher or lower will not call out the response.

IN UNSTRIPED MUSCULAR REACTION

Considerable work has been done upon the conditioning of unstriped muscular tissue. The circular unstriped muscles of the stomach begin their rhythmical contractions after the stomach has been emptied of food. These so-called hunger contractions serve as the most powerful general stimuli we know. They initiate general bodily reactions usually called exploratory. After food has been obtained and eaten the contractions die down. It is perfectly possible to change the rhythm of these reactions and make them dependent upon our regular meal time. The well-brought-up baby fed every three hours wakes up promptly at the end of the three-hour interval and begins to fuss or cry. Change the interval to a

---

[1] In daily life I have seen many times an accidental contact with a hot electric iron or radiator condition a child (substitution of visual for tissue destroying, tactual stimulus) after one joint stimulation. We are shot through with such accidental conditionings from earliest infancy onward.

four-hour one and after a few days the infant wakes up promptly
at the end of the fourth hour.

One of the most interesting pieces of experimental work done in
this field is that of Cason on the pupillary reflexes. There are two
sets of unstriped muscular fibres in the eye. When the radial set
contracts the pupil dilates. When the circular or sphincter set contracts the pupil grows smaller. The unconditioned formula is:

(U) S................................(U) R
Increase in light intensity   Closure of pupil
Decrease in light intensity   Dilatation of pupil

Stimulus substitution takes place here as in the various other reflexes. By stimulating the subject with an electric bell or a buzzer
just as we increase or decrease the intensity of light falling on the
retina, we finally condition the subject so that the sound stimulus
alone will call out either dilation or constriction of the pupil.

SUBSTITUTION IN THE FIELD OF TOTAL BODILY REACTIONS
(CONDITIONED EMOTIONAL REACTIONS)

In chapter VII I will take up some experiments which show that
certain unconditioned stimuli arousing total bodily reactions called
"fear," "rage," "love," can be substituted for just as in the simple
reflex field we have just studied. This accounts for the ever-
increasing number of stimuli that can call out emotional (really
visceral) reactions. This experimental work does away with the
necessity for any "theory" of the emotions such as that of James.

SUMMARY OF EXPERIMENTS ON STIMULUS SUBSTITUTION

In this summary it is impossible to do more than just sketch
in a few general words the way the human body becomes conditioned. The main point to emphasize is that practically every
responding organ of the body can be conditioned; and that this

conditioning takes place not only throughout adult life but can and does take place daily from the moment of birth (in all probability before birth). Most of this organization takes place below the verbalized level. Indeed the glands and unstriped muscular tissue do not belong to our so-called voluntary systems of responses at all. All of us are shot through with stimulus substitutions of one kind or another which we know nothing about until the behaviorist tries us out and tells us about them.

This field of bodily conditioning lies wholly outside the introspectionist's field. He can get no grip on such reactions. This is an added proof that introspection can at best yield only a very meagre and incomplete kind of psychology. Later I shall attempt to show that "introspection" is nothing but another name for talking about obscure bodily reactions which are taking place. It is not a genuine psychological method at all.

The importance of early conditionings in building up bodily attitudes, especially on the emotional side, is almost undreamed of. It is practically impossible for us in adult life to have a "new" stimulus thrust upon us that does not arouse this vestigial organization. This work helps us, too, in understanding why behaviorists are growing away from the concept of instinct and substituting for it bodily sets and attitudes (conditioned).

OTHER EXPERIMENTAL METHODS

In a single chapter we can hardly hope even to mention by name the various methods—even the worth-while objective ones used in psychological studies. We mention a few here to give a little insight into their numbers. Many of the methods centre around learning and retention—methods for studying the effects of drugs, hunger, thirst, loss of sleep,—methods for studying conditions that affect the performance of acts after learning has been completed; methods for studying emotional reactions, such as the various forms of free and controlled word reactions—galvanometric studies of emotional reaction. Methods for studying the relative strength of hunger and sex stimuli (see the work of Moss at George Washington University, and of Warden and his students at Columbia University). Methods of eliminating sense organs and parts of the brain in animals in order to determine sense organ rôles and the rôle of various parts of the nervous system.[1] (In work on humans in this field we have to wait for accident to prepare our subjects.)

THE SO-CALLED "MENTAL" TEST AS A BEHAVIORISTIC METHOD

During the past quarter of a century, in this country especially, there has grown up an enormous number of so-called mental tests. For a time it looked as though psychology would go test mad. Tests grew up with a mushroom-like growth only to flourish for a few days and then be revised by the next experimenter. Recent years have seen a gradual elimination of many of the tests and the gradual development and standardizing of a few.

In building these tests hundreds of thousands of children and adults were used. One can but admire the patience and assiduity of the originators of these tests. The main purpose behind all testing is to find a measuring rod for classifying masses of individuals according to level of performance, according to age, and the like; to discover deficiencies and special abilities, racial and sex differences.

Two rather wild ideas have grown up about tests: (1) The claim has been made that there is such a thing as "general" intelligence *per se;* and (2) that these are tests that enable one to differentiate "native" ability from acquired ability. To the behaviorist tests mean merely devices—quite unsatisfactory at present—for grading and sampling human performance.

---

[1] Lashley's recent book, *Brain Mechanisms and Intelligence,* is an example of a brilliant research in this field.

SOCIAL EXPERIMENTATION

It can be seen at a glance that in all social experimentation we have two general procedures. (1) We attempt to answer the question, "What would happen if we should make such and such changes in social situations? We can't be sure that we will be any better off, but anything is better than what we have now. Let us make a change." Usually social situations when they become intolerable cause us to dash blindly into action without arousing any verbal correlates such as I have indicated here.

We can phrase the other procedure (2) as follows: "We want this individual or this group of individuals to do a certain thing, but we do not know just how to arrange a situation to get him to do it." Here the procedure is somewhat different. Society experiments blindly by trial and error, but the reaction is known and approved. The stimulus is manipulated not for the purpose of seeing what in general will happen but to bring about the specific action. You may not clearly see the difference between the two types of procedure, but a few examples should clear it up. First we all must admit that social experimentation is going on at a very rapid rate at present—at an alarmingly rapid rate for comfortable, conventional souls. As an example of social experimentation under No. 1 above, we have war. No one can predict what changes in reaction will be brought upon a nation when that nation goes to war. It is a blind manipulation of stimuli on a par with the experimentation of the child when he knocks down his house of blocks so patiently and laboriously constructed.

Prohibition was only a blind rearrangement of a situation. The saloon brought a series of actions condemned by society. The conventional individuals in the community, without being able to make any reasonable prediction as to what would occur, tore down the whole of the old situation and created a new one by ratifying the 18th Amendment. It is true that here they expected certain

results—the doing away of drinking, the depletion of prisons of
their inmates, a lessening of extra-marital intercourse, and the
like.[1] But any student of human nature or even of geography
could have predicted that those results could not come although
he might have been unable to predict what would occur. The result, except in the smaller towns, of course, has been quite contrary to these expectations. Certainly in and near the larger cities
(where legal control is less effective and where public opinion is
less of a factor in control) our prisons are more crowded today
than ever. Crime is especially rampant, particularly homicidal
crimes. The latter are beginning to arouse the concern of life
insurance companies. One company in 1924 lost more than three
quarters of a million dollars due to homicides alone. Then, too,
thousands of citizens have been shot while engaged in rum running or have died from alcohol poisoning. In spite of it all, the
prohibition law has been trampled under foot. With the successful breaking of this one law, fear of law has been removed; and
when a taboo has been broken with impunity not only does that
particular taboo of the medicine man lose its grip, but all of the
taboos of that particular medicine man tend to become ineffective.
What occurred in primitive society occurs today. All laws are unquestionably more lightly esteemed.

The destruction of the monarchy in Russia and the formation of
a Soviet government is another example of blind manipulation
of situations. Neither friend nor foe could predict what changes
in behavior would accrue. The facts are that this change has caused
Russia to become an isolated nation socially and industrially and
has thrown back the intellectual and scientific progress of the Rus-

[1] Those adults who drank before prohibition drink now, only they drink a poor
grade of hard liquor because it is easy to transport and can be more easily concealed.
The adults who did not drink before prohibition don't drink now. It would not
surprise me in the least if this blind manipulation of a stimulus led to another
Civil War. We had a war with England over tea—over a principle, we said then.
Almost any day 60,000,000 Wets may say to the 60,000,000 Puritan Drys who don't
drink that the principle of individual rights has been trampled upon and denied them,
for after all the Drys don't have to drink even if prohibition is done away with.

sian people many, many years. Without further elaboration we can formulate several of these problems under our general scheme:

	Reaction—outcome—too
Stimuli given	*complicated for prediction*
S....................................	R
Overthrow of monarchy; formation of Soviet government	?
War	?
Prohibition	?
Easy divorce	?
No marriage	?
Children brought up in ignorance of their parents	?
Substitution of physiological ethics for religion	?
Equalization of wealth	?
Elimination of hereditary wealth	?

In this type of social experimentation society often plunges—does not feel its way out by means of small scale experimentations. It works with no definite experimental program in front of it. Its behavior often becomes mob-like which is another way of saying that the individuals composing the groups fall back upon infantile behavior.

Similarly, social experimentation goes on in (2) above. Here the

S....................................	R
?	Marriage under modern financial pressure
?	Continence in great cities where social control is difficult
?	Joining the church
?	Truthfulness
?	Rapid acquisition of skill in a special line
?	Correct deportment, etc.

reaction is already known and approved by society—marriage, continence in the unmarried, joining the church, the positive actions demanded in the ten commandments and the like are examples of such approved reactions. In fact every ritual and tabu system fits into this scheme.

Our experimentation consists of setting up one set of stimuli after another until the given specified reaction follows from the correct grouping of stimuli. In trying to arrange these situations, society often works as blindly and as haphazardly as does the infra-human animal. Indeed if one were to characterize social experimentation in general during the past 2000 years one would have to call it precipitous, infantile, unplanned, and say that when planned it is always in the interest of some nation, political group, sect or individual, rather than under the guidance of social scientists—assuming their existence. Never, except possibly at certain periods of Grecian history, have we had even an educated ruling class. Our own country today is one of the worst offenders in history, ruled as it is by professional politicians, labor propagandists and religious persecutors.

I call your attention to the fact that behavioristic psychology, taking as it does its problems genetically and going from the simple to the more complex, is amassing a wealth of information on the reactions following stimuli and on the stimuli underlying given reactions, that will prove of inestimable benefit to society. Believing that his science is basal to the organization and control of society, the behaviorist has hoped that sociology may accept its principles and re-envisage its own problems in a more concrete way.

WHAT CAN WE LEARN BY COMMONSENSE OBSERVATIONS?

So far we have talked mainly about technical methods. Cannot we achieve a commonsense psychology personally helpful by merely watching people? The answer is yes, if we will observe them systematically and over a long enough period of time. Indeed every human being already has considerable organization in psychology whether he has studied it or not. Where would we be in our social life if we could not more or less confidently predict responses and puzzle out the possible effect of stimuli? The more observations one makes upon other people, the better psychologist one becomes—the better one can get along with other people—and almost half the battle for a more sanely adjusted life comes from this ability to get along with people. One does not even have to become a student of conditioned responses, helpful as this study is, in order to learn practical psychology.

I visited a man over a week-end to whom I had promised to try to give a little helpful practical psychology. He had not been getting along too well in his work. Monday morning he arose, sore and sleepy from the strenuous exercises engaged in over the week-end. He groaned aloud and complained about the unsatisfactory character of all vacations and was just about ready to take a mournful shave and a hot bath. I said to him, "Sling your arms and legs about a bit and do your daily dozen and take a tepid bath. This will set you up." This verbal stimulus led to the act. He went down to breakfast feeling fit. But his eggs were overdone. He was just ready to "call" the maid but I noticed a certain stiffening of her body and a certain snappiness to her words much as though she said, "I don't like week-end guests anyway and it serves you both right." I whispered to my host, "Have a care; the Irish biddy is just fretting to go on a rampage. You had better call your wife up by phone when she wakes up and let her scold the cook."

We rushed for the train only to miss it by twenty seconds. He stamped his feet and cursed and said aloud, "This is the first time in three months that train has been on time." His reactions were almost infantile in character. He calmed down finally and we took a later train to the office. His whole tone was lowered as anyone could observe by watching him. His day had started

wrong. Previous commonsense observation had given me, as a
behaviorist, a store of data to predict that with his temperament his
day might go very wrong indeed, considering the start he had.
This situation called out from me the overt verbal response: "You'll
have to watch your step all day with the people you come in contact with or you'll hurt somebody's feelings and make a worse
ending to a day that started badly."

This gave him a new start. He smiled when his secretary handed
him the mail. He plunged into his work. It gripped him and soon
he was lost to the world in the technical duties for which he is
peculiarly fitted. When lunch time came he slackened up in his
work and I happened to hear his voice raised in protest while talking with one of his associates. Observation of his family life over
the week-end had taught me a lot. I was able to predict what the
probable situation was that was upsetting him. I thought I could
again change his world for him, and I said, "It's too bad you didn't
ask your wife to come in to town and have lunch with us today.
I heard her break her date yesterday for lunch with Mr. and Mrs.
Jones (his wife, much to his distress, being particularly friendly
with Mr. Jones) while you were out tuning up the car." Being an
unpsychological person, his relief was obvious and his next hour
was his best. Without asking this man to introspect or psycholo-
gize or psycho-analyze himself, I could detect his weak spots, his
strong points, where he went wrong with his children, where he
went wrong with his wife. There can be little doubt but that the
behaviorist, by training him both in principles and in particulars,
could almost remake this very intelligent individual in a few
weeks' time.

But you may say, "I am not a psychologist—I cannot go following people around telling them to go easy here and hard there."
This is true, but has behaviorism nothing to teach you about your
own life? I think you will admit that you have a lot to learn but
you would not try to lay bricks on your own house until you had
learned how to lay bricks. So with personal psychology you have

to watch other people day by day—you have to systematise and classify your data—throw them into logical moulds—and verbalize your results, e. g., "George Marshall is the quietest man I know. He is always even-tempered and he always speaks in a low even tone. I wonder if I could learn how to talk like a gentleman." This verbal formulation serves you as a stimulus (implicit kinaesthetic word stimulus). It may lead to a changed response; for words whether spoken by others or spoken subvocally in your own throat are just as strong stimuli, lead just as swiftly to action, as hurtling stones, threatening clubs and sharp knives. Once you have acquired technical skill in watching the behavior of others, observation of your own behavior becomes much easier.

If I were an experimental ethicist I'd point out to you the importance of maxims—how potently cut and dried verbal formulae serve as stimuli for shaping our own reactions. This is especially true when those formulae are handed down by persons in authority—by parents, teachers, advisers. Again, if we were studying ethics, I'd point out to you the reasonableness of arriving at such formulations from your own abundant observation, rather than blindly accepting them second-hand. But, I think, I would just as quickly tell you not to reject the results of these collective social experiments—now crystallized into verbal formulae and handed down from father to son and mother to daughter, until your own tentative and small scale social experimentation has given you more trustworthy formulations. In other words, I am trying early to convince you that the behaviorist is not a reactionist—not against anything or for anything until it has been tried out and established like other scientific formulations.

To know what is "good" or "bad" for the human organism— to know how to guide man's conduct on experimentally sound lines is beyond us at present. We know far too little of the makeup of the human body and its needs to be dogmatic in our prescriptions or in our proscriptions.

III. The Human Body

WHAT IT IS MADE OF, HOW IT IS PUT TOGETHER, AND HOW IT WORKS

PART I. THE STRUCTURES THAT MAKE BEHAVIOR POSSIBLE

INTRODUCTION:—There are some psychologists who claim that a knowledge of the body is not essential to the study of psychology. Certainly the behaviorist feels the need of some study of the makeup and functioning of the body. Nor is this knowledge so difficult to obtain. In the following two chapters I have tried to put forth in its simplest form the essential facts about the body.

The Behaviorist is Interested in the Way the Whole Body Works: If you will pick up a physiology or an anatomy you will find that the human body is studied part by part—the digestive apparatus, the circulatory apparatus, the respiratory apparatus, the nervous system. The physiologist has to carry out his experimental work first upon one organ and then upon another. The student of human behavior, by contrast, works with the whole body in action.

While the whole body can do many things, there are very definite limitations to its possibilities of functioning and these limitations are due to the material out of which the body is composed and to the way that material is put together. I mean by this merely that there is a limit to the speed with which we can run; to the loads we can lift; to the length of time we can go without food or water and without sleep; that the body needs special types of food—that it can endure only a certain amount of heat for a certain length of time, or a certain amount of cold for a definite period; that it must be supplied with oxygen and other special materials. Even an hour's study will convince one that the human body, while beautifully put together to do many things, is not a treasure house of mystery but a very commonsense kind of *organic* machine (and by organic machine we mean something many millions of times more complicated than anything man has yet succeeded in making).

Should We as Behaviorists Be Especially Interested in the Central Nervous System? Because he places emphasis on the facts of adjustment of the whole organism rather than upon the working of parts of the body, the behaviorist is often accused of not making a place in his scheme for the nervous system. To understand why it hurts the feelings of the introspectionist for the behaviorist to place no more emphasis on the brain and the spinal cord than upon the striped muscles of the body, the plain muscles of the stomach, the glands, you must remember that the nervous system to the introspectionist has always been a mystery box—whatever he couldn't explain in "mental" terms he pushed over into the brain. Many of our so-called physiological psychologies are filled with pictures of brain and spinal cord schemes. As a matter of fact we do not yet know enough about the functioning of brain and spinal cord to draw diagrams about their functions.

For the behaviorist the nervous system is, 1st, a part of the body —no more mysterious than muscles and glands; 2nd, it is a specialized body mechanism that enables its possessor to react more quickly and in a more integrated way with muscles or glands when acted upon by a given stimulus than would be the case if no nervous system were present. There are many animals and free swimming plants without nervous systems. Their range of adjustment is limited and their reactions to touch, light, sound, etc., are slow. You can react almost instantly with your hand when any part of your body is touched. The nervous system speeds up the passage of the message (known scientifically as a *propagated disturb-*

ance) from the sense organ (where the stimulus is applied) to the reacting organ (the muscles and glands). Where there is no nervous system the message still travels but it travels slowly.

The behaviorist then has to be vitally interested in the nervous system but only as an integral part of the whole body.

DIFFERENT TYPES OF CELLS AND TISSUES THAT MAKE UP THE BODY

What is the Body Made Of? Nearly every one knows today that the human individual springs from a single cell. This cell, though, contains elements contributed by both the father and the mother. The egg in the uterus of the mother becomes fertilized by the sperm of the father. This fertilized egg is the original single cell. The cell soon begins to divide. All of the billions of cells of which the adult human body is made up are the result of this process of division.

Professor Jennings in his recent beautiful book, *The Biological Basis of Human Nature,* has told us in a very clear way some of the things every one should know about this cell. He has kindly allowed me to quote extensively from this discussion of the genes (the "bearers" of heredity):

THE GENES

Observation and experiment have shown that the original cell contains a great number of distinct and separable substances, existing as minute particles. The development of an individual is brought about by the interaction of these thousand substances—their interaction with each other, with other parts of the cell, and with material taken from outside. It is known that different individuals start with diverse sets of these substances, and that the way a given individual develops, what he becomes, what characteristics he gets, what peculiarities he shows, depend, other things being equal, on what set of these substances he starts with. Different individuals are made as it were on diverse recipes; and the diverse recipes give different results. Much is known of the results of altering only a single one of the thousand different substances present in the original cell, and of altering several or many. Some combinations of them give imperfect individuals, feeble-minded, deformed, monstrous. Others give normal individuals, others superior individuals. There are combinations giving every intermediate type, some yielding slightly imperfect individuals, lazy, stupid or silly; and there are combinations that produce genius. No two individuals, in such an organism as man, are concocted on the same recipe (save in the rare cases known as identical twins). It is clearly proved experimentally that the diverse combinations yield structural and physiological differences of all types and grades, including diversities in behavior, in what we call mentality.

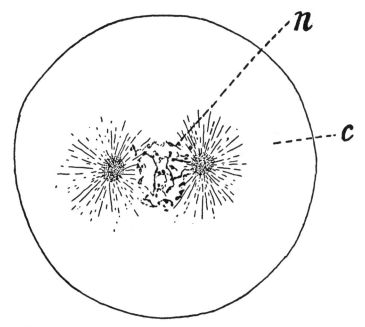

Figure a—Individual in the earliest stage, the fertilized egg of the starfish. c, cytoplasm; n, nucleus, showing the small dark chromosomes. Based on the photograph in Wilson's Atlas of Fertilization, Plate VI, figure 24. (Columbia University Press, 1895.)

(Reprinted by permission from "The Biological Basis of Human Nature" by H. S. Jennings.)

These many diverse substances present at the beginning of development are called the genes. The genes exist in the two pieces that unite to form the new individual. They were present in the two parents from which the two pieces came; so that the genes are transmitted to us directly from our parents.

The genes exist in the egg cell as a great number of extremely minute particles, which are grouped together to form structures that are visible under the microscope, and are known as *chromosomes* (figures c and d). The chromosomes, with their included genes, constitute a vesicle in the interior of the cell, known as the *nucleus*. The egg cell consists of a mass of jelly-like material, known as *cytoplasm,* in which is embedded the nucleus, with its chromosomes and genes (figure a).

The Genetic System

Many of the most important features of development and of individuality result from the way the genes are disposed in the cells, their actual physical arrangement and consequent behavior. The way diverse individuals develop, the peculiarities that they show, the so-called laws of heredity, the extraordinary resemblances and differences between parents and offspring—all these things depend largely on the arrangement and behavior of the genes. The genes in their arrangement and operation constitute a system comparable in importance to the nervous or digestive systems; we may call them the *Genetic System*. To understand heredity and its results we must have in mind a picture of the genetic system and its method of operation. To try to grasp these matters without such a picture is a hopeless task. As well may one attempt to understand the movements and reactions of organisms without a knowledge of their nervous and muscular systems; or to understand digestion, knowing nothing of the digestive organs and their action. Anyone who declines the labor of becoming familiar with the fundamental features of the genetic system and its method of operation cuts himself off from the possibility of understanding the nature of man and the origin of his peculiarities. To a presentation of that system and its action we therefore turn. A knowledge of many details is essential; here as nowhere else great results follow from small causes.

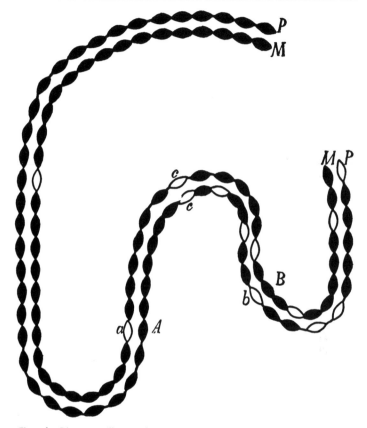

Figure b—Diagram to illustrate the arrangement and action of the genes in the genetic system. The genes, represented by the spindle-shaped bodies, arranged in consecutive order, in long paired strings, the chromosomes. One string (P) of the pair comes from the father, the other (M) from the mother. Thus the genes themselves are in pairs, one member of each pair from the father, one from the mother. The genes shown in white are to be conceived as defective genes.

(Reprinted by permission from "The Biological Basis of Human Nature" by H. S. Jennings.)

The genes are present in the nucleus of the cell with which the individual starts (and in all the cells produced from it). In the nuclei it is known that they are strung up in long strings, like strings of a thousand beads (see figure b). These strings are what are called the chromosomes. The separate chromosomes are pieces into which the total string of beads is divided; separate segments of it, each contain-

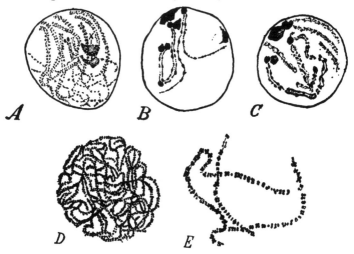

Figure c—Structure of chromosomes as seen under the microscope, showing the minute paired particles (chromomeres) of which they are composed. A, B, C, chromomeres in the chromosomes of the grasshopper, after Wenrich (1916). D, E, chromomeres in the chromosomes of the lily, after Belling (1928). E shows a portion of D at a higher magnification. The chromomeres probably show the position of the genes.

(Reprinted by permission from "The Biological Basis of Human Nature" by H. S. Jennings.)

ing many genes. At certain periods in the life of the cell the strings of genes are unfolded and widely drawn out; then it is that minute particles arranged in consecutive linear order like beads are visible under the microscope (figure c). It appears probable that these particles (known as *chromomeres*) show the position of the genes, if they are not to be looked on as themselves the genes. They show just the paired consecutive arrangement known to be that in which the genes occur. At other periods the strings of genes are coiled or folded into bundles; it is these that are seen as thick chromosomes of various forms (figure d). For an understanding of the behavior and effects of the genes, they must be pictured in linear order, as shown in the diagram of figure b.

It is known that each of the thousand genes is a distinctive substance, having a definite function, a particular work to do in producing the new individual; so that if any one of them is destroyed or changed, de-

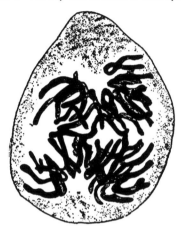

Figure d—Chromosomes in the condensed condition, in a dividing cell of the salamander, Amblystoma.

(Reprinted by permission from "The Biological Basis of Human Nature" by H. S. Jennings.)

velopment is altered in a definite way, and the resulting individual shows a corresponding change in his characteristics: a change perhaps in the color of his eyes, the shape of his nose, his stature; or in his temper or temperament.

It is known that each different kind of a gene has its regular and invariable place in the string. Thus the different genes can be named or numbered, and a particular one, as number 4 or number 47, is always the same gene, with the same rôle to play, and found at the same place in the chromosomes.

A further matter is known concerning the genes and their arrangement—a matter of extreme practical importance—a matter that is the key to many of the puzzles and problems and paradoxes of humanity, and of biology in general. This is the fact that each of our parents gives us a complete set of genes, strung up in the way we have described. So we have in every cell two such strings of genes, each one complete in itself, as represented in the diagram of figure b. We are therefore double with respect to our genes. Each of the two sets in a cell contains all the materials that are necessary for producing an individual; a fact that has strange consequences. The mother gives us all the materials required for producing an individual of a certain type; the father also gives us the materials for producing another individual of another type. So we start life as double individuals. We are each in a sense two individuals, two diverse persons—rather thoroughly blended; but in certain respects not completely blended. This doubleness has a very great effect on life.

The doubleness applies to each of the thousand diverse substances or genes with which we begin life. Each kind is present in every cell in two doses, forming a pair of genes. One gene from each pair is from the father, one from the mother. The order and arrangement of the genes is then that shown in figure b: a set of pairs arranged in longitudinal strings. In some animals, particularly certain insects, the two paired strings seemingly remain side by side during life, as indicated in the diagram. In others the two diverge at times, but become paired again at certain critical periods. For understanding the action of the genes, for understanding heredity, for understanding the nature of man, a picture of this paired arrangement (figure b) must be kept in mind; it is the key to many of the riddles of biology.

The different pairs of genes have different functions in development. The two members of any one pair of genes (as A and a, figure b) have the same general function. If one of the two has to do with producing the color of the eyes, so has its mate. If one has to do with building up some part of the brain, so has the other. If one influences the growth of the body, so does the other. But now a fact of extreme practical importance! Though the two members of a particular pair of genes have the same kind of work to do, they usually differ in the way they do that work. The one from the father may tend to produce a certain eye color, that from the mother to produce a different eye color. One from the father may tend to produce a poor brain and so a stupid individual; its mate from the mother may tend to produce a good brain, and so an intelligent individual. One of a pair may do its work well, another ill. One of the two genes of a pair (from father or mother) may be deficient or defective in some way. If its work is to lay down pigment in hair, skin and eyes, it may fail to do this properly, yielding what is called an albino, with white hair and skin and pink eyes. The other gene, from the other parent, may, however, perform the function fully, so that owing to its presence pigment is properly laid down. A certain gene may fail in laying a proper foundation for the brain; the result will be to produce a feeble-minded individual—unless there is also present, as its mate, a gene that performs fully this function. There are gene defects or deficiencies of every possible degree and kind, from slight differences in acuteness of senses, or in industry or patience, up to such serious defects as result in feeble-mindedness or insanity. It is rare, in organisms reproducing from two parents, for father and mother to give to any of the pairs genes exactly alike in their action. In any individual, therefore, many or most of the pairs will have the two genes somewhat diverse. Gene defects, or at least inequalities, slight or serious, are very common; so that every human being bears a few or many of them.

HOW THE BODY IS BUILT

As the original cell begins to divide, the new cells take on different forms and functions and shapes and are woven into different kinds of patterns (tissues).

Possibly you can understand better the job this parent cell finally performs if you think of yourself as being chemical and physical architect enough to build up a human being out of cells and the tissues formed from them. Obviously to do this job you would need four different kinds of cells and their products to form the four fundamental *tissues* of the body. These four fundamental tissues enter into various combinations to form every organ of the body, such as skin, heart, lungs, brain, muscles, stomach, glands.

(1) *Cells for Covering the Body and Lining All Openings:* In the first place you would want cells which you could weave into a membrane to cover the whole of the body—to form the outside layers of the skin. In places you would want to modify the cells in this tissue to form the nails of the fingers and toes and the hair and the teeth. In other places such as the glassy window of the

eye ball (the cornea) you would want to modify the cells of this
tissue so that they would admit light. Then you would want to
line all of the inside tubes and cavities, such as the whole of the
alimentary tract—mouth, back of throat, stomach, small intestines,
large intestines. You would want to line the blood-vessels and the
openings in the brain (ventricles and spinal canal). You would
want to form or weave these tissues into the structures we call
glands and to modify the cells again so that they would secrete
fluids—such as tears, sweat, wax, saliva, and dozens of other fluids
and chemicals which the body needs for its own use or which the
body must excrete or get rid of. Let us call the cells we use for these
purposes (1) epithelial cells, and the tissues they form *epithelial
tissue*. We shall see further on that we need very highly specialized
forms of these epithelial cells to furnish the sensitive element in
each of our sense organs. Fig. I shows some individual epithelial
cells and Fig. 2 a gland made up of them.

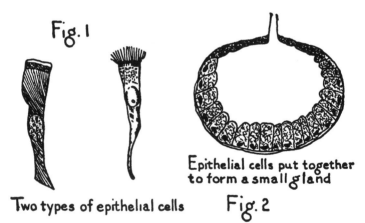

Fig. I

Two types of epithelial cells

Epithelial cells put together
to form a small gland

Fig. 2

(2) *Cells That Form Tissue for Supporting and Connecting
Bodily Parts:* You could not go very far in constructing man with
one type of cell and the tissue it forms. You would quickly need

strong tissue for tying the bodily parts together. You would want elastic tendons to attach muscles to. You would want strong cartilages to give form to your nose and to hold your windpipe open. During the embryonic (intra-uterine) life of your infant you would need sturdy framework upon which mineral salts could be deposited for forming bones (after the bones are formed by these deposits the connective-tissue framework disappears). You would want to sheathe your bones with a tough fibrous coating (*periosteum*) and to put buffers where bones come together and you would want very strong tough fibres (white fibro-cartilage) to tie the movable bones together. All of this supporting connective framework is made up of *connective-tissue* cells. The tissues themselves are called *connective tissues* (cartilage and bone, elastic, fibrous, areolar). Fig. 3 shows two connective-tissue cells that enter into the structure of the bones.

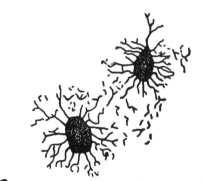

Connective tissue cells (osteoblasts)

Fig. 3

(3) *Cells That Form Our Muscular Tissues:* We would want to build our human so that it would go from place to place; so that its heart could beat and it could breathe; so that its stomach could

get smaller or larger, its blood vessels could expand or contract—
in other words, we need to provide locomotion for the body as a
whole and for changes in the shape and size of the hollow internal
organs (e. g. the stomach must vary considerably in size; the
blood vessels have to vary in size). To perform all of the varied
muscular functions of the body we need really two kinds of muscular cells and two kinds of tissue.

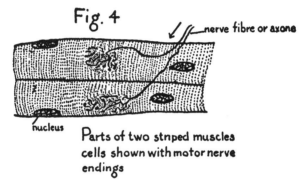

Fig. 4

nerve fibre or axone

nucleus

Parts of two striped muscles
cells shown with motor nerve
endings

(a) *Striped or Skeletal Muscle Cells and Striped Muscle Tissue:*
The striped muscle cells are on the average about 1/500 of an inch
in diameter. They are often an inch or more in length. The cells
are uniform throughout their length and there is no branching.[1]
The cell is made up of alternate dark and light stripes which run
across the length of the cell. This gives the cell its name—cross
striated or striped. Like all other cells, muscle cells are supplied
with a nucleus—usually with several nuclei. Over each cell is a
tough connective-tissue membrane (called sarcolemma). It usually takes hundreds and thousands of these cells to form a single

[1] In the heart we have striped muscle of a slightly different type. Here the individual
cells are short and show short intercommunicating branches. Since this type of muscle
is found only in the heart and is responsible for the rhythmic beat of the heart, we
shall have very little further to say about it. Hereafter where we speak of striped muscles
we shall mean (a) above.

muscle (striped muscle tissue). Over the muscles as a whole there is also a well marked connective-tissue sheath (called the *epimysium*). Intermixed with muscle one finds the blood vessels which feed them.

This is the way the great muscles such as the biceps of the arm, the muscles of the leg and trunk, tongue, the six big muscles that control the eye are made up. Our striped muscles are used whenever movement has to be rapid or where big masses have to be moved. Fig. 4 shows part of two individual striped muscle cells and the way the motor nerve fibres enter them.

Smooth muscle cell with a
nerve fibre entering it. The dark
portion in the center is the nucleus

Fig. 5

(b) *The Unstriped or Smooth Muscle Cells and Smooth Muscle Tissue:* The cells which go to make up the unstriped smooth muscle tissue are thin, elongated, almost hairlike structures. See Fig. 5. These cells are grouped into layers to form muscular coats. Unstriped muscular tissue forms the chief muscular coat of the stomach, intestines, the bladder, sex organs, the iris of the eye (for opening and closing of the pupil), the walls of ducts (tubes) leading from glands, and the arteries and veins.

The Nerve Cells and Nervous Tissue: We still need one other type of cell and the tissue formed from it to perfect our human being. The human animal (as well as all other higher vertebrates) must be able to respond quickly and complexly to stimuli. We know that stimuli are effective only when applied to an appropriate sense organ. We know that the animal must respond with

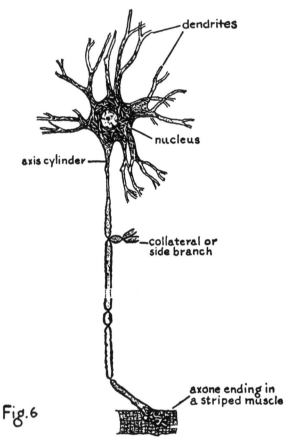

Fig. 6

One type of neurone—the lower motor neurone
(After Barker)

either striped or unstriped muscles, with glands, or with combinations of these. Oftentimes the point where the sensory stimulus is applied is very far distant from the point where the reaction takes place. For example, we may run a thorn into our foot. Immediately we stop, bend over with our trunk, grasp the thorn with our fingers and pull it out. This reaction could not take place unless we had specially differentiated and highly developed nerve cells with their processes—put together in such a way as to form an actual neural pathway extending from the skin of the foot into the spinal cord, then up the spinal cord to the brain, from the brain back to the spinal cord and from the spinal cord out to the muscles of the trunk, hand and fingers. Nerve cells and their processes are the only bodily structures capable of connecting sense organ with muscle in this speedy, intimate way.

So far as general structure goes, nerve cells are not very different from other cells in the body. Each nerve cell consists of a cell body with its outgrowths or processes—sometimes the processes are few in number; sometimes there are hundreds of them. If we take as our example a cell from the spinal cord (Fig. 6, p. 62) (so-

Fig. 7   nodes (of Ranvier)   axis cylinder
                                                      medullary sheath

A diagram of a part of a nerve fibre

The axis cylinder, consisting of a large number of very fine fibrils, makes up the center of the nerve fibre. The dark outside portion represents the medullary sheath. At certain definite intervals the medullary sheath is constricted. These constricted portions are called "nodes" (of Ranvier).

called lower motor neurone), we find a large cell body with a nucleus. Growing out from the cell we find short branches closely matted around the cell body. These are called *dendrites* because they look like the branches of a tree. At one point a slender fibre leaves the cell and extends for a longer or shorter distance (it may vary in length from the merest fraction of an inch to several feet). This slender process is called an axone or *axis-cylinder*. Often during its course it throws out side branches called *collaterals*. A fatty sheath (called the medullary sheath) clothes the whole of the axis-cylinder with its collaterals (for details of axone, see Fig. 7). This fatty sheath is not present on the dendrites. The whole structure so far described is the cell with its processes. The cell

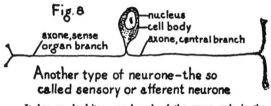

Fig. 8

nucleus
cell body
axone, central branch
axone, sense organ branch

Another type of neurone–the so called sensory or afferent neurone

It has no dendrites—one branch of the axone ends in the sense organ. The other branch ends in the central nervous system (brain or spinal cord).

with all of these processes is usually called a *neurone*. There are many forms of these cells, some with only a single process such as the afferent neurones of the spinal cord (those that connect the sense organs with the spinal cord—for details of this type of neurone see Fig. 8). The neurone is the unit of all nervous tissue such as we find the brain and spinal cord made up of.

The dendrites serve as receiving stations to pick up the various nerve impulses. The impulses pass through the cell body, down the axis-cylinder and the collaterals. The *axis-cylinder* of one neurone always ends by contact around the *dendrites* of another neurone (in neurones that lie wholly in the brain and cord). The neural impulse thus passes from cell body to axis-cylinder and down the axis-cylinder to the dendrites of the next neurone. *Thus there is always forward or one way conduction in the nervous system.*

THE PRINCIPAL ORGANS OF THE BODY

These Elementary Tissues Grouped Together Form the Various Organs of the Body: So far in our discussion we have talked only of cells and the elementary tissues they form. We must now take up some of the organs made up of these tissues. For our purposes we need to consider only a few: (1) The sense organs—where the various stimuli produce their effect on the body; (2) the reacting organs—the whole system of muscles and glands; (3) the nervous or conducting organs, that connect sense organs with reacting organs—they are the brain, spinal cord, and peripheral nerves. By peripheral nerves we mean nerves that run outside in the body from sense organs to brain and spinal cord, and nerves that leave the brain and cord to end (directly) in striped muscles and (indirectly) in smooth muscles and glands.

Your study of the elementary tissues already has taken you a long way toward understanding these organs. They are made up wholly of combinations of the four types of cells and their tissues which you have already studied. For example, in the muscular system you will find connective tissue covering each muscle cell, you will find epithelial tissue and nervous tissue. Let us spend a short time considering the general features in each of these groups of organs.

General Grouping of Organs or Structures: Let us first group the organs we are most in need of studying:

1. The *sense organs*—where the various stimuli produce their effect on the body.
2. The *reacting organs*—consisting of (a) the striped muscular system that moves the skeleton (and the heart); (b) the unstriped muscular system of the viscera; (c) glands.
3. The *nervous system*. It connects the sense organs with the reacting organs. It consists of the *brain, spinal cord* and the *peripheral nerves* which run from sense organs into brain

and spinal cord, and from brain and cord to muscles and glands.

The General Plan of the Sense Organs: The general plan of a sense organ is quite simple and almost uniform. Of course all sense organs contain connective tissue for giving them form—blood vessels for supplying them with nourishment, and muscular fibres of both the striped and unstriped for adjusting them for the reception of stimuli. All of them except sensory nerve endings in muscle and tendon contain epithelial tissue. All of them contain nervous tissue.

These epithelial cells in the sense organs are most astonishing structures, possibly the most interesting of the whole body. *They are sensitive* (in general) *only* to one form of stimulation (selectively sensitive). For example, the two types of epithelial elements in the eye sensitive to light are called *rods* and *cones;* see Fig. 9. The nervous connecting elements (true optic nerve) end around the rods and cones. In the ear there is a whole group of these specialized epithelial cells—(1) a cell that runs across the bony cavity of the inner ear (called basilar membrane fibre); (2) on this are to be found a pair of cells placed so as to form arches, called arches of Corti; (3) on either side of the arches of Corti there is a group of epithelial cells called *hair cells* (inner and outer row). It is around these hair cells that the nervous elements end (auditory nerve). This group of structures as a whole vibrates when a tone of a certain wave length is sounded (it is best not to attempt now to go into theories about the functioning of the ear). The muscle spindles (the sense organs in the muscles, see Fig. 10) act only when the muscle has been shortened or lengthened by the motor nerves; the taste buds act when a fluid (sapid substance) reaches them; the olfactory cells only when gaseous particles strike them; the semi-circular canals only when head movements disturb the fluids in the inner ear; the cells in the skin are selectively sensitive to (i. e. are stimulated by) several forms of stimuli—certain ones are stimulated by gentle touch (hairs, Meissner corpuscles); oth-

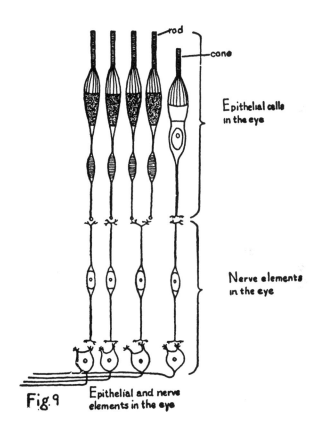

Fig. 9 Epithelial and nerve
elements in the eye

ers by sharp cuts, pricks, electric shocks (here of course the nerve endings may be directly stimulated); others are stimulated by

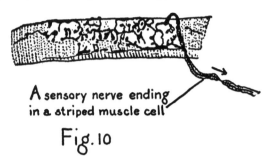

A sensory nerve ending
in a striped muscle cell

Fig. 10

warm objects; others by cold objects. Possibly still others by light stroking (called "tickling," "itching").

Let us conveniently group these facts:

	Sense organ:	*Stimulated by:*
(Visual sense)	Eye	Ether vibration
(Auditory sense)	Ear (cochlea) . . .	Air waves
(Olfactory sense)	Nose	Gaseous particles
(Gustatory sense)	Tongue	Sapid fluids
(Dermal sense—	Skin	
a—temperature		{ Warm objects { Cold objects
b—pressure		Contact with any object
c—pain)		Cutting, burning, pricking
(So-called kinaes- thetic sense)	{ Muscles . . . . { Tendons	Change in position of muscle Change in position of tendon
(Equilibration sense)	Ear (semi-circular canals)	Change in position of head

What happens when the appropriate stimuli strikes or impinges upon a given sense organ? *Some kind of physical and chemical change takes place in the epithelial cell.* Let us look upon these cells constituting the sense organs then as physico-chemical workshops. There are lots of simple things in your own experience that may help to make this clear: When light strikes a photographic plate it (the silver salts) turns black. When you take the damper off the strings of your piano and sing middle C the middle C string begins to "speak" without your having to touch the keyboard (so-called sympathetic vibration).

This physico-chemical process set going in the sense organ by the stimulus, starts another process going. *It sets up a neural impulse in the nerve ending which is in contact with the epithelial cell; this nervous impulse travels over a chain of neurones to the central nervous system (brain and spinal cord) and then out somewhere to a muscle or gland.*

We have now talked about the organs where stimuli produce their effect upon the body (sense organs or receptor organs). Let us now turn to the muscular and glandular organs which move in response to sense organ activity. Later, after finishing our study of the responding side of our body (muscles and glands—called effector organs) we will come back to the nervous system which forms the pathway or bridge between *sense organs* and *effector organs.*

ORGANS OF RESPONSE—MUSCLES AND GLANDS

Introduction: There are three major types of responding organs. They are: (1) the striped or skeletal muscular system; (2) the unstriped muscular system; (3) the glandular system. If it were not for these structures the body could not do anything—could not even take care of itself.

The skeletal muscles: The striped or skeletal muscular system upon the arms, legs or trunk, and you come immediately upon makes up the principal mass of our body. Strip away the skin layers and layers of striped muscles. The variety of arrangement seems endless and confusing and yet each muscle in this system has a definite task to do. Psychologists used to call these "voluntary muscles"—subject to the "will," but if you study their action you will soon discover that what you "will" to do is to raise your arm or crook your finger, to hop, run, or bend your trunk. Now a whole system of muscles responds when each of those acts is accomplished. The muscles always work in large groups. For example, you may reach up to pull down the window shade. You think of the arm and fingers as being the active moving members. But the muscles all over the body are taking part. The whole body has to take on a new *set* or *attitude* before you can do this simple act. The next moment you stoop over to pick up a pin. There is a rapid shift in the tension of every muscle of the body.

Function of the bones: No discussion of the skeletal muscles can be complete without some reference to the bones of the body with which the muscles collaborate so closely. In our body there are about 200 bones. Some of these bones form rigid joints with their neighbors—as the bones of the skull. Others form semi-mobile points capable of a small amount of movement—such as the bones encasing the spinal cord and our ribs. Still others, like the elbow joints, the knee, shoulder and hip are joined in such a way that movement in one direction or several directions is possible. Our striped muscles are attached to these bones by connective tissue (which we have already studied). Most of the muscles are attached at one end to one bone and at the other end (directly or through tendons) to a contiguous bone. They thus cross one joint and a lever is created. The principle of the lever is widely utilized in our bodily construction. Some of our movements require the whole body to be raised slowly a short distance, as when we stand on the ball of the foot and raise the body. Other movements require great speed through a wide arc as the movements of the arms in boxing.

Antagonism between muscular groups: Each of the muscles or muscle groups that tend to move our limbs in a given direction—e. g. to flex or bend the elbow (flexors)—has another opposed set of muscles which tend to extend the arm or keep it straight (extensors). Usually the muscles are kept under some slight tension due to motor impulses coming constantly from the brain or spinal cord. This is proven by the fact that when the belly of a resting muscle is cut across, the two ends draw away from each other. This tension in both a muscle and its antagonist tends to make our movements very fine and smooth. When the motor nerve impulse sent from the brain or cord results in raising the arm, the flexors contract (shorten); but at the same time there occurs a lessening of the tension in the antagonistic muscles. When a given muscular contraction has taken place the muscle gradually assumes its normal size and shape (relaxation).

How efficient are our muscles as working machines? Careful tests have shown that the muscular system as a machine for work is quite as efficient as the steam engine. The net efficiency as determined by the Nutrition Laboratory of the Carnegie Institution is given at slightly above 21%. The steam engine has a net efficiency of about 15–25%.

The food of the muscle: The well nourished muscle contains a quantity of stored food brought in by the blood. In the blood this food has the form of *blood sugar.* Muscle tissue has the power to convert this blood sugar into glycogen (so-called animal starch). This food stored in the muscle in the form of glycogen is gradually used up when the muscle goes into action. After this stored supply is used up, the muscle is dependent upon the blood sugar brought in by the blood for its further supply. The ductless glands help increase the food supply to the muscles as I shall show later.

Waste products and fatigue of muscle: As muscle work is done chemical changes take place in the muscle. Carbon dioxide is formed as are lactic and other acids. Many so-called "fatigue products" are formed. Finally the muscle can no longer do work. The ductless glands here also come to the aid of the muscles by neutralizing the fatigue products (and by increasing the blood supply of the working muscle so that fatigue products are more rapidly washed away). Probably the most important process in working is the using up of stored food material.

Muscle strain: A muscle which has been contracted until it can no longer do work will contract again after a short rest. The rest allows time for the blood to wash away fatigue products and to bring in a fresh food supply. If the muscle has been greatly over-exercised—strained—the period of recovery is very slow indeed. The muscle itself, however, is rarely injured by over-exercise beyond, at least, the point where repair can take place.

The effect of exercise: An unused muscle rapidly weakens and may even atrophy. Lack of exercise means lack of good circulation and lack of good circulation means a deficient supply of nutrition and insufficient elimination of waste products. All hygienists to-day recognize the importance of exercise in keeping the muscles in good condition. To the busiest men and women they recommend simple setting up exercises, to others more severe drills. To those with more leisure, outdoor games. To those who engage steadily in activities where a fixed group of muscles are used they recommend daily exercises which will call the other muscles of the body into play. Social institutions like life insurance companies and business organizations are providing facilities for regular muscular exercise. There is general recognition that the tone of the muscle which is heightened by exercise is conducive to the general well being of the body, especially of the all-important internal organs. There is little question that the heeding of the advice "to exercise often and sensibly" is helping to keep older men and women young for a much longer time than was formerly the case; and to keep even the younger men and women supple and graceful.

The behaviorist is especially interested in these facts because stressing the behavior side as he does he believes that supple, well nourished muscles, regardless of the absolute age of the individual, prolong the period of training—increase really the span of youth.

The system of plain or unstriped muscles: The smooth or plain unstriped muscles—that enter so largely into the formation of our internal organs—are less familiar than are the striped muscles. Before discussing them, let us get a clear picture of what we mean by *viscera*—a term which is playing an ever wider rôle in behavioristic psychology. *Changes in these organs often serve as stimuli to many of the major reactions of the whole body.* Often we can assign no verbal reason for a reaction. When this is the case the stimulus to that act probably must be sought for in the viscera (change in their shape or size or chemical condition).

Let us extend the usual meaning of viscera to include the *mouth*, the *pharynx*, the *oesophagus*, the *stomach*, the *small intestines*, the *large intestine*, the *heart*, the *lungs*, the *diaphragm*, the *arteries* and *veins*, the *bladder*, the *urinary* and *anal passages;* the *sex organs;* the *liver, spleen, pancreas, kidneys*, and all the other *glands* of the body. This is not a strictly scientific classification but we are in need of a term in psychology which will include all of our inside organs.

Smooth or plain muscle tissue dominates this field with the exception of the glands which I shall come to in a moment.[1]

Many of the visceral organs are hollow (they are sometimes called the hollow organs). These hollow organs are always filled or partially filled with something; stomach (food), lungs (air), heart, arteries and blood vessels (blood), small intestine (digested food undergoing absorption), large intestine (waste products on the way toward elimination), bladder (urine and other fluid wastes). This is one reason why the hollow organs are so important—they are always "quarreling" because they are too full or too empty—their contents are constantly in motion, constantly changing. Hence they are *constantly reacting* and each reaction sets up a *visceral stimulus* that may drive the whole body into action. Let me illustrate. The walls of the stomach are lined with several layers of plain muscle. When food is present producing normal extension of the stomach walls the muscles are quiet.

[1] Do not forget that in the viscera we also have connective tissue, epithelial tissue and nervous tissue. Smooth muscle tissue at least quantitatively dominates these organs.

Now in a few hours' time in the adult the food begins to pass into the small intestine. This leaves the stomach empty. Immediately it begins to contract rhythmically. These rhythmical contractions (called hunger contractions) make us search for food—men have been known to steal or even kill to get food. Fig. 11 shows the whole alimentary tract—mouth, stomach, small and large intestines. Fig. 12 shows a cross section of this tract at the level of the stomach.

The reverse process takes place in the bladder and in the colon —when these hollow organs get too full their distended walls serve as powerful stimuli to overt reaction—causing us to seek places where evacuation may take place. Distension of the seminal duct may lead to sex activity in the male.[1]

Fluttering of the heart, palpitation, dropping of beats of the heart, may lead to overt action—lack of oxygen, heat, cold, may lead to marked changes in the movements of our diaphragm and lungs.

It should be clear now that thousands of responses are going on in these smooth muscle organs every second. Every one of these visceral responses may also serve as a stimulus (since the viscera are lined also with *sense organ structures*) for calling out general bodily activity—i. e. they may start activity in the striped muscles.

Our "environment"—our world of stimuli—is thus not only one

[1] In the case of the female there seems to be no pressure or lack of pressure which leads to sex activity in the same way. But we know that in the females of many mammals there is seasonal rut and in the human female there is a menstrual period every lunar month. Probably in the case of the female there are certain chemical bodies released in the blood stream (from ductless glands) during the formation of the egg which may set up periodic changes in smooth muscles which may serve as stimuli to sex activity. I bring out these facts to show that the unconditioned stimulus to sex activity in the case of the female is probably much less definite than in the case of the male. There is probably thus a reason physiologically sound which will account for the difference in sex standards between the human male and female—a difference now not so clearly marked as in former times.

Please do not confuse the issue here between a conditioned response and an un-conditioned one. Both males and females become sex conditioned to visual, auditory and other stimuli. The sight of the male's hat may stir the woman as much as the bonnet may stir the male.

of external objects, sights, sounds and smells; it is one of internal objects as well—hunger contractions, bladder distensions, palpitating heart, rapid breathing, muscular changes and the like.[1]

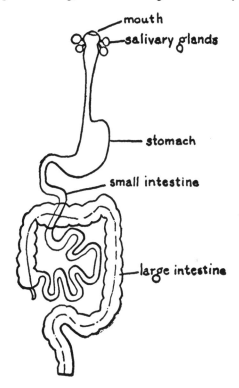

Diagram of alimentary tract

Fig. 11

[1] These powerful visceral stimuli have been called "drives" by a good many psychologists. This is becoming vitalistic in order to be dramatic. Professor R. S. Woodworth of Columbia has especially sinned in this direction.

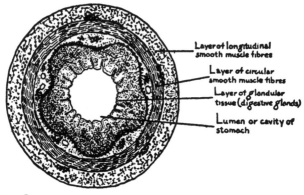

Diagram of cross section of stomach
Fig. 12

Smooth muscle fibres are important parts of the structure of non-hollow organs, e. g. the skin. Stimulation of them there arouses goose-flesh. Each hair has a smooth muscle attached to it. The function of this hair muscle can best be seen in the dog and cat when each sights an enemy. The hair on the back stands up straight. We find these fibres playing an important rôle in the eye —in adjusting the diameter of the pupil to the intensity of the light.

The physiology of plain muscle differs in many particulars from that of striped muscle. The main facts are alike. We have the phenomena of contraction, relaxation, latent period and summation.

In the next chapter we will talk about structures that are fast becoming of general popular interest—the glands.

IV. The Human Body, (CONTINUED)

WHAT IT IS MADE OF, HOW IT IS PUT TOGETHER, AND HOW IT WORKS

PART II. THE RÔLE THE GLANDS PLAY IN EVERYDAY BEHAVIOR

The *Glands as Reacting Organs:* One may not think at first of the glands as being of especial importance as reacting organs. But if I peel an onion in front of an adult or release tear gas near him, his eyes begin to drip water. Likewise if pain stimulation becomes intense, tears begin to flow. Tear responses may become conditioned—sad news may cause a copious flow of tears—the mere *sight* of the doctor may bring honest tears to the eyes of the three-year-old. This type of reaction, feigned or real, has saved many of us from just chastisement at the hands of our parents; has filled the tin cups of beggars and won many elections for politicians. Tears of females have more than once swayed the fate of empires.

If I place a subject in a hot room, the sweat glands in his skin begin to work; again his mouth may water, or become dry, owing to excess or deficient secretion of the salivary glands. *Glands are thus organs with which we behave*—they are important organs of reaction. They are closely associated with the viscera—they really form part of the visceral system. They are not primarily muscular organs (although some smooth muscle fibres may be present). I brought out the fact, you will remember, on page 58 that glands are really organs made up of highly specialized epithelial tissue. Instead of contracting as striped and smooth muscles do when they react, the glands *secrete.*

Duct Glands: Let us divide the glands into *duct* and *ductless glands*. Duct glands have a little opening or tube that leads from the gland to the outside of the body (e. g. the sweat glands) or that leads into the hollow viscera (e. g. the salivary glands). They secrete as a rule an appreciable quantity of one or another kind of fluid or solid (e. g. wax in the external ear). The whole of the alimentary tract is lined with small glands—all of the so-called mucous surfaces, the nasal passages, interior of mouth, throat, sex organs, are kept moist by means of the mucous glands.

Fig. 13

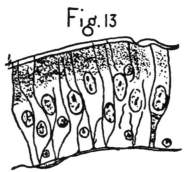

Epithelial cells put together
to form a lining tissue
for the intestines

Then there are many duct glands especially devoted to the digestion of our food. The salivary glands in the mouth give out a secretion that starts the process of digestion. In the stomach there are several different types of glands that continue the process of digestion. Again, nearby or in the small intestine are glands that give out secretions that pour into it to complete the process of digestion. Chief among these glands are the *pancreas* (secreting the pancreatic juice); *glands in the walls of the intestine* (gland cells lining the intestine are shown in Fig. 12); and the *liver* (secreting bile). One of the large glands of the body is the *kidney* which secretes urine.

The unconditioned stimuli that start glandular action are of sense organ origin. In other words, *secretion responses* (one form of behavior) are aroused in the same way that motor responses are aroused (through sense organ stimulation).

Even after this short survey of the duct glands, one must admit that secretion responses are of the utmost importance in human behavior. Our so-called higher forms of behavior are terribly at the mercy of these lowly secretions, especially when something goes wrong with one or more of them. Let the mouth glands begin to over-secrete or under-secrete, as happens at times; or the small mucous glands begin to over-secrete as they do in the nose when we have a cold; let something go wrong with the digestive secretions, or let the throat become irritable and sensitive through lack of secretions; let the kidney over-secrete and keep the bladder overly full, or the secretions from the sex organs become excessive —then our whole conduct may become modified. Even our social behavior may become involved. We may insult or hurt the feelings of a friend, spoil a piece of fine work, even lose our jobs, and, what is worse, if the faulty glands are deep down in the visceral cavity we may be able to give no verbal account of what has gone wrong. I shall return later to a discussion of this lack of ability to put anything in words about visceral and glandular behavior on page 259.

The Ductless Glands (*sometimes called endocrine organs*): During recent years, physiology and medicine have devoted a great deal of effort and thought to the exceedingly interesting and elusive structures we call ductless glands. The duct glands pour out their secretions through an opening, as we have just seen. These secretions are largely *local* in their action. Again relatively large measurable amounts of the secretions are poured out.

The situation is quite different with the ductless glands. While the organ may be very large, e. g. the thyroid, the secretions from it are minute—too small to be collected or directly measured by any known physiological method.

Again these glands have no external opening. How do their products get out into the body? Look upon these (closed or duct-less) glands as a chemical laboratory—each manufacturing a powerful compound or chemical body (some of which we now know) but in minute quantities. As the blood bathes the cells of these glands, it takes up the chemical bodies and carries them to other organs, sometimes remotely removed from the place where the gland gave rise to the secretion. These minute chemical bodies have the power to stir up activity in many other organs of the body. We have a name for these ductless gland secretions—*hormones*—which means literally something to arouse or to stir up. Hormones, then, are the chemical messengers which the glands send to arouse or depress activity in another part of the body (very often it is another ductless gland that is aroused or checked).[1] Everything that we know about ductless gland secretions points to the fact that they act *like drugs upon the body*. They play a vitally important rôle both in the general nutrition of the body and in its growth. They likewise play an extremely important part in the general behavior of human beings, as we shall soon see.

The most important Endocrine Glands: The most important ductless glands are: (1) *The thyroids* and *parathyroids;* (2) the *adrenal bodies;* (3) the *pituitary bodies;* (4) the *pineal body;* (5) the so-called *puberty gland*. There are several other glands that furnish internal secretions, as well as external secretions, such as the pancreas, liver, thymus and others, but the above five are the important ones.

The Thyroid Gland: The thyroid gland in men is located along each side of the windpipe just below the Adam's apple. It is located at the corresponding level in women. It is a fairly large gland. There are two lobes to it connected by a bridge that crosses in front

---

[1] Sometimes the ductless gland secretions which depress activities in other organs are called *chalones*.

of the windpipe. It is made up largely of specialized epithelial cells. It has no duct. It is richly supplied with blood vessels and with nerve fibres which run directly to the secreting gland cells.

In this workshop a most powerful chemical body is secreted. This chemical body has been experimentally isolated and can now be made in the laboratory. It is called *thyroxin*. It contains 60% iodine.

Effect of thyroid secretion upon growth: If a child is born with deficient or faulty thyroid apparatus it becomes a *Cretin:* growth is arrested and stunted, bones fail to become hard (incomplete ossification), the skin becomes thick and dry and the hair dry and colorless, the reproductive organs fail to develop. General behavior is markedly affected. Only the simplest things can be learned. Age improves its condition not at all. It remains infantile in all of its reactions.

If the thyroid is removed from the adult because of disease there is no change in stature but the other disturbing symptoms occur— the pasty, clammy appearance of the skin, the dry, falling hair. The individual rapidly puts on weight. General activity becomes low.

Thanks to modern advances in physiological science, relief from this condition can often be obtained both by the adult and by the child. Indeed, normal growth can often be restored in the child by feeding it the dried thyroid gland of sheep or by feeding at stated intervals a small amount of thyroxin. In both cases feeding of this substance must continue throughout life.

Sometimes the gland is overdeveloped and gives out an over-secretion. The body then works too fast—at too high a level. All vital processes are speeded up (Graves' disease). Blood pressure becomes high, the heart speeds up in its action. The individual shows general overactivity, irritableness, oftentimes insomnia. Formerly surgical treatment was resorted to in such cases—part of the gland was removed. Now "special care and feeding" are more often resorted to. Iodine-free diet is prescribed—as are rest and freedom from occupational strain.

In general it may be said that the thyroid seems to act as a kind of governor for the whole body. If it over-secretes every cell in the body speeds up its action. If it under-secretes every cell in the body slows down its rate.

Is it any wonder that all behaviorists are interested in everything the physiologist can teach us about this gland?

The Parathyroid Glands: Situated close to each lobe of the thyroid, and sometimes imbedded in it, are two little structures about the size of a pea (four structures in all). These structures are made up of solid masses of specialized epithelial cells. The positive functions of the parathyroids are still in the realm of speculation, but we know what happens when these glands are removed. Occasionally when removing diseased thyroids in man the parathyroids are accidentally excised. Their complete removal brings death both in man and in practically all other mammals. Following their loss the animal shows muscular tremor—then spasms, uncoördinated contractions, a rise in body temperature, rapid gasping respiration, vomiting and diarrhoea. Finally death ensues. It is now believed that the parathyroids give rise to a *secretion which tends to keep in check or restrain overactivity of the nervous system (restrains the discharge of nerve cells).* Secretions from this gland seem also to exert some influence upon the deposits of calcium for the bony tissue and the formation of the teeth. In a few cases young animals have survived the removal of these glands for several weeks. These animals showed poorly formed bones and poorly formed teeth. Extract of parathyroid (made from dried parathyroids of sheep) help to keep animals alive which have suffered removal of the glands, but no satisfactory way of keeping such animals alive for any length of time has been found. The chemical body given out by these glands has never been isolated.

The Adrenal Bodies or Glands: The adrenal glands, of which there are two (left and right) lie very close to the kidneys. Death follows the removal of both glands. After removal of both, the animal begins to show signs of muscular weakness. The body temperature drops, the heart beat becomes slow. Death usually occurs by the end of the third day.

The active secretion from this gland (that is from one portion of it—the medulla) has been chemically isolated by Abel at the Johns Hopkins Hospital, and others. It is called *epinephrin,* or *adrenin.*

Under emotional excitement relatively large quantities of adrenin are released and find their way into the blood vessels. It is during strong emotional excitement ("fear," "rage" and "pain") that we find great and long continued muscular effort exhibited.

The reason for this increase in the muscular output in the presence of exciting stimuli is to be sought for in the following factors: I showed on page 71 that there is a stored food supply in the liver called *glycogen.* We have just seen that under emotional excitement there is an increased supply of adrenin in the blood. Now adrenin has the power to split up the glycogen in the liver and set it free in the blood stream in the form of blood sugar. The blood sugar is carried to the working muscles giving them a readily utilizable food supply. The free adrenin in the blood also causes the arteries to expand and pour through the working muscles a larger and faster stream of blood. This has the additional effect of rapidly washing out the fast accumulating waste products that come from the working muscles. Professor Cannon, of Harvard, whose discovery this is, claims that this adrenal gland mechanism which makes the animal fight harder and longer, run faster and farther, has been of great biological service to man in his struggles with a hostile environment.

The Pituitary Body: This very small body is situated underneath the brain. If you make a small opening in the back part of the roof of the mouth, you come upon it just before you reach the brain. It is made up of a *posterior division* and an *anterior division.* Each of its divisions must be looked upon as a separate gland each giving rise to a characteristic hormone (or possibly several).

The Anterior Division or Lobe: If the anterior division (or lobe) is removed, death occurs within a very few days. There is a fall in body temperature, unsteadiness in gait, emaciation and diarrhoea. When, owing to disease early in life, the anterior portion begins to over-secrete, there comes a peculiar development of the whole body known as *gigantism* (one can see these overgrown giants in circuses). When the over-secretion occurs in later life there is very great enlargement of the bones of the face and of the hands and feet (acromegaly).

No one has yet succeeded in chemically isolating this hormone. Extracts made from the dried anterior portion of the pituitary seem to have very little effect. There can be no doubt from all of the medical evidence we have that the secretions from the anterior portion exert a profound effect upon the growth of the skeleton and upon the growth of the connective tissue of the body.

The Posterior Division or Lobe: Removal of the posterior lobe does not produce death but it brings about a very marked change in metabolism (the way food is handled by the body). The body becomes very tolerant of sugars. Fat is taken on rapidly. When the posterior lobe is removed in young animals the growth of the sex glands is arrested and the animal becomes almost like a eunuch in behavior.

While the chemical bodies set free by the posterior gland have not been isolated, extracts of the dried gland when administered produce a marked effect. The heart is slowed and the blood pressure is raised (an effect somewhat similar to that of adrenin). The main effect can be seen in the *increased tone that comes to all unstriped muscles.* It has an especially marked effect in causing the muscles of the uterus to contract (used frequently in hastening childbirth). Extracts from this portion have a distinctly stimulating effect upon the kidneys and upon the mammary glands. Like adrenin again the extract hastens the process of breaking up the stored glycogen in the liver, thus releasing it in the form of blood sugar for the use of active muscles.

The Pineal Gland: This is a very small gland situated in the brain itself. It reaches its most active stage of development about the seventh year and then begins to atrophy. The glandular tissue gradually disappears. It is supposed that this gland furnishes a secretion early in life which holds the development of the sex organs in check until puberty. It shares this function with the *thymus*— another ductless gland in the neck which also gradually disappears around puberty or even earlier.

The So-Called Puberty Gland: The sex glands in addition to furnishing the external secretions for reproduction, furnish also a ductless gland secretion or hormone. The cells furnishing the external secretion are called gonads (true sex cells). Lying among the sex cells or gonads are numbers of small cells called *interstitial cells*. The latter cells furnish the ductless gland secretion or hormone that gets into the blood and is distributed all over the body. This group of interstitial cells makes up the so-called puberty gland. This gland is much in the public and medical eye. All of the so-called *rejuvenation operations* are concerned with it.

If this gland (or rather this group of interstitial cells) is removed in the male youth, as it always has to be when castration occurs (removal of testes), the youth grows to be tall, the face is beardless, the voice never deepens. There is no sex aggressiveness. The effect of castration upon the female (removal of ovaries) is not so marked as in the case of the male.

The evidence is growing that it is the removal of the hormones coming from the puberty glands which robs the castrated individual of sex aggressiveness and all positive forms of sex behavior, rather than the removal of the gonads or true sex cells.

In other words the *hormone coming from the puberty glands* seems to activate the whole sex life of both male and female. Lacking this hormone there is a lack of sex vigor and what we call youthfulness of sex life.

This has led to the thought, in recent years, that there may be a way of restoring sex life to older men and women by operative methods. The one method—that of Dr. Serge Voronoff of Paris

—is to graft into the old male small pieces of testes from a young hardy animal of the same (or closely allied) species. He claims that the graft "takes"—i. e. lives, and begins to send its hormone out into the blood, restoring sex aggressiveness and sex vitality. You can see that no matter in what part of the body the gland tissue is grafted, it has to give out its secretion to the blood and thus give sex tone to all the necessary tissues of the body. The question whether such a rejuvenated old individual could impregnate the female would depend upon whether the gonads or true sex cells remained functional or not—upon the presence of live sperm in the testes. At any rate erection would take place and an orgasm would occur (the essentials of the male sex act). Sex life would thus be prolonged.

Another operation for increasing the production of the ductless gland hormone from the puberty gland is employed by Steinach, the Viennese surgeon. He finds that if the tube carrying the spermatozoa (the cell passing from the male that fertilizes the female egg) is tied off so that the spermatozoa cannot escape, it causes the true sex cells to atrophy,[1]—*but not the interstitial* cells. These increase in size and in number apparently—thus causing an increase in their activity. Males having lost sex vigor when operated upon in this way have apparently a renewal of their sex life. They are sterile, of course, because the spermatozoa do not form nor could they get out if they did form.

It is too early yet to forecast the real effects upon society of these attempts to prolong the period of the sex life. The effects of these operations, or the allied ones, on the female are still very much in doubt. In the case of the male we know little yet of their permanency. If the chemical body constituting the hormone could be experimentally isolated and if it were found that it could exert its effect when taken through the mouth as does thyroxin, it might

[1] Some physiologists claim that the gonads (sex cells) do not atrophy when the vas (duct) is tied off.

considerably alleviate the inferiorities and anxieties of advanced middle age.

Can the Activity of Ductless Glands be Conditioned? We saw in our study of the other reacting organs, the striped and unstriped muscles and the *duct* glands, that their activity could be conditioned—i. e. that habits could be set up in them. No secure evidence is at hand to show that the *activity* of ductless glands can be conditioned. Since these hormones act like powerful drugs—since they control growth and development and regulate the speed at which the body runs—it is of utmost importance to know whether or not they are conditioned. If they are, society is more than ever under obligation to watch carefully the early home training of the infant and child. Too much or too little of these secretions or a lack of balance of secretions may even prevent the possibility of the child's developing along normal behavior lines.

While experimental proof is lacking, I for one am convinced that these glands can be and always are conditioned. We know that unconditioned stimuli arousing the reactions we call fear and rage (e. g. where cats are tied down and harried and worried by a barking dog) bring about an increase of adrenin. We now know that fear and rage behavior can be conditioned. We have some reason, too, to think that the thyroid is directly thrown into activity by unconditioned sex stimuli and since we know that positive sex behavior can be conditioned we have good theoretical grounds for holding that thyroid activity can be conditioned. The evidence is fair for holding *that in the whole bodily process we call conditioning the ductless glands are intimately involved—that conditioned stimuli may bring about both over-secretion (hyperactivity) and under-secretion (hyposecretion) of the ductless glands.*

This may explain in part why it is that psychopathological disturbance of behavior may result from constant contact with an environment in which a multitude of unfortunate conditioned stimuli are ever assailing us, and why it is that we very often get well as soon as we straighten out that environment or else get away from it. Sometimes we carry the old environment along with us to the new environment by means of our *verbal organization*. There is thus a good reason when going into the new environment for us to build up new activities with new verbalization—letting the old world of overt activity die out and the old words lose their hold upon us by the well known process we call *disuse*. Many a youthful psychopath and many a youthful criminal have been reclaimed in this way—even when we were working blindly and without any clear plan as to what we hoped to accomplish. I think that it is becoming possible now to work more definitely along these lines, especially in the field of childhood—with the difficult child—with the youthful criminal.

Résumé: We started out in these two chapters on the body to study the elementary cells and the elementary tissues they form. We then took up the *organs* formed by these tissues. We found that there are sense organs—where the stimuli are applied. We found that there are reacting organs—striped muscles, unstriped muscles, duct glands and ductless glands. But there is one more set of organs—the *conducting organs*—the nervous system. *Its function is to conduct a nervous impulse from the sense organs over to the reacting organs—the muscles and the glands. To do this there must be an actual chain of nerve cells (and their fibres) running from each sense organ to the central nervous system (the brain and spinal cord) and out from the central nervous system to the muscles and glands.* Before finishing our study of the body let us look for a moment at this enormously important part of our body.

How the Nervous System is Made Up: On page 63 we described the nerve cells and their fibres, the individual neurones that make up the nervous system. The nervous system is made up of these neurones placed together in such a way as to form actual permanent pathways from sense organs to reacting organs—the central organs of the brain and spinal cord form no exception to this rule since we must look upon them as just a part of the system of pathways running from sense organs to reacting organs. Naturally in the nervous system as a whole and especially in the brain and spinal cord there are supporting structures—connective-tissue membranes—blood vessels.

The Simplest Pathway From Sense Organ to Reacting Organ—The Short Reflex Arc: The simplest functional pathway from a sense organ to a reacting organ is called a *short reflex arc.* Sup-

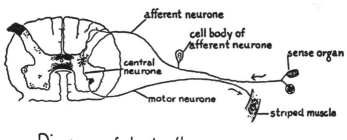

Diagram of short reflex arc

Fig 14

pose the tip of my finger is burnt as my hand touches an electric flat-iron which has been left standing with the current on! Immediately before "ouch!" or some swear word can be spoken the hand is jerked back—reflexly jerked back so we say. Only three neurones (theoretically) are involved in this act—one extending from the skin to the spinal cord—the so-called *afferent* neurone; one inside the spinal cord (and which does not run outside of the cord) called the *central* neurone; one extending from the spinal cord to the muscles of the hand, called the *motor* neurone. There are hundreds of thousands of these simple direct short reflex pathways. There are many thousands of them connecting the skin alone with the reacting organs. These afford a direct connection—a segmental arrangement—for getting prompt response to dangerous stimuli.

The Long Reflexes: No matter how complicated the pathway for the neural impulse may be, two elements of the above described short reflex arc are always involved—viz: the afferent neurone running from sense organ to cord or brain (please note now that the brain is connected with some of the sense organs by these short reflex arcs, e. g. the eye, ear, nose, tongue, semi-circular canals, the skin of the head and face, and indeed with some of the sense organ structures in the viscera and striped muscles); and the motor neurone running from the cord or brain to the muscles and glands. Whenever we respond to a stimulus these two elements of the reflex arc are always involved.

Now the longer and more complicated neural pathways are made longer and more complicated by the fact that sometimes *more than one central neurone is included in the arc. Sometimes the pathway in the cord and brain is very complicated.* Suppose this reaction is demanded of us: I go downstairs to find a pencil in the dark. I left it lying on the library table. I reach out my hand; it strikes something round and smooth. I feel for its point; it has none. I say aloud: "My oldest boy's pea-shooter." I drop it and continue my search. I come upon another round object. It has a point. I touch the other end. It has no eraser on it. I say again: "This is a stick belonging to the baby's meccano set." I drop it and search further. Finally I come upon a round object; it is pointed; it has an eraser on it. I grasp it, turn upon my heels and go upstairs and begin to write. Notice that this kind of response involves a wide range of adjustments: muscles of hands, legs and trunk are all called into action; earlier learned speech reactions are called into play; more than one segment of the body is involved; many segments have to coöperate, to function together. There is *integration* —a tying up of one bodily part with another. *For this process of integration we need a central nervous system*—something more than an open connection between some sense organ point and a single set of muscles—we need a complicated system of neural pathways—we need a brain and spinal cord.

Nature of Nervous Impulse: What is it that passes over the neural pathways? A *neural impulse* that starts in the chemical workshop of the sense organ. By nature it is something like a series of local electric currents (one would scientifically describe it as a rapid passage of a wave of chemical decomposition essentially electrical in nature). We know that it travels at a rate of about 125 metres per second. We know further that if the nerve elements are deprived of oxygen they will not conduct the impulse—we know that when the nervous elements are actively at work they give off CO_2 (carbon dioxide) more rapidly than when at rest. While we do not know everything about the nature of the nervous impulse we know enough to be sure that it is a normal physico-chemical process that is rapidly losing its mysteriousness by being brought under laboratory control.

Summary: Let us now recapitulate in a hundred words or so the principal results of our study of the body: The body is built of cells and their products. These cells are woven into elementary tissues and the tissues are built up into larger structures, organs, each possessing a certain unity and performing definite functions. One such group of organs is (1) the sense organs—skin, eye, ear, nose, etc. (don't forget that some of the sense organs are hidden from the direct observation—e. g. those in the muscles and tendons and those in the viscera); another set is (2) the reacting organs—the striped or skeletal muscles; the unstriped muscles and glands (making up largely the viscera). A third set is (3) the connecting organs, namely, the nervous system consisting of nerve paths running from sense organ to brain or cord and from brain or cord to the reacting organs—and please do not forget that there are very complicated, but not mysterious, pathways in the brain and cord themselves. The whole body of man is built around the keynote "rapid—and when needed, complicated—reactions to simple and complex stimuli."

In the next chapter we shall study some of man's *unlearned embryological reactions*—some of the things he does in advance of training—some of the things he does just because he comes here equipped to behave in that way. We used to call such reactions *instincts*. We seriously doubt now that they are "inborn" and "native" reactions. They apparently grow up (modifying the structure as they grow up, just as exercise structurally modifies the blacksmith's arm and whole body) as a result of the complicated stimuli that are offered throughout intra-uterine life.

V. Are There Any Human Instincts?

PART I. ON THE SUBJECT OF TALENT, TENDENCIES AND THE
INHERITANCE OF ALL SO-CALLED "MENTAL" TRAITS

INTRODUCTION:—In the next four chapters we shall try to find
out how man is equipped to behave at birth—a subject that
touches the very heart of human psychology.

When the array of facts about any subject is not very complete
it is customary to announce a thesis, that is, state what one is going to try to prove and then try to prove it by a logical argument.
We are all in that position today about man's equipment at birth.
We have not the full complement of facts about the so-called "instinctive" nature of man; hence, please look upon the next few
chapters both as logical presentations of what facts there are in
the case and as a thesis which the behaviorist is trying to defend.
I shall present the behaviorist's thesis first.

THE THESIS PRESENTED

Man is an animal born with certain definite types of structure.
Having that kind of structure, he is forced to respond to stimuli at
birth in certain ways (for example: breathing, heart beat, sneezing,
and the like. A fairly full list will be given later on). This repertoire of responses is in general the same for each of us. Yet there exists a certain amount of variation in each—the variation is probably merely proportional to the variation there is in structure
(including in structure, of course, chemical constitution). It is
probably the same repertoire now that it was when the *genus homo*

first appeared many millions of years ago. Let us call this group of reactions man's *unlearned behavior*.

In this relatively simple list of human responses there is none corresponding to what is called an "instinct" by present-day psychologists and biologists. There are then for us no instincts—we no longer need the term in psychology. Everything we have been in the habit of calling an "instinct" today is a result largely of training —belongs to man's *learned behavior*.

As a corollary from this we draw the conclusion that there is no such thing as an inheritance of *capacity, talent, temperament, mental constitution* and *characteristics*. These things again depend on training that goes on mainly in the cradle. The behaviorist would *not* say: "He inherits his father's capacity or talent for being a fine swordsman." He would say: "This child certainly has his father's slender build of body, the same type of eyes. His build is wonderfully like his father's. He, too, has the build of a swordsman." And he would go on to say: "—and his father is very fond of him. He put a tiny sword into his hand when he was a year of age, and in all their walks he talks sword play, attack and defense, the code of duelling and the like." A certain type of structure, plus early training—*slanting*—accounts for adult performance.

THE ARGUMENT IN ITS DEFENSE

Let us start by saying that from now on man for us is a *whole animal. When he reacts he reacts with each and every part of his body.* Sometimes he reacts more strongly with one group of muscles and glands than with another. We then say he is doing something. We have named many of these acts such as breathing, sleeping, crawling, walking, running, fighting, crying. But please do not forget that each of these named acts involves the whole body.

We must begin, too, to think of man as a mammal—a primate— a two-legged animal with two arms and two delicate mobile hands.

As an animal that has a nine-month embryonic life, a long helpless infancy, a slowly developing childhood, eight years of adolescence and a total life span of some three score years and ten.

We find this animal living in the tropics almost without shelter; going naked, living upon easily caught animals and upon fruit and herbs that require no cultivation. We find him in temperate regions, but dwelling here in well built, steam heated houses. We find the male always heavily clad even in summer, wearing a hat upon his head—the only naturally protected part of his body. We find the female of this species dressed in the scantiest of clothes. We find the male working frantically (the female rarely) at almost every kind of vocation, from digging holes in the ground, damming up water like beavers, to building tall buildings of steel and concrete. Again we find man in Arctic regions, clad in furs, eating fatty foods and living in houses built of snow and ice.

Everywhere we find man, we find him doing the strangest things, displaying the most divergent manners and customs. In Africa we find the blacks eating one another; in Southern China we find men eating rice and throwing it towards the mouth with dainty chopsticks. In other countries we find man using a metal knife and fork. So widely different is the adult behavior of the primitive Australian bushmen from that of the dwellers in internal China, and both of these groups differ so widely in behavior from the cultivated Englishman, that the question is forced upon us—*Do all members of the species homo wherever they are found in biological history start at birth with the same group of responses and are these responses aroused by the same set of stimuli?* Put in another way, is the *unlearned,* birth equipment of man, which we have been in the habit of calling *instincts,* the same wherever he is found, be it in Africa or in Boston, be it in the year six million B. C. or in 1930 A. D.? Has he the same unlearned equipment, whether born in the cotton fields of the South, in the Mayflower or beneath the silken purple quilts of European royalty?

THE GENETIC PSYCHOLOGIST'S ANSWER

The genetic psychologist—the student best qualified to answer this question—hates to be faced with it because his data are limited. But since he is forced to answer he can give his honest conviction. His answer is, "Yes, within the limits of individual variation, all men are born alike regardless of the station of their parents, regardless of the geological age in which they are born and regardless of the geographical zone in which they are born."

But one may say: "Is there nothing in heredity—is there nothing in eugenics—is there no advantage in being born an 'F. F. V.'— has there been no *progress* in human evolution?" Let us examine a few of the questions which excite so many people almost to the point of combat.

Certainly black parents will bear black children if the line is pure (except possibly once in a million years or so when a sport or "mutant" is born which theoretically may be white, yellow or red). Certainly the yellow skinned Chinese parents will bear a yellow skinned offspring. Certainly Caucasian parents will bear white children. But these differences are relatively slight. They are due among other things to differences in the amount and kind of pigments in the skin. It would be very difficult to take these infants at birth, study their behavior, and mark off differences in behavior that would characterize white from black and white or black from yellow. There will be differences in behavior but the burden of proof is upon the individual, be he biologist or eugenicist who claims that these racial differences are greater than the individual differences.

Again one hears the question: "How about children born from parents who have large hands, with short stiff fingers, extra fingers or toes? It can be shown that children from these parents inherit these peculiarities of structure." Our answer is: Yes, thousands of variations are laid down in the germ plasm and will always appear (other factors being equal) in the offspring. Other inheritances are color of hair, color of eyes, texture of skin, Albinism (very light individuals with little or no pigment in hair and eyes—vision always being defective). The biologist, knowing the makeup of the parents and grandparents, can predict many of even the finer structural characteristics of the offspring.

So let us hasten to admit—yes, there are heritable differences in form, in structure. Some people are born with long slender fingers, with delicate throat structure; some are born tall, large, of prizefighter build; others with delicate skin and eye coloring. These differences are in the germ plasm and are handed down from parent to child. More questionable is the inheritance of such things as the early or late graying of hair, the early loss of hair, the span of life, the bearing of twins, and the like. Many of these questions have already been answered by biologists and many others are in the process of being answered. But do not let these undoubted facts of inheritance lead us astray as they have some of the biologists. The mere presence of these structures tells us not one thing about function. This has been the source of a great deal of confusion. Much of our structure laid down in heredity would never come to light, would never show in function, unless the organism were put in a certain environment, subjected to certain stimuli and forced to undergo training. Our hereditary structure lies ready to be shaped in a thousand different ways—the same structure—depending on the way in which the child is brought up. To convince oneself, measure the right arm of the blacksmith, look at the pictures of strong men in our terrible magazines devoted to physical culture. Or turn to the poor bent back of the ancient bookkeeper. These people are structurally shaped (within limits) by the kinds of lives they lead.

ARE "MENTAL" TRAITS INHERITED?

But every one admits this about bone and tendons and muscles —"now how about mental traits? Does the behaviorist mean to say that great talent is not inherited? That criminal tendencies are not inherited? Surely we can prove that these things can be inherited." This was the older idea, the idea which grew up before we knew as much about what early shaping throughout infant life will do as we now know. The question is often put in specific form: "Look at the musicians who are sons of musicians; look at Wesley Smith, the son of the great economist, John Smith—surely a chip off the old block if ever there was one." The behaviorist recognizes no such things as mental traits, dispositions or tendencies. Hence, for him, there is no use in raising the question of the inheritance of talent in its old form.

Wesley Smith was thrown into an environment early in life that fairly reeked with economic, political and social questions. His attachment for his father was strong. The path he took was a very natural one. He went into that life for the same reason that your son becomes a lawyer, a doctor, or a politician. If the father is a shoemaker, a saloonkeeper, or a street cleaner—or is engaged in any other socially unrecognized occupation, the son does not follow so easily in the father's footsteps, but that is another story. Why did Wesley Smith succeed in reaching eminence when so many sons who had famous fathers failed to attain equal eminence? Was it because this particular son inherited his father's talent? There may be a thousand reasons, not one of which lends any color to the view that Wesley Smith inherited the "talent" of his father. Suppose John Smith had had three sons who by hypothesis all had bodies so made up anatomically and physiologically that each could put on the same organization (habits) as the other two.[1] Suppose further that all three began to work upon economics at the age of six years. One was beloved by his father. He followed in his father's footsteps and due to his father's tutorship this son overtook and finally surpassed his father. Two years after the birth of Wesley, the second son was born; but the father was taken up with the elder son. The second son was beloved by the mother who now got less and less of her husband's time, so she

[1] And by this statement we do *not mean that their genetic constitution is identical.*

devoted her time to the second son. The second son could not follow so closely in the footsteps of his father; he was influenced naturally by what his mother was doing. He early gave up his economic studies, entered society and ultimately became a "lounge lizard." The third son, born two years later, was unwanted. The father was taken up with the eldest son, the mother with the second son. The third son was also put to work upon economics, but receiving little parental care, he drifted daily towards the servants' quarters. An unscrupulous maid had taught him to masturbate at three. At twelve the chauffeur made a homosexual of him. Later falling in with neighborhood thieves he became a pickpocket, then a stool-pigeon and finally a drug fiend. He died of paresis in an insane asylum. There was nothing wrong with the heredity of any one of these sons. All by hypothesis had equal chances at birth. All could have been the fathers of fine, healthy sons if their respective wives had been of good stock (except possibly the third son *after* he contracted syphilis).

Objectors will probably say that the behaviorist is flying in the face of the known facts of eugenics and experimental evolution —that the geneticists have proven that many of the behavior characteristics of the parents are handed down to the offspring—they will cite mathematical ability, musical ability, and many, many other types. Our reply is that the geneticists are working under the banner of the old "faculty" psychology. One need not give very much weight to any of their present conclusions. We no longer believe in faculties nor in any stereotyped patterns of behavior which go under the names of "talent" and inherited "capacities."

DIFFERENCES IN STRUCTURE AND DIFFERENCES IN EARLY TRAINING WILL ACCOUNT FOR ALL DIFFERENCES IN LATER BEHAVIOR

We have already asserted that even though there is individual variation in structure we can find no real proof that man's unlearned repertoire of acts has differed widely through the ages or that he has ever been either more or less capable of putting on complex training than he is in 1930. The fact that there are marked individual variations in structure among men has been known since biology began. But we have never sufficiently utilized it in analyzing man's behavior. I want to utilize another fact only recently brought out by the behaviorists and other students of animal psychology. Namely, that *habit formation starts in all probability in embryonic life and that even in the human young, environment shapes behavior so quickly that all of the older ideas about what types of behavior are inherited and what are learned break down*. Grant variations in structure at birth and rapid habit formation from birth, and you have a basis for explaining many of the so-called facts of inheritance of "mental" characteristics. Let us take up these two points:

(1) HUMAN BEINGS DIFFER IN THE WAY THEY ARE PUT TOGETHER

In our study of the makeup of the body, we obtained a faint idea of the complexity of the material and the processes that enter into the makeup of a human being. It enabled us to tolerate the fact too that there must be variation in the way these complicated tissues are put together. We have just brought out the fact that some human beings are born with long fingers, some with short; some with long arm and leg bones, some with short; some with hard bones, and some with soft; some with over-developed glands; some with poorly functioning glands. Again we know that we can identify human beings by differences in their finger-prints. No two human beings have ever had the same finger-prints, yet one can mark off man's hand and footprints from the tracks of all other animals. No two human beings have bones exactly alike, yet any good comparative anatomist can pick out a human bone (and there are over 200 of them) from the bones of any other mammal. If so simple a thing as the markings on the fingers differs in every individual, we have absolute proof that general behavior will and must be different. Infants crawl differently, cry differently, differ in the frequency with which defaecation and urination occur, differ in early vocal efforts, in requirements for food, in the speed and rapidity with which they use their hands—even identical twins show these differences—because they differ structurally and differ slightly in their chemical makeup. They differ, likewise in the finer details of sense organ equipment, in the details of brain and cord structure, in the heart and circulatory mechanisms and in the length, breadth, thickness and flexibility of the striped muscular systems.

Yet with all of these structural differences "a man's a man for a' that"—he is made up of the same material as other men and has the same general architectural plan regardless of habit.

(2) DIFFERENCES IN EARLY TRAINING MAKE MAN STILL MORE DIFFERENT

There are then admittedly these slight but significant differences in structure between each human being and every other human being. Differences in early training are even more marked. We now know that conditioned reflexes start in the human child at birth (and probably before)—we know that there is no such thing as giving two children, even though belonging to the same family, the same training. A doting young married couple have twins—a boy and a girl—the children are dressed alike and fed alike. But the father pets and fondles the girl, surrounds her with love; the mother treats the boy in the same way, but the father wants the boy to follow in his own footsteps. He is stern with him—he can't help shaping the boy his way. The mother wants the girl to be modest and maidenly. Soon these children show great differences in behavior. They receive different training from infancy. The next children are born. Now the father is more taken up with affairs—he has to work harder. The mother is more taken up with social duties; servants are brought in. The younger children have brothers and sisters; they are brought up in a world wholly different from that of the older childen. One child falls ill. Strict training is abandoned, all rules are off with a sickly child. Again, one child gets badly frightened—becomes conditioned—shows fear at everything; he becomes timid and his regular course of boyish activity is interfered with. Indeed we may take an actual case. Two girls, aged nine, live in adjoining houses. They have the "same" training (mothers are close friends and bring up children according to the same rules). One day they took a walk. The girl on the left looked at the street and saw only street activity, the one on the right looked towards the houses and saw a man exposing his sex organs. The girl on the right was considerably troubled and disturbed and reached equanimity only after months of discussion with her parents.

THE CONCLUSION WE DRAW

How will these two points explain the so-called facts of inheritance of talent or mental characteristics? Let us take a hypothetical case. Here are two boys, one aged 7, the other 6. The father is a pianist of great talent, the mother an artist working in oil, a portrait painter of note. The father has strong large hands but with long, flexible fingers (it is a myth that all artists have long, tapering, finely formed fingers). The older son has the same type of hand. The father loves his first born, the mother the younger. Then the process of "creating them in his own image" begins. The world is brought up on the basis largely of shaping the young you are attached to as you yourself have been shaped. In this case the older becomes a wonderful pianist, the younger an indifferent artist. So much for different training or different slanting in youth. But what about different structure? Please note this. The younger son, under ordinary conditions, could not have been trained into a pianist.

His fingers were not long enough and the muscular arrangement of the hand was not flexible enough. But even here we should be cautious—the piano is a standard instrument—a certain finger span and a certain hand, wrist and finger strength are needed. But suppose the father had been fond of the younger child and said, "I want him to be a pianist and I am going to try an experiment— his fingers are short—he'll never have a flexible hand, so I'll build him a piano. I'll make the keys narrow so that even with his short fingers his span will be sufficient, and I'll make a different leverage for the keys so that no particular strength or even flexibility will be needed." Who knows—the younger son under these conditions might have become the world's greatest pianist.

Such factors, especially those on the training side, have been wholly neglected in the study of inheritance. We have not the facts to build up statistics on the inheritance of special types of behavior, and until the facts have been brought out by the study of the human young, all data on the evolution of different forms of human behavior and eugenics must be accepted with the greatest possible caution.

Our conclusion, then, is that we have no real evidence of the inheritance of traits. I would feel perfectly confident in the ultimately favorable outcome of careful upbringing of a *healthy, well-formed baby* born of a long line of crooks, murderers and thieves, and prostitutes. Who has any evidence to the contrary? Many, many thousands of children yearly, born from moral households and steadfast parents become wayward, steal, become prostitutes, through one mishap or another of nurture. Many more thousands of sons and daughters of the wicked grow up to be wicked because they couldn't grow up any other way in such surroundings. But let one adopted child who has a bad ancestry go wrong and it is used as incontestable evidence for the inheritance of moral turpitude and criminal tendencies. As a matter of fact, there has not been a double handful of cases in the whole of our civilization of which records have been carefully enough kept for us to draw any such conclusions—mental testers, Lombroso, and all other students of criminality to the contrary notwithstanding. As a matter of fact adopted children are never brought up as one's own. One cannot use statistics gained from observations in charitable institutions and orphan asylums. All one needs to do to discount such statistics is to go there and work for a while, and I say this without trying to belittle the work of such organizations.

I should like to go one step further now and say, "Give me a dozen healthy infants, well-formed, and my own specified world to bring them up in and I'll guarantee to take any one at random and train him to become any type of specialist I might select—doctor, lawyer, artist, merchant-chief and, yes, even beggar-man and thief, regardless of his talents, penchants, tendencies, abilities, vocations, and race of his ancestors." I am going beyond my facts and I admit it, but so have the advocates of the contrary and they have been doing it for many thousands of years. Please note that when this experiment is made I am to be allowed to specify the way the children are to be brought up and the type of world they have to live in.

Where there are structural defects that are inherited, as apparently is the case in certain glandular diseases; in "mental" defectives; where there is intra-uterine infection as in syphilis and in gonorrhea, troublesome behavior of one kind or another may develop early and rapidly. But some of these children haven't the structural possibilities to be trained—as when fundamental connections in body and brain are lacking. Again, where there are structural defects more easily observed as in deformities, loss of digits, possession of extra digits, there is social inferiority—competition on equal grounds is denied. The same is true when "inferior" races are brought up along with "superior" races. We have no sure evidence of inferiority in the negro race. Yet, educate a white child and a negro child in the same school—bring them up in the same family (theoretically without difference) and when society begins to exert its crushing might, the negro cannot compete.[1]

The truth is society does not like to face facts. Pride of race has been strong, hence our Mayflower ancestry—our Daughters of the Revolution. We like to boast of our ancestry. It sets us apart. We like to think that it takes three generations to make a gentleman (sometimes a lot longer!) and that we have more than three behind us. Again, on the other hand, the belief in the inheritance of tendencies and traits saves us from blame in the training of our young. The mother says when her son goes "wrong"—"Look at his father" or "Look at his grandfather" (whichever one she hates). "What could you expect with that ancestry on his father's side?" And the father, when the girl shows wayward tendencies—"What can you expect? Her mother has always let every man she came in contact with make love to her." "If these tendencies are inherited we can't be much blamed for it. Traits in the older psychologies are God-given and if my boy or girl goes wrong, I as a parent can't be blamed."

During the past five years considerable light has been thrown upon the relative influence of environment and heredity by the study of identical twins. Let us examine this material at some length.

DOES THE EXPERIMENTAL WORK ON IDENTICAL TWINS NEGATE OUR
EMPHASIS ON THE RELATIVELY GREATER INFLUENCE OF ENVIRON-
MENT IN THE EARLY DIFFERENTIATION OF BEHAVIOR?

Dr. Arnold Gesell is the strongest advocate of heredity and growth factors. In his article, "Behavior Resemblance in Identical Infant Twins" (*Eugenical News,* Vol. XIV, No. 5, May, 1929)

[1] I say nothing here on the inheritance of acquired behavior characteristics. The evidence in biology is all against it. An infant descended from a long line of blacksmith ancestors starts with approximately the same puny upper right arm girth as his original blacksmith forebear—and with one no larger than his own left arm. The facts for and against have been beautifully summarized in Jennings' *The Biological Basis of Human Nature,* page 338 ff.

he states very positively that the behavior pattern of monozygotic twins shows a special degree of resemblance in behavior. For example, "The postural, perceptual, prehensory, exploitive and imitative responses to one, two and three one-inch red cubes placed before each child were described and photographed to provide objective data for a detailed study of the development of behavior patterns." Twins T and C under these test conditions showed a marked degree of resemblance in behavior patterns. These correspondences in behavior patterning were literally uncountable. For example, there were 99 items of minor disparity and 513 items of identical or nearly identical correspondence.

While these experiments are interesting, they constitute no proof that identity of patterns in these two youngsters was any closer than would have been the case had he investigated infants of the same age and kept under relatively the same environmental conditions, namely residence in the clinic, provided the children had been of the same general weight and physical makeup and previous conditioning. So far as I have seen from the report, no controls were introduced in the experiment. Dr. Gesell concludes: "During the course of our simultaneous observation of the behavior patterns of Twins T and C, the correspondence frequently was so striking as to recall Galton's metaphor about clocks and necessitarian whirring wheels!"

That Dr. Gesell is not supported in this conclusion by any other similar study appears from the work of Muller and of Newman. H. G. Muller, *Journal of Heredity*, December 1925, describes his tests upon identical twins, B and J. They were 30 years old at the time of the test. They were separated at two weeks of age. One (B) lived in Wyoming at the time but had lived in New York, Washington and other places, and the other in Arizona (J).

B was brought up by foster parents who did mining, logging and hauling. As a child B was out with the teams all day and had only four years of formal schooling all told, including nine months in a business college. At 15 B obtained a clerical job. Her business career was not very successful—she tried in addition to clerical work, administrative and secretarial work.

J was also brought up by foster parents who owned a ranch and a roadhouse where things were lively. She was also out of doors a great deal and like B was a tomboy. She went through school including high school and then had some summer university work. She taught school and had a child.

Neither of the twins had been very well and their illnesses had been quite similar.

Their scores on the general intelligence tests (Otis and Army Alpha) were not very different but on some sections J was good where B was poor and *vice versa*. In other tests, for example, Kent Rosanoff's Association Test, J, on account of greater schooling responded almost twice as fast. On the tapping test, B because of the typewriting experience had a score of 207 against J's 164 in the same period of time. In the crossing test B had a score of 63 to J's 55. Muller concluded that all tests on motor reaction time, "will temperament" emotions and social attitudes "give results in striking contrast with those of the intelligence tests, in that the twins made markedly different scores on all these tests. *The differences* were, on the average, slightly greater than the median differences between the scores of two individuals chosen at random from the group in which the 'norms' of the tests had been established."

Newman in his article, "Mental Traits of Identical Twins Reared Apart," *Journal of Heredity,* April, 1929, gives an even more striking case of identical twin boys reared apart—one in the city, the other in the country. Twins C and O were born in 1925. They are almost indistinguishable in physical appearance. I quote him: "In this case the environment and training of the twins were closely similar in general, at least insofar as we were able to ascertain the facts. Yet the 'personalities' of the two boys are utterly different. So opposite is the impression made by them upon all the observers that we were forcibly struck by it from the beginning."

On the Pressey test of emotional reaction, C's (city boy's) total score was 29; O's (country boy's) was 55, O thus being decidedly more neurotic. On the international group intelligence test, C's score was 156, while O's was 146. On Thurstone's Psychological Examination, C's score was 101 and O's 84. This test involves completion, artificial language, analogies, arithmetic, and opposites.

Newman studied also two pairs of identical twin sisters. The first pair, separated at the end of 18 months, were tested after 18 years (they had lived together one year before the psychological tests were made). During the separation the environments were very different. "The twins dealt with in this paper differed tremendously in mental capacity—the difference being three times as great as the average of 50 pairs of identical twins reared together." In this case the twins showed considerable resemblance in emotional characteristics (which was to be expected, due to the fact that the first 18 months of their lives were spent together—so early are emotional patterns laid down).

In the case of the second pair of identical twin girls studied by Newman, the environments were also different. One attended school seven years longer than the other. They also were separated after living together 18 months. They were tested after 19 years of separation. The more highly educated twin, G, gave a very superior performance in every test of "mental" ability and "native" performance. In emotional tests they too were quite similar.

In all these tests on identical twins, I see not one scintilla of evidence for the contention of the biologist that the number and the relation of the genes are the determining factors in behavior patterns. In identical twins we are dealing with the same set of genes, and yet the outcome of different training yields different individuals.

Just to emphasize our point here again—after all, life outside the laboratory has a good deal of similarity. Suppose now we were to take identical twins into the laboratory and begin rigidly to condition them from birth to the twentieth year along utterly different lines as diverse as possible. We might even condition one of the children to grow up without language. Those of us who have spent years in the conditioning of children and animals cannot help but realize that the two end products would be as different as day is from night.

Yet in face of this evidence, Jennings, who is by all odds the fairest and most scientific of the biologists interested in genetics, in *"The Biological Basis of Human Nature"* says:

"Thus the study of the four cases of identical twins reared separately is favorable to the claims of those who hold that environment and experience may have a great effect on mental and on temperamental characteristics, producing marked difference in these respects, even in individuals that are genetically alike. The four cases, however, support equally the view that the genetic constitution likewise affects greatly these matters. For in all cases the twins reared under diverse environments were much more alike in certain respects—in some cases in mental processes, in others in temperament—than can be accounted for on any basis except their identity in genetic constitution. The results of the study agree thoroughly with the conclusion, practically certain on other grounds, that both the genetic constitution and the environment deeply influence mental and temperamental characteristics; and that effects produced in one case by genetic constitution may be produced in another case by environment."

I am sure that Jennings, if he were to take account of the fact that in several of the above cases the children had had their early conditioning together, that the tests were by no means sufficient to bring out all or even a large part of the actual differences in behavior patterns, and that in the study of these cases the behaviorist had had no opportunity to train the children experimentally along different lines, would have to agree that my position, which I have outlined above, is the only one which has any reasonable facts and hypotheses to support it. And we must remember here that in identical twins we are taking the biologically hardest case for the behaviorist to cope with in his emphasis on environment.

Let us, then, lay aside the thought of inheritance of aptitudes, of "mental" characteristics, of special abilities (not based upon favorable structure such as throat formation in singing, hand formation in playing, structurally sound eyes and ears) and take up the more general question of what the world has been in the habit of calling instincts.

ARE THERE ANY INSTINCTS?

It is not easy to answer this question. Up to the advent of the behaviorist man was supposed to be a creature of many complicated instincts. A group of older writers, under the sway of the newly created theories of Darwin, vied with one another in finding new and perfect instincts in both man and animals. William James made a careful selection from among these asserted instincts and gave man the following list: *Climbing, imitation, emulation, rivalry, pugnacity, anger, resentment, sympathy, hunting, fear, appropriation, acquisitiveness, kleptomania, constructiveness, play, curiosity, sociability, shyness, cleanliness, modesty, shame, love, jealousy, parental love.* James states that no other mammal, not even the monkey, can lay claim to so large a list.

The behaviorist finds himself wholly unable to agree with James and the other psychologists who claim that man has unlearned activities of these complicated kinds. We have all been brought up on James or possibly even on a worse diet, and it is hard to run counter to him. James says an instinct is "a tendency to act in such a way as to bring about certain ends without having foresight of those ends." Surely this formulation fits a lot of the early behavior of children and young animals. At first this formulation looks convincing. But when one tests it out in terms of one's own observations on young animals and children, one finds that one has not a scientific definition but a metaphysical assumption. One gets lost in the sophistry of "foresight" and "end."

No subject in psychology today is more written about than the so-called instincts. In the past few years many hundreds of articles have been written about instincts. The articles in general are of the armchair variety written by men who have never watched the whole life history of animals and the early childhood of the human young. Philosophy will never answer any questions about instincts. The questions asked are factual ones—to be answered only by genetic observation. Let me hasten to add that the behaviorist's knowledge of instinct also suffers from lack of observed facts but one cannot accuse him of going beyond natural science in his inferences. Before attempting to answer the question "What is an instinct?" let us take a little journey into mechanics. Possibly we may find that we do not need the term after all.

A LESSON FROM THE BOOMERANG

I have in my hand a hardwood stick. If I throw it forward and upward it goes a certain distance and drops to the ground. I retrieve the stick, put it in hot water, bend it at a certain angle, throw it out again—it goes outward, revolving as it goes for a short distance, turns to the right and then drops down. Again I retrieve the stick, reshape it slightly and make its edges convex. I call it a boomerang. Again I throw it upward and outward. Again it goes forward revolving as it goes. Suddenly it turns, comes back and gracefully and kindly falls at my feet. It is still a stick, still made of the same material, but it has been shaped differently. *Has the boomerang an instinct to return to the hand of the thrower?* No? Well, why does it return? Because it is made in such a way that when it is thrown upward and outward with a given force it must return (parallelogram of forces). Let me call attention to the fact here that all well made and well thrown boomerangs will return to or near to the thrower's feet, but no two will follow exactly the same forward pathway or the same return pathway, even if shot mechanically with the same application of force and at the same elevation, yet they are called boomerangs. This example may be a little unusual. Let us take one a little easier. Most of us have rolled dice now and again. Take a die, load it in a certain way, roll it, and the face bearing "six" will nearly always come up when the die is thrown. Why? The die must roll that way because of the way it was constructed. Again take a toy soldier. Mount it on a semi-circular loaded rubber base. No matter how one throws this soldier, he will always bob upright, oscillate a bit, then come to a steady vertical position. *Has the rubber soldier an instinct to stand erect?*

Notice that not until the boomerang, the toy soldier and the die are hurled into space do they exhibit their peculiarities of motion. Change their form or their structure, or alter greatly the material out of which they are made (make them of iron instead of wood or rubber), and their characteristic motion may markedly change. But man is made up of certain kinds of material—put together in certain ways. If he is hurled into action (as a result of stimulation) may he not exhibit movement (in advance of training) just as peculiar as (but no more mysterious than) that of the boomerang? [1]

CONCEPT OF INSTINCT NO LONGER NEEDED IN PSYCHOLOGY

This brings us now to our central thought. If the boomerang has no instinct (aptitude, capacity, tendency, trait) to return to the hand of the thrower; if we need no mysterious way of accounting for the motion of the boomerang, if the laws of physics will account for its motions—cannot psychology see in this a much needed lesson in simplicity? Can it not dispense with instincts? Can we not say that man is built of certain materials put together in certain complex ways, and *as a corollary of the way he is put together and*

[1] One may argue that in mechanics action and reaction are equal—that the thrower imparts to the boomerang a quantity of energy equal to so many dynes and that just that same quantity of energy is used up by the boomerang in returning to the thrower (including the heat loss to the air). When I touch a man with a hair, though, and he jumps two feet, the reaction is out of all proportion to the energy in the stimulus. The explanation is that in man the energy used in the reaction was stored. In dynamics you find the same thing when a match touches off a powder blast or when a breeze blows a rocking boulder from a cliff and the boulder destroys a house in the valley.

of the material out of which he is made—he must act (until learning has reshaped him) as he does act?

But one may argue: "That gives your whole argument away—you admit he does a lot of things at birth which he is forced to do by his structure—this is just what I mean by *instinct*." My answer is that we must now go to the facts. We can no longer postpone a visit to the nursery. I think the student will find there, in the study of the infant and child, *little that will encourage him to keep sacred James' list of instincts.* In the next chapter we shall study just what the human offspring does do at birth.

VI. Are There Any Human Instincts?

INTRODUCTION: In the preceding chapter we brought out the fact that most of the problems concerned with the *unlearned equipment* of man can be solved only by a study of his life history. This means beginning our study on the newborn human infant. It is an unfortunate fact but true that we know a great deal more about the young of other species of animals than we know about the human young. During the past 25 years the students of animal behavior have been gathering a sound body of facts about the young of nearly every species except man. We have lived with young monkeys, we have watched the growth of young rats, rabbits, guinea pigs, and birds of many species. We have watched them develop daily in our laboratories from the moment of birth to maturity. To check our laboratory results we have watched many of them grow up in their own native habitat—in a natural environment.

These studies have enabled us to reach a fair understanding of both the *unlearned* and *learned* equipment of many species of animals. They have taught us that no one by watching the performance of the adult can determine what part of a complicated series of acts belongs in the *unlearned* category and what part belongs in the category of the *learned*. Best of all they have given us a method that we can apply to the study of the human young. Finally animal studies have taught us that it is not safe to generalize from the data we gather on one species as to what will be true in another species. For example, the guinea pig is born with a heavy coat of fur, and with a very complete set of motor responses. It becomes practically independent of the mother at three days of age. The white rat, on the other hand, is born in a very immature state, has a long period of infancy; it becomes independent of the mother only at the end of thirty days. Such a wide divergence of birth equipment in two animal species so closely related (both rodents) proves how unsafe it is to generalize on the basis of infra-human animal studies, as to what the unlearned equipment of man is.

RESISTANCE TO THE STUDY OF THE HUMAN YOUNG

Until very recently we have had little reliable data on what happens during the first few years of human infancy and childhood. Indeed there has been very great resistance to studying the behavior of the human young. Society is in the habit of seeing them starve by hundreds, of seeing them grow up in dives and slums, without getting particularly wrought up about it. But let the hardy behaviorist attempt an experimental study of the infant or even begin systematic observation, and criticism begins at once. When experiments and observations are made in the maternity wards of hospitals there is naturally also considerable misunderstanding of the behaviorist's aims. The child is not sick, the behaviorist is not advancing clinical methods—therefore what good are such studies? Again, when the parents who have children under observation learn of it they become excited. They are ignorant of what the psychologists are doing. The psychologists have great difficulty in making the medical people understand what they are doing. It is almost impossible to make satisfactory studies continuous in nature over long periods of time unless the psychologist is put in complete charge of the experimental nursery (working with a physician on the staff but not in charge). Several such nurseries are now in operation, at the University of California under Dr. Mary Jones, at the University of Minnesota under Prof. Anderson, at Johns Hopkins under Prof. Buford Johnson, and at Yale under Dr. Gesell. A vast deal of research work can still be carried out in maternity hospitals if the medical men in charge will arrange affairs in such a way that psychological examination of the infants shall become a part of the regular routine of the care of all infants born in the hospital.

STUDYING THE BEHAVIOR OF THE HUMAN INFANT

No one should attempt to make studies upon the infant until he has had considerable training in physiology and in animal psychology. *He should have practical training in the nursery of the hospital where the work is to be done.* In this way he can learn what is safe to do with a baby and what is not. Before recording observations he should watch a few deliveries. By watching deliveries he will speedily learn that the human infant can stand considerable *necessary* hard usage without breaking under the strain!

WHAT WE KNOW ABOUT INTRA-UTERINE BEHAVIOR

Our knowledge of the intra-uterine life of the human young is very meagre indeed. Intra-uterine life begins with the fertilization of the ovum. Recent observations by M. Minkowski, at the University of Zurich, upon embryos which have had to be taken from the uterus show that the foetus two to two and one-half months of age exhibits considerable movement of the head, the trunk, and the extremities. The movements are slow, asymmetrical, arhythmic and uncoördinated. Their amplitude is small. Response to cutaneous stimulation is present, as is also response to changes in position of the limbs. The heart beat in the foetus begins to show at a much earlier time, often as early as the third week. There is some evidence that the stomach glands begin to function at the end of the fifth month.

The position of the foetus in the uterus is not without significance since it affects the movements and posture of the infant for a considerable time after birth. Dr. J. Whitridge Williams describes the intra-uterine position of the foetus as follows: "Irrespective of the relation which it may bear to the mother, the foetus in the later months of pregnancy assumes a characteristic posture, which is described as its *attitude* or *habitus;* and, as a general rule, it may be said to form an ovoid mass, which roughly corresponds with the shape of the uterine cavity. Thus, it is folded or bent upon itself in such a way that the back becomes markedly convex, the head is sharply flexed so that the chin is almost in contact with the breast, the thighs are flexed over the abdomen, the legs are bent at the knee-joints, and the arches of the feet rest upon the anterior surfaces of the legs. The arms are usually crossed over the thorax or are parallel to the sides, while the umbilical cord lies in the space between them and the lower extremities. This attitude is usually retained throughout pregnancy, though it is frequently modified somewhat by the movements of the extremities, and in rare instances the head may become extended, when a totally different posture is assumed. The characteristic attitude results partly from the mode of growth of the foetus, and partly from a process of accommodation between it and the outlines of the uterine cavity." (*Obstetrics,* p. 180.) The extent to which slight differences in the intra-uterine position of the foetus may possibly later influence or even determine right and left handedness of the individual is not known. Attention is called to the fact that the liver is on the right side in about 80% of the observed cases. Whether this large organ may swing the foetus slightly so that the right side is constantly under less restraint than the left is not known. If this is true the infants with the liver on the right side should be right-handed from birth. My own Johns Hopkins records on hundreds of infants prove that this is not the case.

In general we get our best information on foetal structures ready to function by study of infants prematurely born. At 6 months (lunar) the infant may draw a few gasping breaths and make a few abortive movements. It never lives. From the 7th month on to full term infants may live. At birth they display the usual birth equipment. This proves that from the beginning of the 7th month many structures exist in the foetus ready to function as soon as the appropriate stimulus is applied: e. g. breathing as soon as the air strikes the lungs; complete and independent circulation and purification of the blood as soon as the umbilical cord is severed; independent metabolism showing the visceral system is ready to function, etc.

THE BIRTH EQUIPMENT OF THE HUMAN YOUNG

Almost daily observation of several hundred infants from birth through the first thirty days of infancy and of a smaller number through the first years of childhood has given us the following set of (rough) facts on unlearned responses: [1]

Sneezing: This apparently can begin in a full-fledged way from birth. Sometimes it appears even before the so-called birth cry is given. It is one of the responses that stays in the activity stream throughout life (see p. 138); habit factors apparently affect it very little indeed. No experiments so far have ever been made to see if the mere sight of the pepper box may not after a sufficient number of conditioning experiments call out sneezing. The normal intra-organic stimulus calling out sneezing is not very well defined. Sometimes it occurs when the baby is taken from a cooler room into an overheated room. With some babies carrying them out into the sunshine apparently will produce sneezing.

Hiccoughing: This usually does not begin at birth but can be noticed in children from 7 days of age on with great ease. Over 50 cases have been observed carefully. The earliest noted case of hiccoughing was 6 hours after birth. So far as is known this re-

[1] Mrs. Margaret Gray Blanton, working in the psychological laboratory of the Johns Hopkins Hospital, has given us valuable data upon this subject (*Psychological Review*, Vol. 24, p. 456). Dr. Mary Cover Jones' study, "The Development of Early Behavior Patterns in Young Children," *Ped. Sem., and Jr. Genetic Psychology*, 33, 4, 1926, has been borrowed from freely in this text.

sponse is rarely conditioned in the course of the ordinary happenings of life. The stimulus most commonly calling it out apparently is the pressure on the diaphragm coming from a full stomach. Decrease in body temperature is another cause, according to Professor Prescott Lecky.

Crying: The so-called birth cry takes place at the establishment of respiration. The lungs are not inflated until the stimulus of the air is present. As the air strikes the lungs and mucous membranes of the upper alimentary tract, the mechanism of breathing is gradually established. To establish breathing, the infant has sometimes to be plunged into icy water. Coincident with the plunge into the icy water, the cry appears. It usually appears during the vigorous rubbing and slapping of the infant's back and buttocks—a method invariably employed to establish respiration. The birth cry itself differs markedly in different infants.

Hunger will bring out crying. Noxious stimuli such as rough handling, circumcision, or the lancing and care of boils will bring out cries even in extremely young infants. When the baby suspends itself with either hand crying is usually elicited.

Crying as such very shortly becomes conditioned. The child quickly learns that it can control the responses of nurse, parents and attendants by the cry, and uses it as a weapon thereafter. Crying in infants is not always accompanied by tears, although tears can sometimes be observed as soon as 10 minutes after birth. Owing to the almost universal practice now of putting silver nitrate into the eyes shortly after birth, the normal appearance of tears is hard to determine. Tears have been observed, though, on a great many babies from the 4th day on. Tears, in all probability, are also conditioned very quickly since they are a much more effective means of controlling the movements of nurses and parents than is dry crying.

Numerous experiments have been carried out to see whether the crying of one infant in a nursery will serve as a stimulus to set off the rest of the children in the nursery. Our results are entirely negative. In order to control the conditions more thoroughly, we made phonographic records of a lusty crier. We would then reproduce this sound very close to the ear of, first, a sleeping infant, then a wakeful but quiet infant. The results again were wholly negative. Hunger contractions and noxious stimuli (also loud sounds, see p. 152) are unquestionably the unconditioned stimuli which call out crying. We shall take up crying again on p. 177.

Colic, bringing a set of noxious stimuli, may and usually does call out a cry and apparently one slightly different from other types. This is due to the pressure in the abdominal cavity caused by the formation of gas. The full set of muscles used in the hunger cry is thus not available for the colic cry. The cries of infants are so different that at night in a nursery of 25 it does not take very long to be able to name the child which is crying, regardless of its location in the nursery.

Erection of Penis: This can occur at birth and from that time on throughout life. The complete set of stimuli calling out this response is not known. Apparently radiant heat, warm water, stroking of the sex organs, possibly pressure from the urine, are the main factors operative at birth. This, of course, is conditioned later on in life through visual stimulation and the like. The stimulus to the later appearing orgasm is possibly different. Short rhythmical contacts as in coition and in masturbation lead to the orgasm (and after puberty to its attendant ejaculation). Probably the orgasm itself both in men and women can be hastened or slowed through stimulus substitutions (through words, sounds, etc.—a factor of the utmost sociological importance).

At what age tumescence becomes a conditioned response is not known. Masturbation (a better term with infants is manipulation of the penis or vagina respectively) can occur at almost any age. The earliest case I have personally observed was a girl around 1 year of age (it often begins much earlier). The infant was sitting up in the bathtub and in reaching for the soap accidentally touched the external opening of the vagina with her finger. The search for the soap stopped, stroking of the vagina began and a smile overspread the face. In the case of neither infant boys nor infant girls have I seen masturbation carried to the point where the orgasm takes place (it must be remembered that the orgasm can occur without ejaculation in the male before the age of puberty is reached). Apparently a great many of the muscular responses later to be used in the sex act such as pushing, climbing, stroking, are ready to function in the male at least at a very much earlier age than we are accustomed to think. In one observed case which came into the clinic, a boy of 3½ years of age would mount his mother or nurse, whichever one happened to be sleeping with him. Erection would take place and he would manipulate and bite her breasts, then clasping and sex movements similar to those of adults would ensue. In this case the mother, who was separated from her husband, had deliberately attempted to build up this reaction in her child.

Voiding of Urine: This occurs from birth. The unconditioned stimulus is unquestionably intra-organic due to the pressure of the fluid in the bladder. Conditioning of the act of urination can begin as early as the second week. Usually, however, conditioning at this age requires almost infinite patience. Anywhere from the third month on, the infant can be conditioned easily by a little care. If the infant is observed closely at intervals of a half hour or so, it will occasionally be found dry. When this occurs, place it upon the chamber. If the bladder is quite full, the increased pressure which comes from putting the infant in a sitting position will be stimulus enough to release the act. After repeated trials the conditioned response is perfected. Young children can be so thoroughly conditioned in this act that the response can be called out without awakening them.

Defaecation: This mechanism seems to be perfect from birth and in all probability the mechanism was perfected several weeks before birth. The stimulus probably is pressure in the lower colon. Pressing a clinical thermometer into the anus often brings about the passage of faeces.

Defaecation can also be conditioned at a very early age. One of the methods of course is to introduce a glycerine or soap suppository at the time the infant is placed upon the chamber. After considerable repetition of this routine, contact with the chamber will be sufficient to call out the response.

Early Eye Movements: Infants from birth when lying flat on their backs in a dark room with their heads held horizontally will slowly turn their eyes towards a faint light. Movements of the eyes are not very well coördinated at birth, but "cross eyes" are not nearly so prevalent as most people seem to believe. Right and left coördinated movements of the eyes are the first to appear. Upward and downward movements of the eyes come at a slightly later period. Still later on a light can be followed when revolved in a circle over the baby's face.

As is well known, habit factors almost immediately begin to enter into fixation and other eye responses. I have already brought out the fact that movements both of the lids and of the pupils can be conditioned.

Smiling: Smiling is due in all probability at first to the presence of kinaesthetic and actual stimuli. It appears as early as the fourth day. It can most often be seen after a full feeding. Light touches on parts of the body, blowing upon the body, touching the sex organs and sensitive zones of the skin are the unconditioned stimuli that will produce smiling. Tickling under the chin and a gentle jogging and rocking of the infant will often bring out smiling.

Smiling is the response in which conditioning factors begin to appear as early as the thirtieth day. Dr. Mary Cover Jones has made an extensive study of smiling. In a large group of children she found that conditioned smiling—that is, smiling when the experimenter smiles or says babyish words to the infant (both auditory and visual factors)—begins to appear at around the 30th day.

In her total study of 185 cases, the latest age at which the conditioned smile first appeared was 80 days.

Manual Responses: By manual responses we mean different movements of the head, neck, legs, trunk, toes, as well as of the arms, hands and fingers.

Turning the Head: A great many infants at birth if placed stomach down with chin on the mattress can swing their heads to right or left and lift their heads from the mattress. We have noticed these reactions from 30 minutes of age on. On one occasion 15 babies were tested one at a time in succession. All except one could make these head reactions.

Holding up Head when the Infant is held in Upright Position: This seems to vary with the development of the head and neck musculature. Some newborn infants can support their heads for a few seconds. The infant is held in the experimenter's lap with stomach and back supported. There seems to be a rapid improvement in this response due apparently to the development of structure rather than to training factors. The head can be held up in most infants from the 6th month on.

Hand Movements at Birth: Marked hand movements in many children can be observed even at birth, such as closing the hand, opening it, spreading the fingers, stretching the fingers of one hand or both hands at the same time. Usually in these hand movements the thumb is folded inside the palm and takes no part in hand response. It does not begin to participate in the movements of the hand until a much later period—around the 100th day. I shall speak of grasping, which is also present at birth, later on (p. 128).

Arm Movements: The slightest stimulation of the skin anywhere will usually bring out marked arm, wrist, hand, and shoulder responses. Apparently kinaesthetic and organic stimuli may bring out these responses as well as tactual, auditory and visual stimuli. The arms can be thrown up to the face and even as far as the top of the head and down to the legs. Usually, however, the first movements of the arms, no matter where the stimulus is applied, are towards the chest and head (probably a remnant of the intra-uterine habit). One of the most characteristic ways of producing violent movements of arms and hands is to hold the nose. In a very few seconds one or the other arm or both arms fly upward until the hand actually comes in contact with the hand of the experi-menter. If one hand is held, the other hand will go up just the same.

Leg and Foot Movements: Kicking is one of the most pro-nounced movements to be seen at birth. It can be brought out by touching the soles of the feet, by stimulation with hot or cold air, by contact with the skin and directly through kinaesthetic stimula-tion. One characteristic way of producing leg and foot movements is to pinch the skin over the knee. If the left leg is held out straight and the knee cap pinched, the right foot comes up and in contact with the experimenter's fingers. When the inside of the right knee is pinched, the left leg goes up and strikes the experimenter's fingers. This will appear perfectly at birth. Sometimes it takes only a few seconds for the foot to be brought up as far as the ex-perimenter's fingers.

Trunk, Leg, Foot and Toe Movements: When an infant is sus-pending itself with either right or left hand, marked "climbing" motions in the trunk and hips are noticeable. There seems to be a wave of contraction pulling the trunk and legs upward followed by a relaxation period, then another wave of contraction sets in. Tickling the foot, stimulating the foot with hot water, will pro-duce marked movements in foot and toes. Usually if the bottom of the foot is stimulated with a match stick, the characteristic Babinski reflex appears in nearly all infants. This is a variable re-flex. The usual pattern is an upward jump of the great toe (ex-tension) and a drawing down of the other toes (flexion). Occasion-ally the Babinski takes the form merely of "fanning," that is, spreading of all the toes. The Babinski reflex usually disappears around the end of the first year although it may continue longer even in normal children. Infants cannot suspend themselves with their toes. A wire or other small round object placed under the toes will often produce flexion, that is, a closing of the toes, but the slightest pressure will release the rod or wire.

Many infants almost from birth can turn over from face to back when placed naked face downward on an unyielding surface. Mrs. Blanton describes one case as follows: Subject T, at 7 days of age, turned repeatedly from face to back when not impeded by clothing. Placed face downward on an unyielding surface, her arms in line with her body, she would immediately start crying. Relaxing and contracting of the muscles of the legs, arms, abdomen and back are natural accompaniments of crying. During the act she pulled her knees under her and contracted her muscles generally, then relaxed them. Gradually, owing to the unequal activity of the two sides of the body, she would finally come to lie nearer to one side of the body—a final spasm of muscular effort would put her over. In one case it took 10 minutes to effect the turn and 9 separate spasms.

Picture here all of the hundreds of partial responses called out in the general larger act of turning over. Here again, habit very quickly sets in and the response becomes sharper and sharper with the dropping away of many of the part reactions. It takes many weeks and months for an infant to learn to turn over quickly and with a minimum of muscular effort.

Feeding Responses: Touching the face of a hungry baby at the corners of the mouth or on the cheek or on the chin, will cause quick, jerky head movements which result in bringing the mouth near the source of stimulation. This has been observed many, many times from 5 hours of age onward. The lip or sucking reflex is another characteristic response. Tapping slightly with the tip of the finger below or above the corner of the mouth of a sleeping baby may bring the lips and tongue almost immediately into the nursing position. Suckling as such varies tremendously in young infants. It can be demonstrated in practically every infant within the first hour after birth. Occasionally when there is marked injury during birth suckling is retarded. The feeding response as such includes sucking, tongue, lip and cheek movements and swallowing. With most newborn infants this mechanism, unless there is birth injury (or possibly when the parents are "feeble-minded") is fairly perfect.

The whole group of feeding responses can be conditioned easily. Conditioning can be most easily observed in a bottle fed baby. Even before reaching (occurring around the 120th day) the infant will get extremely active in its bodily "squirmings" the instant the bottle is shown. After reaching has developed, the mere sight of the bottle will call out the lustiest kind of bodily movements and crying begins immediately. So sensitive do infants become to the visual stimulus of the bottle that if it is shown from 12 to 15 feet away, the response begins to appear. There are many, many other conditioned factors in connection with feeding that are well worth studying—negative reactions to food, food tantrums, and the like. Most of these seem to fall within the class of purely conditioned responses.

Crawling: Crawling is an indeterminate kind of response. Many infants never crawl at all, and all of them exhibit different behavior in crawling. After many experiments I am inclined to believe that crawling comes largely as a result of a habit formation. When the infant is placed face downward, the contact and kinaesthetic stimuli bring out very general bodily activity. Oftentimes one side of the body is more active than the opposite side; circular (circus) motions result. In one 9 months old infant, turning in a circle resulted for days but no forward progress could be observed. In this gradual twisting and turning of the body, the child sometimes moves right, sometimes left, sometimes forward, and sometimes backward. If, in these movements, it manages to reach and manipulate some object, we have practically a situation like that of the hungry rat in a maze that has food at its center. A habit of crawling toward objects results. Crawling probably could always be taught if teaching were regularly instituted with the milk bottle as the stimulus. Our daily test is conducted as follows: The naked infant is placed on the carpet. His legs are extended and a mark is set at the furthest reach of the toes. Then a nursing bottle or a lump of sugar (previously conditioning him on sugar so that he will struggle for it) is put just out of reach of the hands. Five minutes is enough for the test. Sometimes at the end of the test if crawling does not appear an electric heater is placed a few feet behind him. This merely hastens general bodily activity.

Lenoir H. Burnside has recently made at the Hopkins laboratory a very careful study of the coördination in the locomotion of infants (*Genetic Psychology Monographs* Vol. II, No. 5) by means of motion pictures, and *camera lucida* drawings. Lenoir divides locomotion into *crawling, creeping,* and *walking.*

Standing and Walking: The whole complex mechanism of standing upright first with support, then without support, then walking, then running, then jumping, is a very slowly developing one. The start of the whole mechanism seems to lie in the development of the so-called "extensor thrust." The extensor thrust is not usually present during the first few months of infancy. Some months after birth if the infant is gradually lifted up by the arms to nearly a standing position with a part of its feet in contact with the floor at all times, there comes, as weight falls on the feet, a stiffening of the muscles of both legs. Soon after the appearance of this reflex, the child begins to attempt to pull itself up. Between 7 and 8 months of age many infants can pull themselves up with very little help and can support themselves in a standing position holding on to some object for a short space of time. After this feat has been accomplished, the next stage in the general process is walking around holding on to an object. The final stage is the first step alone. The first step alone occurs at very variable times, depending upon the weight of the baby, its general health, whether or not it has had serious mishaps through falling (conditioning). Often the first step is taken at 1 year of age and sometimes slightly earlier. In the most completely observed case in my records the first step was taken at the end of 11 months and 3 days. After the first step is taken the remainder of the act has to be learned just as the youth learns to "balance" himself in bicycle riding, swimming, skating, and tight rope walking. Two factors seem to go hand in hand in the development of this mechanism. One is the actual growth of body tissue, the other is habit formation. The act can be hastened by coaching (positive conditioning); it can be markedly retarded at almost any of these stages if the infant falls and injures itself (negative conditioning).

Vocal Behavior: The early sounds made by infants and the conditioning and organization of these sounds into words and speech habits, will be taken up in detail on page 226.

Swimming: Swimming is very largely a process of learning. By the time the child first attempts to swim, the well organized habits of using arms, legs, hands and trunk are well established. "Balancing," breathing, removal of fear, are the remaining important factors.

When the newborn infant is placed in water at body temperature with head only supported above the water, almost no general response is called out. If plunged into cold water, violent general bodily response is called out but no movements *even approximating* swimming appear.

Grasping: With few exceptions infants at birth can support their full weight with either right or left hands. The method we use in testing them is to place a small rod about the diameter of a pencil in one or the other hand and close the fingers on the rod. This stimulus causes the grasping reflex to appear. It usually starts a cry at the same time. Then fingers and hands clamp tightly on the rod. During the reaction the infant can be completely lifted from the pillow upon which it lies. An assistant places her two hands below the infant ready to catch it as it falls back to the pillow. The length of time the infant can support itself varies all the way from a fraction of a second to more than a minute. The time in a given case may vary considerably on different days.

The reaction is almost invariable from birth until it begins to disappear around the 120th day. The time of disappearance of this response varies considerably—in observed cases from 80 days to well over 150 days. There seems to be a continuance of the reflex in defective infants long after the period of disappearance in normal infants.

Prematurely born infants of 7 and 8 months' gestation exhibit the reflex in a normal manner. Infants born without cerebral hemispheres exhibit the same reaction: in one observed case this was tested from birth to death 18 days later.

How much more than their own weight the infants can support has never been tested out, but we have made these tests when the infants were fully clothed and sometimes slightly weighted.

This primitive reaction of course finally disappears from the stream of activity never to reappear. It gives place as we shall show to the *habit* of handling, holding, and *manipulation*.

Blinking: Any newborn infant will close the lids when the eye (cornea) is touched or when a current of air strikes the eye. But no infant at birth will "blink" when a shadow rapidly crosses the eye as when a pencil or piece of paper is passed rapidly across the whole field of vision. The earliest reaction I have noted occurred on the 65th day. Dr. Mary Cover Jones noted the reaction in one infant at 40 days.

It apparently appears quite suddenly—it is at first easily "fatigued" and is quite variable. Even up to the age of 80 days some infants will not blink every time the stimulus is applied. Usually at 100 days the infant will blink whenever the stimulus is applied if at least one minute is allowed between stimulations. This reaction stays in the activity stream until death. We cannot prove it yet but this reaction looks to us very much like a conditioned visual eyelid response, as follows:

$$(U)S\dots\dots\dots\dots\dots\dots\dots\dots\dots(U)R$$

Contact with cornea   blink but objects which touch the eye often cast a shadow, hence

(C)S..(U)R
Shadow   blink

If this reasoning is correct, blinking at a shadow is not an *un-learned* response.

Handedness: We have already pointed out the possibility of handedness being due to the long enforced intra-uterine position of the child (really a habit). Studies of handedness can be made from birth on in several different ways.

1. Measurements of right and left anatomical structures such as width of right and left wrist, palm, length of forearm, etc. With specially devised instruments the measurements have been made upon several hundred children. The results show that there is no significant difference in the right and left measurements. The average error of the measurement is greater than each observed difference.

2. By recording the time of suspension (see *Grasping*) with left and right hand. Care is taken in all such tests to begin work with the right hand on one day and with the left on the following day. Chart I (left two columns) shows that there is no constancy in time of suspension from day to day.

3. By recording approximately the total amount of work done with right and left hands for a given period of time. For this work we use an especially devised work adder. This in principle is an escapement wheel that works in such a way that no matter how the baby slashes its arms about it turns the wheel always in one direction. As the wheel revolves it winds up a small lead weight attached to the wheel by a cord. Of course there is a separate instrument in use for each hand. At the beginning of the work period the two weights are let down until they just touch the table top. The hands of the baby are then attached. His slashing movements begin to wind the ball up. Usually the baby lies naked on its back, unstimulated by the observer. At the end of 5 minutes the baby is

taken out of the apparatus and the height in inches of the two weights above the table top is measured.

Again when we face the records obtained in this way we find little significant difference between the work of the two hands.

Subject J

Chart I

showing daily record of results on the two hands:

AGE IN DAYS	Time of suspension (in seconds)		Work done on adders (in inches)	
	RIGHT	LEFT	RIGHT	LEFT
1	1.2	5.6	16.16	13.75
2	2.2	3.0	25.00	15.00
3	.6	1.4	37.50	36.25
4	.6	.4	12.00	15.00
5	1.2	1.0	15.00	27.00
6	1.0	1.6	17.16	16.00
7	.6	3.2	21.25	29.37
8	1.0	2.2	24.16	18.37
9	1.8	1.8	17.25	13.00
10	1.4	.6	28.00	9.00
Average	1.16	2.08	21.34	19.27

Longer with right 3   More work with right 7
Longer with left 6   More work with left 3
Equal 1   Equal 0

Chart I (right two columns) gives the record of one infant for the first ten days of its life. The table as a whole shows the results obtained both from the work adder and from suspension. Note that the average time of suspension for J was with right hand 1.16 seconds; with the left 2.08 seconds. The average work done (average height weight was wound up) with right hand was 21.34 inches; with left hand 19.27 inches. On 3 days he suspended himself longer with right hand; on 6 days with left hand; on 1

day the time of suspension was equal. Note, too, that he wound
the weight up faster with right hand on 7 days and with left
3 days.

Thus we see how handedness can vary during the first few days
of infancy. No dependence can be placed in the records of one
child. We give one record here simply to show the type of results
to expect. When a distribution curve is made by plotting a large
number of such records no significant difference can be found
between the hands either when time of suspension is charted or
when total work done on work adders is charted. Evidently habit
(or some hitherto undetermined structural factor) must come in
to stabilize it.

4. *Testing handedness by presenting objects after the act of
reaching has been established:* Learning to reach for and to manipulate small objects will be taken up on page 201. At the moment we
are concerned with the earliest reaching reactions of the infant because of its bearing upon handedness. At the age of approximately
120 days we can begin to get the baby to reach for a stick of gaudily
striped peppermint candy. We had first to condition him positively
upon candy. This was done, long before the habit of reaching was
established, by visually stimulating the infant with the stick of
candy and then putting the candy in the mouth or else putting it
in the baby's hands. If the latter is done the baby puts the candy in
its mouth. Usually by the 160th day the infant will reach readily for
the candy as soon as it is exhibited. The infant is then ready to test
for handedness.

In all we have worked with about 20 babies during this interesting period. In making the test the baby is held in the mother's lap
so that both hands are equally free. The experimenter stands in
front of the baby and extends the candy slowly towards the baby at
the level of its eyes using care to advance the stimulus on a line
between the two hands. When the candy gets just within reach
(and usually not much before) the two hands get active, then one

or the other or both are lifted and advanced towards the candy. The hand touching it first is noted.

The results of all our tests of this nature extending from the age of 150 days to one year show no steady and uniform handedness. Some days the right is used more often, some days the left.

THE CONCLUSION WE DRAW

Our whole group of results on handedness leads us to believe that there is no fixed differentiation of response in either hand until social usage begins to establish handedness. Society soon thereafter steps in and says "Thou shalt use thy right hand." Pressure promptly begins. "Shake hands with your right hand, Willy." We hold the infant so that it will wave "bye-bye" with the right hand. *We force it to eat with the right hand. This in itself is a potent enough conditioning factor to account for handedness.* But you say "Why is society right-handed?" This possibly goes back to primitive days. One old theory often advanced is probably the true one. The heart is on the left side. It was easy enough for our most primitive ancestors to *learn* that the men who carried their shields with the left hand and jabbed with or hurled their spears with the right were the ones who more often came back bearing their shields rather than being borne upon them. If there is any truth in this it is easy enough to see why our primitive ancestors began to teach their young to be right-handed.

Long before the shield was put aside the day of manuscripts and books had come; and long before that the strolling bards and minstrels had orally crystallized the tradition. The strong right arm has become a part of our legends of the hero. All of our implements —candle snuffers, scissors and the like—were and are made for right-handed people.

If handedness is a habit socially instilled, should we or should we not change over the left-handers—those hardy souls who have resisted social pressure? I am firmly convinced that if the job is done early enough and wisely enough not the slightest harm results. I should want to do it before language develops very much. In a later chapter I will attempt to show that from the beginning we begin to *verbalize our acts*—that is, put acts into words and *vice versa*. Now changing over a left-handed, talking child suddenly into a right-handed child is likely to reduce the child to the level of a 6 months old infant. By interfering constantly with his acts we break down his manual habits and *we may simultaneously interfere with speech* (since the word and the manual act are simultaneously conditioned). In other words, while he is relearning he will fumble not only with his hands but also with his speech. The child is reduced to sheer infancy again. The unorganized (emotional) visceral control of the body as a whole again becomes predominant. It takes wiser handling to change the child over at this age than the average parent or teacher is prepared to give.

The main problem is, I believe, settled: handedness is not an "instinct." It is possibly not even structurally determined. It is socially conditioned. But why we have 5% of out and out left-handers and from 10–15% who are mixtures—e. g. using right hand to throw a ball, write or eat, but the left hand to guide an axe or hoe, etc.—is not known.[1]

SUMMARY OF UNLEARNED EQUIPMENT

At birth or soon thereafter we find nearly all of the so-called clinical neurological signs or reflexes established such as the reac-

---

[1] There are several factors which must be noted and followed through. Thumb, fingers and hand sucking are present in many infants and often unless very wisely handled last into late childhood. Usually but not always one or the other hand is fairly steadily used. One would expect the hand not used in thumb sucking to quickly become more facile in the manipulation of objects.

Again, sometimes for months the infant reaching the standing stage holds on with one or the other hand—possibly indeed with the better trained, stronger hand! During this period the other hand is left free. It may overtake or even surpass the hand slowed up from non-use. Questionnaires and statistical studies upon adults will never throw any light upon the problem.

tion of the pupil to light, the patellar reflex and many others.

We find the birth cry followed by breathing; the heart beat and all circulatory phenomena, such as vasomotor constriction (decrease in diameter of vessels) and dilatation, pulse beat. Beginning with the alimentary tract we find sucking, tongue movements, and swallowing. We find hunger contractions, digestion, necessitating glandular reactions in the whole alimentary tract, and elimination (defaecation, urination, sweat). The acts of smiling, sneezing, hiccoughing belong in part at least to the alimentary canal system. We find also erection of the penis.

We find general movements of the trunk, head and neck best observed so far as the trunk is concerned when the infant suspends himself with the hands. Rhythmical "climbing" movements then appear. We can see the trunk at work in breathing, when the infant cries, during defaecation and urination, when turning over or when the head is raised or turned.

We find the arms, wrists, hands and fingers in almost ceaseless activity (the thumb rarely taking part until later). In this activity especially are to be noted, grasping, opening and closing hands repeatedly, "slashing" about of whole arm, putting hand or fingers into mouth, and throwing arm and fingers to face when nose is held.

We find the legs, ankles, feet and fingers in almost ceaseless movement except in sleep and even during sleep if external (and internal) stimuli are present. The knee can be bent, leg moved at hip, ankle turned, toes spread, etc. If the bottom of the foot is touched there is a characteristic movement of the toes (Babinski reflex); if the left knee is pinched the right foot is brought up to the point of stimulation and *vice versa.*

Other activities appear at a later stage—such as blinking, reaching, handling, handedness, crawling, standing, sitting up, walking, running, jumping. *In the great majority of these later activities it is difficult to say how much of the act as a whole is due to training or conditioning. A considerable part is unquestionably due to the growth changes in structure, and the remainder is due we believe to training or conditioning.*

WHAT HAS BECOME OF INSTINCTS?

Are we not ready to admit that the whole concept of instinct is thus academic and meaningless? Even from the earliest moment we find habit factors present—present even in many acts so apparently simple that we used to call them physiological reflexes. Now let us turn back to James' list of instincts on p. 110 or turn to some other list of instincts. The infant is a graduate student in the subject of *learned responses* (he is multitudinously conditioned) by the time behavior such as James describes—imitation, rivalry, cleanliness, and the other forms he lists—can be observed.

Actual observation thus makes it impossible for us any longer to entertain the concept of instinct. We have seen that every act has a genetic history. Is not the only correct scientific procedure then to single out for study whatever act is in question and to watch and record its life history?

Take smiling. It begins at birth—aroused by intra-organic stimulation and by contact. Quickly it becomes conditioned, the sight of the mother calls it out, then vocal stimuli, finally pictures, then words and then life situations either viewed, told or read about. Naturally what we laugh at, whom we laugh at and with whom we laugh are determined by our whole life history of special conditionings. No theory is required to explain it—only a systematic observation of genetic facts. All the elaborate nonsense the Freudians have written on humor and laughter is just so much chaff which will be blown aside as observation and experiment bring out the facts.

Again take manipulation. It starts at 120 days, becomes smooth, sharp and facile at 6 months. It can be built up in a thousand ways, depending upon the time allowed for it, the toys the infant plays with, whether the infant is hurt by any of its toys, whether it is frightened by loud sounds often at the time it is handling its toys. To argue for a so-called "constructive building instinct" apart from early training factors is to leave the world of facts.

Again there is a similar printed collection of meaningless material in educative propaganda—taking the form of "let the child develop its own inward nature." Other phrases expressive of this mystical inner life of bents and instincts are "self-realization," "self-expression," "untutored life" (of the savage, for example), the "brute instincts," "man's baser self," "elemental facts." Such writers as Albert Payson Terhune, Jack London, Rex Beach and Edgar Rice Burroughs, owe the response they call out from their public to the organization laid down by social traditions (especially through taboos upon sex) aided and supported by the misconceptions of the psychologists themselves.

In order that one may more easily grasp the central principle of behaviorism—viz: that all complex behavior is a growth or development out of simple responses, let us introduce here the notion of "activity stream."

THE ACTIVITY STREAM AS A SUBSTITUTE FOR JAMES' "STREAM OF CONSCIOUSNESS"

Nearly every one is familiar with William James' classic chapter on the stream of consciousness. We have all loved that chapter. Today it seems as much out of touch with modern psychology as the stage-coach would be on modern New York's Fifth Avenue. The stage-coach was picturesque but it has given place to a more effective means of transportation.

We have passed in review many of the known facts on the early behavior of the human infant. Let us draw a diagram to represent the *increasingly* complex whole of man's organization. This picture is very incomplete. In the first place we have room on the chart to show only few activities. In the second place our studies are not complete enough to afford the data for an adequate chart.

Timeline axis labels: BIRTH, 60 DAYS, 120 DAYS, 180 DAYS, 240 DAYS, 300 DAYS, 360 DAYS, 2 YEARS, 3 YEARS, 4 YEARS, 5 YEARS

FERTILIZATION

LOVE BEHAVIOR — COND. LOVES
RAGE BEHAVIOR — COND. RAGES
FEAR BEHAVIOR — COND. FEARS
SNEEZING
HICCOUGHING
FEEDING REACTIONS — CONDITIONED FEEDING RESPONSES
TRUNK AND LEG MOVEMENTS — CRAWLING [COND] — WALKING [COND]
VOCAL RESPONSES — TALKING [COND] — THINKING [SILENT TALKING]
CIRCULATION AND RESPIRATION — COND. RESPIRATION AND CIRCULATION
GRASPING — REACHING AND MANIPULATION, ACTS OF SKILL, VOCATIONS, ETC. COND — HANDEDNESS [COND]
DEFAECATION AND URINATION — COND. ELIMINATION RESPONSES
CRYING AND OTHER DUCT GLAND ACTIVITY
ERECTION AND OTHER SEX ORGAN RESPONSES — COND. GLANDULAR ACTIVITY
SMILING AND LAUGHTER
"DEFENSIVE" MOVEMENTS — COND. SMILING AND LAUGHTER — COND. SEX ORGAN RESPONSES
BABINSKI REFLEX
BLINKING
FIGHTING, BOXING, ETC. [COND]

THE ACTIVITY STREAM

Rough diagram showing increasing complexity of certain human action systems. The black solid line shows the *unlearned beginning* of each system. The dotted line shows how each system is made complex by conditioning.

Some of the systems apparently are not modified. They exist in the stream throughout life without increasing in complexity.

The chart is neither complete nor accurate. Until more thorough genetic work has been done, a chart of this kind cannot be used as a measuring rod of what to expect of infants at different ages.

Finally our knowledge of visceral and emotional reactions and stimuli that call them forth is far from adequate.

In spite of these handicaps, let us try to think of a complete life chart—of the ceaseless stream of activity beginning when the egg is fertilized and ever becoming more complex as age increases. Some of the unlearned acts we perform are shortlived—they stay in the stream only a little time—such, for example, as suckling, unlearned grasping (as opposed to learned grasping and manipulation), extension of the great toe (Babinski), then disappear forever from the stream. Try to think of others beginning later in life, e. g. blinking, menstruation, ejaculation, and remaining in the stream—blinking until death, menstruation until from, say, 45–55 years, then disappearing; the act of ejaculation remaining on the chart of the male until the 70th–80th years or even longer.

It is very essential to get the point of view that each unlearned act becomes conditioned shortly after birth—even our respiration and circulation. We should remember, too, that the unlearned movements of arms, hands, trunk, legs, feet and toes become organized quickly into stabilized habits, some of which remain in the stream throughout life, others staying in only a short time and then disappearing forever. For example, our 2-year habits must give place to 3- and 4-year habits.

This chart gives quickly in graphic form the whole scope of psychology. Every problem the behaviorist works upon has some kind of setting in this stream of definite, tangible, actually observable happenings. It presents, too, the fundamental point of view of the behaviorist—viz. that in order to understand man we have to understand the life history of his activities. It shows too most convincingly that psychology is a natural science—a definite part of biology.

In the next two chapters we shall see whether at the hands of the behaviorist the case for human emotions fares better than that for instincts.

VII. Emotions

WHAT EMOTIONS ARE WE BORN WITH—HOW DO WE ACQUIRE
NEW ONES—HOW DO WE LOSE OUR OLD ONES?

PART I. A GENERAL SURVEY OF THE FIELD AND SOME
EXPERIMENTAL STUDIES

THE last two chapters have shown us that the current psychological view of instincts is not in harmony with the experimental findings of the behaviorist. Can the case for the present conception of emotions be made out any better? Probably no subject, unless it be that of instinct, has been more written about than emotions. Indeed the awe-inspiring number of volumes and papers and journals produced by Freudians and post-Freudians in the last 20 years would fill a good-sized room. And yet the behaviorist, as he reads through this great mass of literature, cannot but feel in it a lack of any central scientific viewpoint. Not until his own genetic studies, started less than 15 years ago, began to bear fruit, did it become apparent to the behaviorist that he could simplify the problems of emotion and apply objective experimental methods to their solution. Since most of us have been brought up on James' "theory" of the emotions, let us start with him. Pointing out the weakness of his position is the easiest way to convince one that the behaviorist has something genuine to contribute both on methods and in results.

JAMES' INTROVERTED VIEWPOINT ABOUT EMOTIONS

Nearly 40 years ago James gave to the psychology of the emotions a setback from which it has only recently begun to recover.

It is to be regretted that James, physiologist and physician as he was, in addition to being the most brilliant psychologist the world has ever known, should have diverged so far from Darwin who preceded him by many years. Darwin and also Lange emphasized the stimulus arousing the emotional response and the reaction to it. Their objective descriptions of fear reactions are classical and thoroughly objective and behavioristic.

But James was bored with the objective pictures of emotional reactions. He says in commenting upon the objective treatment of the emotions: "The result of all this flux is that the merely descriptive literature of the emotions is one of the most tedious parts of psychology. And not only is it tedious, but you feel that its subdivisions are to a great extent either fictitious or unimportant and that its pretenses to accuracy are a sham." James sought for a formula—a verbal container into which he could toss every separate emotion. To use his own simile, he sought to capture the goose that lays the golden eggs, "for then," says he, "the description of each egg laid is a minor matter."

JAMES' GOOSE THAT LAYS THE GOLDEN EGGS

James found such a formula. Here it is. "My theory, on the contrary, is that the *bodily changes follow directly the perception of the exciting fact, and that our feeling of the same changes as they occur IS the emotions."* His proof for this formulation? Merely a bit of introspecting that leads him to make the further statement which he says is the vital point of his whole theory: *"If we fancy some strong emotion, and then try to abstract from our consciousness of it all the feelings of its bodily symptoms, we find that we have nothing left behind,* no 'mind-stuff' out of which the emotion can be constituted, and that a cold and neutral state of intellectual perception is all that remains." Thus we see that according to James the best way to study emotions is to stand stock-still while having one and begin to introspect. The result of your introspection might take the following form: "I have a 'sensation' of a slowed heart beat—a 'sensation' of dryness in my mouth—a group of 'sensations' coming from my legs. This group of 'sensations'—this conscious state—*IS* the emotion of fear." Each man has to make his own introspections. No experimental method of approach is possible. No verification of observations is possible. In other words, no scientific objective study of emotions is possible.

Apparently it never occurred to James, or to any of his followers for that matter, to speculate, much less experiment, upon the genesis of the emotional forms of response. To him they were true heritages from our primitive ancestors. By this empty, verbal formulation, James robbed psychology of perhaps its most beautiful and most interesting field of research. He saddled upon the study of the emotions a condition from which it can scarcely recover because his formula has been swallowed by practically all the leading psychologists in the country who will continue to teach it for a greater number of years than I can think of with equanimity.

THE CURRENT LIST OF EMOTIONS

Without attempting to use any other method than the introspective one, James gives us a list of, first, what he calls the coarser emotions—grief, fear, rage, love; and a list of subtler emotions which he says may be grouped under the heading of moral, intellectual and aesthetic feelings. The latter are entirely too numerous to be separately listed.

McDougall has made a different grouping. He finds that every principal instinct has a primary emotion coupled with it; for example, the *emotion of fear* is coupled with the instinct of flight; the *emotion of disgust* is coupled with the instinct of repulsion; the *emotion of wonder* with the instinct of curiosity;

the *emotion of anger* with the instinct of pugnacity; the *emotions* of *subjection and elation* with the instincts of self-abasement and self-assertion; the *tender emotions* coupled with the parental instincts. In addition there is a whole group of emotional tendencies less marked in character. Since we have already shown that this elaborate group of McDougallian instincts does not exist (as instincts) it would be futile for us to consider it further, nor can we spend the time examining all of the lists of emotions in other current psychological texts. They are valueless because no objective method was used in determining them.

THE BEHAVIORIST'S APPROACH TO THE PROBLEM OF EMOTION

During the last few years the behaviorist has approached the problem of emotions from a new angle. His observation of adults told him that mature individuals, both men and women, display a wide group of reactions which go under the general name of emotions. The negro down South whines and trembles at the darkness which comes with a total eclipse of the sun, often falling on his knees and crying out, begging the Deity to forgive him for his sins. These same negroes will not pass through graveyards at night. They cringe and shrink when charms and relics are shown. They will not burn wood which has been struck by lightning. In rural communities adults and children collect around the home as soon as dusk begins to fall. They often rationalize it by saying that they will get the "misery" from the night air. Situations of the most ordinary kinds judged from our more sophisticated standpoint arouse the strongest kinds of emotional reactions in them.

But let us be even more specific and bring the matter closer home. Here is the list of things a 3-year-old youngster in our laboratory fears: darkness, all rabbits, rats, dogs, fish, frogs, insects, mechanical animal toys. This infant may be playing excitedly with blocks. When a rabbit or other animal is introduced, all constructive activity ceases. He crowds towards one corner of his pen and begins to cry out "take it away," "take it away." Another child examined the same day shows a different set. Another may show no fear reactions.

The more the behaviorist goes about examining the sets of reactions of adults, *the more he finds that the world of objects and situations surrounding people brings out more complex reactions than the efficient use or manipulation of the object or situation would call for.* In other words, the object seems to be "charged," seems to bring out thousands of accessory bodily reactions which the laws of efficient habit do not call for. I can illustrate this by the negro's rabbit foot. For us the rabbit foot is something to be cut off from the carcass of the animal and thrown away. One might toss it to one's dog as a part of its food. But to many of the negroes the rabbit foot is not an object to be reacted to in this simple way. It is dried, polished, put into the pocket, cared for and guarded jealously. He examines it now and then; when in trouble he calls upon it for guidance and aid, and in general reacts to it not as to a rabbit's foot but in the same way that a religious man reacts to a Deity.

Civilization to some extent has stripped from man these superfluous reactions to objects and situations. Bread is something to be eaten when hungry. Wine is something to be drunk with meals or on festive occasions. But these simple, commonplace, unemotional objects call out kneeling, prayer, bowing of the head, closing of the eyes, and a whole mass of other verbal and bodily responses, when fed to the individual at church under the guise of communion. The bones and relics of the saints may call out in devout religious individuals a set of reactions different from those the rabbit foot calls out in the negro but entirely homologous (from the standpoint of origin). The behaviorist even goes further and investigates his colleagues' everyday behavior. He finds that a noise in the basement at night may reduce his next door neighbors to reactions quite infantile; that many of them are shocked when the Lord's name is "taken in vain," giving as a rationalization that it is irreverent, that punishment will be visited upon the individual so misbehaving. He finds many of them walking away from dogs and horses, even though they have to turn back or cross the street to avoid coming near them. He finds men and women picking out impossible mates without being able to rationalize the act at all in any way. In other words, if we were to take all of life's objects and situations into the laboratory and were to work out a physiologically sound and scientific way of reacting to them (experimental ethics may approach this some day) and call these forms the norms or standards, and were then to examine man's everyday behavior in the light of such norms, we would find divergence from them the rule. Divergence takes the form of accessory reactions, slowed reactions, non-reactions (paralysis), blocked reactions, negative reactions, reactions not sanctioned by society (stealing, murder, etc.), reactions belonging properly to other stimuli (substitute).[1]

---

[1] Examples:

Of accessory reactions: The subject does the task quickly and correctly *but he becomes pale, he may even cry, urinate or defaecate, his mouth glands may become inactive.* He reacts steadily and correctly in spite of his emotional state. Other examples of accessory reactions are whistling, talking, singing, while at work.

Of slowed reactions: He does the act but his reaction time is increased—he may fumble and drop his work, or react with too much or too little energy. Response to questions comes slowly or very rapidly.

Of negative reactions: He may show fear at food—push it away or run away from it himself. Instead of the ordinary reactions to dog or horse, the subject may walk away from them. Phobias belong in this group.

Of reactions not sanctioned by society: The subject may in "heat of anger," for example, commit murder, injure property. I have in mind here all acts which the law punishes but for which it tempers justice with mercy because of emotional factors.

Of reactions belonging to other stimuli: All homosexual reactions; all sex attacks by sons upon their mothers; all sex reactions to fetishes, etc. Emotional responses of parents to children masquerading under the guise of natural affection.

There are, of course, legions of responses we call "emotional," that cannot be listed under any one of these headings.

It seems fair to call all of this group *emotional* without further defining the word at the present time.

We have no physiologically standardized norms of reactions as yet. There is some approach to it. Progress in physical sciences has done much towards standardizing our way of reacting to day and night, the seasons, the weather. We no longer react to a tree struck by lightning as if it were accursed. We no longer think that we have any advantage over our enemy when we come into possession of his nail parings, hair and excrement. We no longer look upon the blue of the heavens above as a kingdom in which super-mundane beings play harps and sing hymns for no reason at all. We no longer react to distant and almost invisible mountains as if they were the bones of gnomes and fairies. Science, geography and travel have standardized our responses. Our reactions to foods are becoming standardized through the work of the food chemist. We no longer think of any particular form of food as being "clean" or "unclean." We think of it now as fulfilling or not fulfilling definite bodily requirements.

Our social reactions, however, remain unstandardized. There is even no historical guide. Professor Sumner, of Yale, has well pointed this out. According to him, every conceivable kind of social reaction has at one time or another been considered the "normal" and unemotional way of acting. One woman could have many husbands; one man many wives; the offspring could be killed in times of famine; human flesh could be eaten; sacrifice of offspring could be made to appease deities; you could lend your wife to your neighbor or guest; the wife was acting properly when she burned herself on the pyre that consumed her husband's body.

Our social reactions are not standardized any better today. Think of our 1930 accessory responses when we are in the presence of our parents, in front of our social leaders. Think of our hero worship, our veneration for the intellectual giant, the author, the artist, the church! Think of the way we behave in crowds, at masked parties (Ku Klux as well as social)—at football and baseball games, at elections, in religious revivals (conversions, antics of the holy rollers), in grief at the loss of loved objects and people. We have a host of words to cover these accessory reactions—reverence, love of family, of God, of church, of country; respect, adulation, awe, enthusiasm. When in the presence of many of these emotional stimuli we act like infants.

How the Behaviorist Works: The complicated nature of all these adult responses makes it hopeless for the behaviorist to begin his study of emotion upon adults. He has to start with the infant where his problems are simpler.

Suppose we start with three-year-olds—we will go out into the highways and byways and collect them; and then let us go to the mansions of the rich. We bring them into our laboratory. We put them face to face with certain situations. Suppose we first let a boy go alone into a well lighted playroom and begin to play with his toys. Suddenly we release a small boa constrictor or some other animal. Next we may take him to a dark room and suddenly start a miniature bonfire with newspapers. We can set the stage so that we can duplicate almost any kind of life situation.

But after testing him alone in all these situations we must test him again when an adult, possibly father or mother, is with him—when another child of his own age and sex is nearby, when another child of opposite sex accompanies him, when groups of children are present.

In order to get a picture of his emotional behavior, we have to test separation from his mother. We have to test him with different and uncustomary foods, with strange people to feed him, with strange nurses to bathe him, clothe him and put him to bed. We must rob him of his toys, of things he is playing with. We must let a bigger boy or girl bully him, we must put him in high places, on ledges (making injury impossible, however), on the backs of ponies or dogs.

I am giving you a picture of how we work just to convince you of the simplicity, naturalness and accuracy of our methods—that there is a wide field for objective experimentation.

BRIEF SUMMARY OF RESULTS OF SUCH TESTS

One of the things we find by such tests is that even at three years of age many (but not all) of the children are shot through with all kinds of useless and actually harmful reactions which go under the general name *emotional*.

They are afraid in many situations.[1] They are shy in dozens of others. They go into tantrums at being bathed or dressed. They go into tantrums when given certain foods—or when a new nurse feeds them. They go into crying fits when the mother leaves them. They hide behind their mother's dress. They become shy and silent when visitors come. A characteristic picture is to have one hand in the mouth and the other grasping the mother's dress. One fights every child who comes near. He is called a bully, a ruffian, sadistic. Another cries and runs away if a child half his size threatens him. His parents call him a coward and his playmates make him the scapegoat.

WHENCE ARISE THESE VARIED FORMS OF EMOTIONAL RESPONSE?

A child three years of age is very young. Must we conclude that emotional reactions are hereditary? Is there an hereditary pattern of love, of fear, rage, shame, shyness, humor, anger, jealousy, timidity, awe, reverence, admiration, cruelty? Or are these just *words* to describe general types of behavior without

[1] Dr. Mary Cover Jones reports that in the work with the older children at the Heckscher Foundation, the frog especially, when it suddenly jumps, is the most potent stimulus of all in bringing out fear reactions. The most pronounced reactions were called out from the children by an animal when it was come upon suddenly. For this reason the smaller animals were often left around the room concealed in boxes. General manipulation of objects in the room led the child sooner or later to the sudden uncovering of the animal. Dr. Jones has given a recent summary of all her work on emotional reactions in *The New Generation*, 1930, p. 445 ff.

implying anything as to their origin? Historically they have been considered hereditary in origin. To answer the question scientifically we need new methods of experimentation.

In our experimental work we early reached the conclusion that young children taken at random from homes both of the poor and of the well-to-do do not make good subjects for the study of the origin of emotions. Their educational behavior is too complex. Fortunately we have been able to study a number of strong healthy children belonging to wet-nurses in hospitals, and other children brought up in the home under the eye of the experimenters. Several of these children were observed from approximately birth through the first year, others through the second year and two or three children through the third year.

In putting these hospital-reared children through emotional situations we usually had the older ones sit in small infants' chairs. If the infant was very small—too young to sit up—we allowed it to sit in the lap of the mother or in that of one of the attendants.

(a) *Reactions to Animals in the Laboratory*: We first took the children to the laboratory and put them through the routine of tests with various animals. We had the laboratory so arranged that they could be tested in the open room, alone; with an attendant; with the mother. They were tested in the dark room, the walls of which were painted black. This room was bare of furniture. It offered an unusual situation in itself. In the dark room we had conditions so arranged that we could turn on a light behind the infant's head or illuminate the room with the light in front of and above the infant. The infants were always tested one at a time. The following group of situations was usually presented:

First, a lively black cat invariably affectionately aggressive, was shown. The cat never ceased its purring. It climbed over and walked around the infant many times during the course of each test, rubbing its body against the infant in the usual feline way. So many false notions have grown up around the response of infants to furry animals that we were surprised ourselves to see these youngsters *positive always* in their behavior toward this proverbial 'black cat.' Reaching out to touch the cat's fur, eyes and nose was the invariable response.

A rabbit was always presented. This, likewise, in every case called out manipulatory responses and nothing else. Catching an ear of the animal in one hand, attempting to put it in the mouth, was one of the favorite responses.

Another furry animal invariably used was the white rat. This, possibly on account of its size and whiteness, rarely called out continued fixation of the eyes of the infant. When, however, the animal was fixated, reaching occurred.

Airedale dogs, large and small, were also presented. The dogs were also very friendly. The dogs rarely called out the amount of manipulatory response that an animal the size of the cat and rabbit called out. Not even when the children were tested with these animals in the dark room, either in full illumination or with a dim light behind the head of the child, was any fear response evoked.

These tests on children not emotionally conditioned proved to us conclusively that the classical illustrations of hereditary responses to furry objects and animals are just old wives' tales.

Next a feathery animal was used, usually a pigeon. The pigeon was presented first in a paper bag. This was a rather unusual situation even for an adult. The bird struggled and in struggling would move the bag around the couch. Oftentimes it would coo. While the pigeon was rattling and moving the paper bag about, the child rarely reached for the bag. The moment, however, the pigeon was taken into the experimenter's hands, the usual manipulatory responses were called forth. We have even had the pigeon moving and flapping its wings near the baby's face. This can be done easily by holding the pigeon by its feet, head down. Under these conditions even an adult will sometimes dodge and flinch a bit. When the wings fanned the infant's eyes, blinking was usually called out. Hesitation in response and failure to reach occur. When the bird quieted down, reaching began.

Another form of test which we have often made under these same conditions, was the lighting of a small newspaper bonfire both out in the open room and in the dark room. In several cases when the paper first caught fire, the infant reached eagerly toward the flame and had to be restrained. As soon, however, as the fire became hot, reaching and manipulatory responses died down. At such times the infant may sit with hands partly up in a position that looks almost like the start of the shading reaction that the adult uses when coming too close to a fire. There isn't much question that this type of habit would have developed if the experiment had been repeated often. It probably is entirely similar to the reaction animals and humans make to the sun. When the sun gets too hot and they are not active they move into whatever shade is available.

(b) *To Animals in Zoological Parks:* On several occasions hospital reared children and home reared children whose emotional history was known, have been taken to zoological parks—always as a first experience. The children under observation were not pronounced in any of their reactions in the zoological park. Every effort was made to give them a good presentation of those animals which apparently have played considerable part in the biological history of the human. For example, a great deal of time was spent in the primates' house. Considerable time was spent also in the rooms where reptiles, frogs, turtles, and snakes were kept. In such tests I have never got the slightest negative reaction to frogs and snakes, although the jumping frog, to children who have been conditioned, is an extremely strong stimulus in bringing out fear responses as I pointed out above (p. 148).

I feel reasonably sure that there are three different forms of emotional response that can be called out at birth by three sets of stimuli. For convenience we may call them "fear," "rage" and "love." Let me hasten to add that while I use the words fear, rage and love, I want to strip them of all their old connotations. Please look upon the reactions we designate by them just as you look upon breathing, heart beat, grasping and other unlearned responses studied in the last chapter.

The facts follow.

Fear: The panicky state into which the primitive individual falls when limbs of trees break and crash around him, and when thunder and other loud sounds occur in his presence, thus has a reasonable genetic basis. Our work upon infants, especially those without cerebral hemispheres where the reaction to noise is more pronounced, early taught us that loud sounds almost invariably produce a marked reaction in infants from the very moment of birth. For example, the striking of a steel bar with a hammer will call out a jump, a start, a respiratory pause followed by more rapid breathing with marked vasomotor changes, sudden closure of the eye, clutching of hands, puckering of lips. Then occur, depending upon the age of the infant, crying, falling down, crawling, walking or running away. I have never made a very systematic study of the range of sound stimuli that will call out fear responses. Not every type of sound will do it. Some extremely low pitched, rumbling noises will not call them out, nor will the very high tones of the Galton whistle. In the half sleeping infant of 2 or 3 days of age I have called them out repeatedly by suddenly crinkling a half of a newspaper near its ear, and by making a loud, shrill, hissing sound with the lips. Pure tones, such as those obtained from the tuning fork at any rate, are not very effective in calling them out. Considerably more work must be done upon the nature of the auditory stimulus as well as upon the separate part reactions in the response before the whole stimulus-response picture is complete.[1]

The other stimulus calling out this same fear reaction is loss of support—*especially when the body is not set to compensate for it.* It can best be observed in newborns just when they are falling asleep. If dropped then, or if the blanket upon which they lie is suddenly jerked, pulling the infant along with it, the response usually occurs.

In infants only a few hours old this fear reaction is quickly "fatigued." In other words, if the same sound or the same kind of loss of support stimulus is frequently applied, the reaction usually appears only on the first and second applications of the stimuli, at times only on the first. After a few moments' rest those same stimuli are again effective.

Even in the case of the adult human and higher mammals, loss of support when the individual is not set for it calls out a strong fear reaction. If we have to walk across a slender plank, naturally as we approach it the muscles of the body are all set for it, but if we cross a bridge which remains perfectly steady until the middle has been reached and then suddenly begins to bend, our response is very marked. When this happens in the case of a horse one can with difficulty get him to cross any bridge again. There are many horses in the country bridge shy. I am sure the same principle is operative when a child is rapidly led out into deep water for the first time. The buoyancy of the water actually throws him off his balance. Even when the water is warm there is a catching of the breath, clutching with the hands and crying.

[1] I have found only one child out of many hundreds worked with in whom a fear response could not be called out by loud sounds. She is well developed, well nourished, and normal in every way. There were no fear reactions to any other stimuli. The nearest approach to fear I saw was at the sight and sound of an opening and closing umbrella. I have no explanation to offer for this exception.

Rage: Have you ever had the experience when proudly walking across a crowded street holding your two-year-old daughter's hand, of having her suddenly pull you in some other direction? And when you quickly and sharply jerked her back and exerted steady pressure on her arm to keep her straight did she then suddenly stiffen, begin to scream at the top of her voice and lie down stiff as a ramrod in the middle of the street, yelling with wide open mouth until she became blue in the face, and continuing to yell until she could make no further sound? If you have not, any picture of rage behavior must appear lifeless to you.

Possibly you have seen the large village bully take some child, down him and hold his arms and legs so closely to his body that the child could not even struggle. Have you watched the youngster stiffen and yell until he became blue in the face?

Did you ever notice the sudden changes that come into the faces of men when they are jostled and suddenly and unduly crowded in the street cars and railway trains? *Hampering of bodily movement* brings out the series of responses we call rage. This can be observed from the moment of birth but more easily in infants 10 to 15 days of age. When the head is held lightly between the hands; when the arms are pressed to the sides; and when the legs are held tightly together, rage behavior begins. The unlearned response elements in rage behavior have never been completely catalogued. Some of the elements, however, are easily observed, such as the stiffening of the whole body, the free slashing movements of hands, arms and legs, and the holding of the breath. There is no crying at first, then the mouth is opened to the fullest extent and the breath is held until the face appears blue. These states can be brought on without the pressure in any case being severe enough to produce the slightest injury to the child. The experiments are discontinued the moment the slightest blueness appears in the skin. All children can be thrown into such a state and the reactions will continue until the irritating situation is relieved and sometimes for a considerable period thereafter.

We have had this state brought out when the arms were held upward by a cord to which was attached a lead ball not exceeding an ounce in weight. The constant hampering of the arms produced by even this slight weight is sufficient to bring out the response. When the child is lying on its back the response can occasionally be brought out by pressing on each side of the head with cotton wool. In many cases this state can be observed quite easily when the mother or nurse has to dress the child somewhat roughly or hurriedly.

Love: The study of this emotion in the infant is beset with a great many difficulties on the conventional side. Our observations consequently have been incidental rather than directly experimental. The stimulus to *love responses* apparently is stroking of the skin, tickling, gentle rocking, patting. The responses are especially easy to bring out by the stimulation of what, for lack of a better term, we may call the erogenous zones, such as the nipples, the lips and the sex organs. The response in an infant depends upon its state; when crying the crying will cease and a smile begin. Gurgling and cooing appear. Violent movement of arms and trunk with pronounced laughter occur in even 6–8 months old infants when tickled. It is thus seen that we used the term "love" in a much broader sense than it is popularly used. The responses we intend to mark off here are those popularly called "affectionate," "good natured," "kindly." The term "love" embraces all of these as well as the responses we see in adults between the sexes.

ARE THERE OTHER UNLEARNED RESPONSES THAN THESE THREE GENERAL TYPES?

Whether these three types of response are all that have an hereditary background we are not sure. Whether or not there are other stimuli which will call out these responses we must also leave in doubt. If our observations are in any way complete, it would seem that emotional reactions are quite simple in the infant and the stimuli which call them out quite few in number.

These reactions which we have agreed, then, to call fear, rage and love, are at first quite indefinite. Much work remains to be done to see what the various part reactions are in each and how much they differ. They are certainly not the complicated kinds of emotional reactions we see later on in life but at least I believe *they form the nucleus out of which all future emotional reactions arise.* So quickly do they become conditioned, as we shall show later, that it gives a wrong impression to call them hereditary modes of response. It is probably better just to keep to the actual facts of observation thus:

(Ordinarily called Fear:)

(U)S	(U)R
Loud sounds Loss of support [1]	Checking of breathing, "jump" or start of whole body, crying, often defaecation and urination (and many others not worked out experimentally. Probably the largest group of part reactions are visceral).

(Ordinarily called Rage:)

(U)S	(U)R
Restraint of bodily movement	Stiffening of whole body, screaming, temporary cessation of breathing, reddening of face changing to blueness of face, etc. It is obvious that while there are general overt responses, the greatest concentration of movement is in the visceral field. Blood tests of infants so manhandled show that there is an increase in blood sugar. This means probably an increase in the secretion of the adrenal glands.

[1] I am uncertain what the relationship is between the fear reactions we have been describing and the reactions called out by very hot objects, ice cold water, blows, cutting, pricking, burns and other noxious stimuli.

(Ordinarily called Love:)

(U)S........................(U)R

Stroking skin and sex organs, rocking, riding on foot, etc.

Cessation of crying; gurgling,
cooing and many others not determined. That visceral factors predominate is shown by changes in
circulation and in respiration, erection of penis, etc.

If we think of these *unlearned* (so-called emotional) responses in the terms of these simple formulae, we cannot go very far wrong.

RECENT CRITICISMS OF THIS VIEW

E. S. Robinson is apparently not convinced of the objective character of my results. He says (*Jr. of Genetic Psychology,* September 1930, p. 433): "It has required Mandel and Irene Sherman, with their statistical conscience, to give us some idea of the difference between what Watson observed and what he read into infantile behavior." Let us look at their work for a moment.

Dr. and Mrs. Sherman, *The Process of Human Behavior* (1929) do seem at first sight by their experiments to throw some doubt upon the simplicity of our analysis of the emotions. Reactions of various kinds—to noise, deprivation of food, pricking with a needle, restraint, dropping and others were induced in infants. Motion pictures of these reactions were taken and then the picture was displayed before a group of graduate students. They were asked to *name the emotion displayed.* As could have been predicted by any one experienced in the reactions of infants, the graduate students showed great diversity in naming the observed reaction. It is hard for me to see the purpose of this investigation. Only an experienced investigator watching a child day in and day out reacting under a given stimulus or situation would have been in a position "given the reaction to predict the stimulus" or *vice versa.* If Dr. and Mrs. Sherman had carefully followed my work, they should have recalled that I suggested that we probably should not call these re-actions fear, rage and love, but rather reactions X, Y, and Z. Any one working for a long period of time upon infant A would certainly come to see the very great difference in its X, Y, Z re-actions. This is all I claimed on the identification side. The real business of the behaviorist was to see whether he could attach reaction X to some other stimulus, Y to another, Z to still another, and if so, by what technique. Again if such emotional attachment could be established to new stimuli, could they be again broken down and if so by what technique? Too many investigators have confirmed this work—any one I believe can confirm it who fol-lows the technique I followed.[1]

HOW OUR EMOTIONAL LIFE BECOMES COMPLICATED

How can we square our own observations with those which show the enormous complexity in the emotional life of the adult? We know that hundreds of children are afraid of the dark, we know that many women are afraid of snakes, mice and insects, and that emotions are attached to many ordinary objects of almost daily use. Fears become attached to persons and to places and to general situations, such as the woods, the water. In the same way the number of objects and situations which can call out rage and love become enormously increased. Rage and love at first are not produced by the mere sight of an object. We know that later on in life the mere sight of persons may call out both of these primi-tive emotions. How do such "attachments" grow up? How can ob-jects which at first do not call out emotions come later to call them out and thus greatly increase the richness as well as the dangers of our emotional life?

We were rather loath at first to conduct experiments in this field,

[1] Still more recently C. W. Valentine, (*Jr. of Genetic Psychology*, Sept. 1930) argues for an innate basis for several forms of fear.

but the need of study was so great that we finally decided to attempt to build up fears in the infant and then later to study practical methods for removing them. We chose as our first subject Albert B., an infant weighing twenty-one pounds, at eleven months of age. Albert was the son of one of the wet nurses in the Harriet Lane Hospital. He had lived his whole life in the hospital. He was a wonderfully "good" baby. In all the months we worked with him we never saw him cry until after our experiments were made!

Before turning to the experiments by means of which we built up emotional responses in the laboratory, it is necessary to recall the technique of establishing conditioned reflexes. In building in a conditioned reflex there must be a fundamental stimulus to start with which will call out the response in question. The next step is to get some other stimulus to call it out. For example, if your purpose is to make the arm and hand jerk away every time a buzzer sounds, you must use the electric shock or other noxious stimulus each time the electric buzzer is sounded. Shortly, the arm will begin to jump away when the buzzer is sounded just as it jumps away when the electric shock is given. We already know now that there is an unconditioned or fundamental stimulus which will call out the fear reaction quickly and easily. It is a loud sound. We determined to use this just as we used the electric shock in the experiments discussed on p. 23.

Our first experiment with Albert had for its object the conditioning of a fear response to a white rat. We first showed by repeated tests that nothing but loud sounds and removal of support would bring out fear response in this child. Everything coming within twelve inches of him was reached for and manipulated. His reaction, however, to a loud sound was characteristic of what occurs with most children. A steel bar about one inch in diameter and three feet long, when struck with a carpenter's hammer, produced the most marked kind of reaction.

Our laboratory notes [1] showing the progress in establishing a conditioned emotional response are given here in full:

Eleven months, 3 days old. (1) White rat which he had played with for weeks was suddenly taken from the basket (the usual routine) and presented to Albert. He began to reach for rat with left hand. Just as his hand touched the animal the bar was struck immediately behind his head. The infant jumped violently and fell forward, burying his face in the mattress. He did not cry, however.

(2) Just as his right hand touched the rat the bar was again struck. Again the infant jumped violently, fell forward and began to whimper.

On account of his disturbed condition no further tests were made for one week.

Eleven months, ten days old. (1) Rat presented suddenly without sound. There was steady fixation but no tendency at first to reach for it. The rat was then placed nearer, whereupon tentative reaching movements began with the right hand. When the rat nosed the infant's left hand the hand was immediately withdrawn. He started to reach for the head of the animal with the forefinger of his left hand but withdrew it suddenly before contact. It is thus seen that the two joint stimulations given last week were not without effect. He was tested with his blocks immediately afterwards to see if they shared in the process of conditioning. He began immediately to pick them up, dropping them and pounding them, etc. In the remainder of the tests the blocks were given frequently to quiet him and to test his general emotional state. They were always removed from sight when the process of conditioning was under way.

(2) Combined stimulation with rat and sound. Started, then fell over immediately to right side. No crying.

(3) Combined stimulation. Fell to right side and rested on hands with head turned from rat. No crying.

(4) Combined stimulation. Same reaction.

(5) Rat suddenly presented *alone.* Puckered face, whimpered and withdrew body sharply to left.

[1] See the original paper by Rosalie Rayner and John B. Watson, *Scientific Monthly,* 1921, p. 493.

(6) Combined stimulation. Fell over immediately to right side and began to whimper.

(7) Combined stimulation. Started violently and cried, but did not fall over.

(8) Rat alone. *The instant the rat was shown the baby began to cry. Almost instantly he turned sharply to the left, fell over, raised himself on all fours and began to crawl away so rapidly that he was caught with difficulty before he reached the edge of the mattress.*

Surely this proof of the conditioned *origin* of a fear response puts us on natural science grounds in our study of emotional behavior. It is a far more prolific goose for laying golden eggs than is James' barren verbal formulation. It yields an explanatory principle that will account for the enormous complexity in the emotional behavior of adults. We no longer in accounting for such behavior have to fall back upon heredity.

THE SPREAD OR TRANSFER OF CONDITIONED EMOTIONAL RESPONSES

Before the above experiment on the rat was made Albert had been playing for weeks with rabbits, pigeons, fur muffs, the hair of the attendants, and false faces. What effect will conditioning him upon the rat have upon his response to these animals and other objects when next he sees them? To test this we made no further experiments upon him for five days. That is, during this five day period he was not allowed to see any of the above objects. At the end of the 6th day we again tested him, first with the rat to see if the conditioned fear response to it had carried over. Our notes are as follows:

Eleven months, fifteen days old.

(1) Tested first with blocks. He reached readily for them, playing with them as usual. This shows that there has been no *general* transfer to the room, table, blocks, etc.

(2) Rat alone. Whimpered immediately, withdrew right hand and turned head and trunk away.

(3) Blocks again offered. Played readily with them, smiling and gurgling.

(4) Rat alone. Leaned over to the left side as far away from the rat as possible, then fell over, getting up on all fours and scurrying away as rapidly as possible.

(5) Blocks again offered. Reached immediately for them, smiling and laughing as before.

This shows that the conditioned response was carried over the five-day period. Next we presented in order a *rabbit,* a *dog,* a *sealskin coat, cotton wool, human hair* and a *false face:*

(6) *Rabbit* alone. A rabbit was suddenly placed on the mattress in front of him. The reaction was pronounced. Negative responses began at once. He leaned as far away from the animal as possible, whimpered, then burst into tears. When the rabbit was placed in contact with him he buried his face in the mattress, then got up on all fours and crawled away, crying as he went. This was a most convincing test.

(7) The blocks were next given him, after an interval. He played with them as before. It was observed by four people that he played far more energetically with them than ever before. The blocks were raised high over his head and slammed down with a great deal of force.

(8) *Dog* alone. The dog did not produce as violent a reaction as the rabbit. The moment fixation of the eyes occurred the child shrank back and as the animal came nearer he attempted to get on all fours but did not cry at first. As soon as the dog passed out of his range of vision he became quiet. The dog was then made to approach the infant's head (he was lying down at the moment). Albert straightened up immediately, fell over to the opposite side and turned his head away. He then began to cry.

(9) Blocks were again presented. He began immediately to play with them.

(10) *Fur coat* (seal). Withdrew immediately to the left side and began to fret. Coat put close to him on the left side, he turned immediately, began to cry and tried to crawl away on all fours.

(11) *Cotton wool.* The wool was presented in a paper package. At the ends the cotton was not covered by the paper. It was placed first on his

feet. He kicked it away but did not touch it with his hands. When his hand was laid on the wool he immediately withdrew it but did not show the shock that the animals or fur coat produced in him. He then began to play with the paper, avoiding contact with the wool itself. Before the hour was up, however, he lost some of his negativism to the wool.

(12) Just in play W., who had made the experiments, put his head down to see if Albert would play with his hair. Albert refused to touch it. The two other observers did the same thing. He began immediately to play with their hair. A Santa Claus mask was then brought and presented to Albert. He reacted strongly against it, although on all previous occasions he had played with it.

Our notes thus give a convincing proof of spread or transfer.

We have here further proof in these transfers that conditioned emotional responses are similar to other conditioned responses. Please recall what I said on p. 32 about *differential* responses. I brought out the fact that if one conditions an animal, say, to a *tone A* of a given pitch almost any other tone will at first call out the response. I stated further, that by continuing the experiment —say by always feeding when tone A is sounded but *never* when any other tone is sounded—one soon gets the animal to the point where it will respond only to A.

I am sure that in these cases of transfer or spread of conditioned emotional responses the same factors are at work.

I believe, although I have never tried the experiment, that we could set up just as sharp a differential reaction in the emotional field as we can in any other. I mean by this merely that if the experiment were long continued we could bring the fear reaction out sharply whenever the rat was shown but never when any other furry object was shown. If this were the case, we should have a *differential conditioned emotional response*. This seems to be what happens in real life. Most of us in infancy and in early youth are in the undifferentiated emotional state. Many adults, especially women, remain in it. All primitive peoples remain in it (superstitions). But educated adults by the long training they get in manipulating objects, handling animals, working with electricity, reach the second or differentiated stage of the conditioned emotional reaction.

There is thus, if my reasoning is correct, a thoroughly sound way of accounting for transferred emotional responses—and for the Freudian's so-called "free-floating affects." When conditioned emotional responses are first set up, a wide range of stimuli (in this case all hairy objects) physically similar will at first call out a response and so far as you know will continue to call it out unless experimental steps (or a very fortunate series of environmental settings take place) are taken to bring the undifferentiated conditioned response up to the differentiated stage. *In the differentiated stage, only the object or situation one is conditioned upon originally will call out the response.*

SUMMARY

We must see that there is just as little evidence for a wholesale inheritance of those complicated patterns of response commonly called *emotional* as there is for the inheritance of those called *instinctive*.

Possibly a better way to describe our findings is to say that in working over the whole field of the human infant's reaction to stimuli, we find that certain types of stimuli—loud sounds and removal of support—produce a certain general type of response, namely, momentary checking of breath, a start of the whole body, crying, marked visceral responses, etc.; that another type of stimulus—holding or restraint—produces crying with wide open mouth, prolonged holding of breath, marked changes in circulation and other visceral changes; that a third stimulus—stroking the skin, especially in sex-sensitive areas—produces smiling, changes in respiration, cessation of crying, cooing, gurgling, erection and other visceral changes. Attention is called to the fact that responses to these stimuli are not mutually exclusive—many of the part reactions are the same.

These unconditioned stimuli with their relatively simple unconditioned responses are our starting points in building up those complicated conditioned habit patterns we later call our emotions. In other words, emotional reactions are built in and to order like most of our other reaction patterns. Not only do we get an increase in the number of stimuli calling out the response (substitution) through direct conditioning and through transfers (thus enormously widening the stimulus range) but also we get marked additions to the responses and other modifications of them.

Another set of factors increasing the complexity of our emotional life must be taken into account. The same object (for example, a person) can become a substitute stimulus for a fear response in one situation and a little later a substitute stimulus for a love response in another, or even for a rage response. The increasing complexity brought about by these factors soon gives us an emotional organization sufficiently complicated to satisfy even the novelist and the poet.

I am loath to close this chapter until I have introduced, parenthetically at least, a thought which I shall take up later in describing some of the human being's more complicated types of reaction. The thought is that notwithstanding the fact that in all emotional responses there are overt factors such as the movement of the eyes and the arms and the legs and the trunk, *visceral and glandular factors predominate.* The "cold sweat" of fear, the "bursting heart," the "bowed head" in apathy and grief, the "exuberance of youth," the "palpitating heart" of the swain or maiden, are more than mere literary expressions; they are bits of genuine observation.

I want to develop the thesis later on that society has never been able to get hold of these implicit concealed visceral and glandular reactions of ours, or else it would have schooled them in us, for society has a great propensity for regulating all of our reactions.

Hence most of our adult overt reactions—our speech, the movements of our arms, legs and trunk—are schooled and habitized. Owing to their concealed nature, however, society cannot get hold of visceral behavior to lay down rules and regulations for its integration. It follows as a corollary from this that we have no names, no words with which to describe these reactions. They remain unverbalized. One can describe in well chosen words every act of two boxers, two fencers, and can criticize each individual detail of their responses, because there are verbal manuals of procedure and practice in the performance of these skillful acts. But what Hoyle has laid down the rules by which the separate movements of our viscera and glands must take place when in the presence of an emotionally exciting object?

Because, then, of the fact that we have never verbalized these responses, a good many things happen to us *that we cannot talk about. We have never learned how to talk about them. There are no words for them.* The theory of the unverbalized in human behavior gives us a natural science way of explaining many things the Freudians now call "unconscious complexes," "suppressed wishes" and the like. In other words, we can now come back to natural science in our study of emotional behavior. Our emotional life grows and develops like our other *sets of habits*. But do our emotional habits once implanted suffer from disuse? Can they be put away and outgrown like our manual and verbal habits? Until very recently we had no facts to guide us in answering these questions. Some are now available. In the next chapter I shall attempt to present them.

VIII. Emotions

WHAT EMOTIONS ARE WE BORN WITH—HOW
DO WE ACQUIRE NEW ONES—HOW
DO WE LOSE OUR OLD ONES?

PART II. FURTHER EXPERIMENTS AND OBSERVATIONS ON HOW
WE ACQUIRE, SHIFT AND LOSE OUR EMOTIONAL LIFE

INTRODUCTION: The experiments discussed in the last chapter were completed in 1920. Until the fall of 1923 no further experiments were undertaken. Finding that emotional responses could be built in with great readiness, we were eager to see next whether they could be broken down, and if so by what methods. No further tests could be made upon Albert B., the youngster in whom the conditioned responses had been built up, because he was shortly afterwards adopted by an out-of-town family.

The matter of further experimentation rested until the fall of 1923. At that time a sum of money was granted by the Laura Spelman Rockefeller Memorial to the Institute of Educational Research of Teachers College, a part of which was used for continuing the study of the emotional life of children. We found a place for work—the Heckscher Foundation. Approximately 70 children are kept there ranging in age from 3 months to 7 years. It was not an ideal place for our experimental work because we were not allowed full control of the children and because of the frequency with which work had to be stopped on account of unavoidable epidemics of one kind or another. In spite of these handi-

caps much work was accomplished. The actual experimentation
was done by Dr. Mary Cover Jones who also wrote up the results.[1]

Locating the Conditioned Fear Responses in Children: We began our experiments by putting a number of children of different
ages through a group of situations designed to bring out fear
responses if any were present. As has already been mentioned, children brought up in the home are prone to show fear reactions.
These we have every reason to believe are conditioned. By passing
each individual through these situations we were able not only to
locate the children possessing the most pronounced conditioned
fear reactions but also to locate the objects (and the general situations) that called out those reactions.

We worked here of course under one disadvantage. We did not
know the genetic history of their fear responses. Hence we did not
know whether a given fear reaction when observed was directly
conditioned or merely transferred. This is always a handicap—
an especially hard one in this work as I shall show you later.

Elimination of Fear Responses Through Disuse: Having located
a child with a fear response and the stimulus calling it out, our
next step was to attempt to remove it.

It has commonly been supposed that the mere removal of the
stimulus for a sufficient length of time will cause the child or
adult to "forget his fear." All of us have heard the expressions
"Just keep him away from it and he'll outgrow it. He will forget
all about it." Laboratory tests were made to determine the efficacy
of this method. I quote from Dr. Jones' laboratory notes.

Case 1.—Rose D. Age 21 months. General situation: sitting in play-
pen with other children none of whom showed specific fears. A rabbit
was introduced from behind a screen.

[1] See The Elimination of Children's Fears, by Mary Cover Jones, Jr. *Exp. Psychology,*
1924, p.382.

Jan. 19. At sight of the rabbit, Rose burst into tears, her crying lessened when the experimenter picked up the rabbit, but again increased when the rabbit was put back on the floor. At the removal of the rabbit she quieted down, accepted a cracker, and presently returned to her blocks.

Feb. 5. After 2 weeks the situation was repeated. She cried and trembled upon seeing the rabbit. E. (the experimenter) sat on the floor between Rose and the rabbit; she continued to cry for several minutes. E. tried to divert her attention with the peg-board; she finally stopped crying, but continued to watch the rabbit and would not attempt to play.

Case 8.—Bobby G. Age 30 months.

Dec. 6. Bobby showed a slight fear response when a rat was presented in a box. He looked at it from a distance of several feet, drew back and cried. A 3-day period of training followed, bringing Bobby to the point where he tolerated a rat in the pen in which he was playing, and even touched it without overt fear indications. No further stimulation with the rat occurred until

Jan. 30. After nearly two months of no experience with the specific stimulus, Bobby was again brought into the laboratory. While he was playing in the pen, E. appeared, with a rat held in her hand. Bobby jumped up, ran outside the pen, and cried. The rat having been returned to its box, Bobby ran to E., held her hand, and showed marked disturbance.

Case 33.—Eleanor J. Age 21 months.

Jan. 17. While playing in the pen, a frog was introduced from behind her. She watched, came nearer, and finally touched it. The frog jumped. She withdrew and when later presented with the frog, shook her head and pushed the experimenter's hand away violently.

Mar. 26. After two months of no further experience with animals, Eleanor was taken to the laboratory and offered the frog. When the frog hopped she drew back, ran from the pen and cried.

These tests and many others similar in character incline us to believe that the *method of disuse in the case of emotional disturbance is not as effective as is commonly supposed.* It is admitted, however, that the tests were not extended over long enough time to yield complete evidence.

METHOD OF VERBAL ORGANIZATION

Most of the subjects in the Heckscher Foundation were under 4 years of age and the possibility of verbally organizing the children about the objects that called out fear responses was very limited. Naturally nothing can be accomplished by the use of this method until the child has a fairly wide language organization. However, one satisfactory subject—Jean E., a girl in her 5th year, was found sufficiently well organized to be used in an extended test. At the initial presentation of the rabbit, marked fear responses were shown. The rabbit was not shown again for some time, but ten minutes' daily conversation was given her on the subject of rabbits. The experimenter introduced such devices as the picture book of Peter Rabbit, toy rabbits and rabbits modeled from plasticine. Brief stories about rabbits were told. During the telling of these stories, she would say "Where is your rabbit?" or "Show me a rabbit"; and once she said "I touched your rabbit and stroked it and never cried" (which was not true). At the end of one week of verbal organization, the rabbit was shown again. *Her reaction was practically the same as at the first encounter.* She jumped up from her play and retreated. When coaxed she touched the rabbit while the experimenter held it, but when the animal was put down on the floor she sobbed "Put it away—take it." Verbal organization when not connected with actual manual or visceral adjustments to the animal had little effect in removing her fear responses.

METHOD OF FREQUENT APPLICATION OF STIMULUS

While experiments with this method have not been extended, the results have not been very hopeful. The routine adopted in applying this method was to have the animal calling out the fear reaction brought in many times each day. While in some cases no actual negative responses were made, this was the only form of improvement noted—no *positive* reactions developed from the use of this method. In some cases a summation effect rather than an adjustment was obtained.

METHOD OF INTRODUCING SOCIAL FACTORS

Most of us are familiar both in the school and on the playground with what happens among groups of children. If one shows fear of any object of which the group does not show fear, the one showing fear is made a scapegoat and is called a " 'fraidy cat." We attempted to use this social factor in the case of some of the children. One case is given here in detail:

Case 41.—Arthur G. Age 4 years.

Arthur was shown the frogs in an aquarium, no other children being present. He cried, said "they bite," and ran out of the play-pen. Later, however, he was brought into the room with four other boys; he swaggered up to the aquarium, pressing ahead of the others who were with him. When one of his companions picked up a frog and turned to him with it, he screamed and fled; at this he was chased and made fun of, but with naturally no lessening of the fear on this particular occasion.

This is probably one of the most unsafe methods in common use for eliminating fears. It tends to breed negative reactions not only to the animal feared but to society as a whole.

Where milder social methods are used, ordinarily called social imitation, better results are obtained. Dr. Jones gives two cases which I quote:

Case 8.—Bobby G. Age 30 months.

Bobby was playing in the pen with Mary and Laurel. The rabbit was introduced in a basket. Bobby cried "No, no," and motioned for the experimenter to remove it. The two girls, however, ran up readily enough, looked in at the rabbit and talked excitedly. Bobby became promptly interested, said "What? Me see," and ran forward, his curiosity and assertiveness in the social situation overmastering other impulses.

Case 54.—Vincent W. Age 21 months.

Jan. 19. Vincent showed no fear of the rabbit, even when it was pushed against his hands or face. His only response was to laugh and reach for the rabbit's fur. On the same day he was taken into the pen with Rosey, who cried at the sight of the rabbit. Vincent immediately developed a fear response; in the ordinary play room situation he would pay no attention to her crying, but in connection with the rabbit, her distress had a marked suggestion value. The fear transferred in this way persisted for over two weeks.

Feb. 6. Eli and Herbert were in the play-pen with the rabbit. When Vincent was brought in, he remained cautiously standing at some distance. Eli led Vincent over to the rabbit, and induced him to touch the animal. Vincent laughed.

As will be noted, however, there are difficulties in the way of the use of this method. Occasionally the children showing no fear to the object become conditioned by the behavior of the child showing fear reactions to the object.[1]

While all of these methods are suggestive and while none of them has been worked out to a final conclusion, none seems especially fruitful or free from danger.

THE METHOD OF RECONDITIONING OR UNCONDITIONING

The most successful method so far discovered for use in removing fears is the method of *unconditioning* or reconditioning. Reconditioning would be a little more satisfactory word to use except for the fact that it has been used by the physical culturists in various types of health propaganda. Unconditioning seems the only other available word.

The method we employed in unconditioning and the results we obtained are best shown by citing the work done on Peter.

Peter was an active eager child approximately 3 years of age.[2]

[1] In her recent article, "The Prevention and Treatment of Children's Fears" in *The New Generation*, 1930, Dr. Jones seems to place more reliance upon this method than I do. Dr. Jones in this article discusses also the therapeutic measures used in the Habit Clinic of the University of California. Finally she gives a set of rules and conditions for handling fear cases at home.

[2] A full report on Peter is given by Mrs. Jones in the December, 1924, number of the *Pedagogical Seminary*.

This child was well adjusted to ordinary life situations except for his fear organization. He was afraid of white rats, rabbits, fur coats, feathers, cotton wool, frogs, fish and mechanical toys. From the description of his fears, one might well think that Peter was merely Albert B. grown up (see p. 162). Only one must remember that Peter's fears were "home grown," not experimentally produced as were Albert's. Peter's fears, though, were much more pronounced, as the following description will show:

Peter was put in a crib in a play room and immediately became absorbed in his toys. A white rat was introduced into the crib from behind. (The experimenter was behind a screen.) At sight of the rat, Peter screamed and fell flat on his back in a paroxysm of fear. The stimulus was removed, and Peter was taken out of the crib and put into a chair. Barbara, a girl of two, was brought to the crib and the white rat introduced as before. She exhibited no fear but picked the rat up in her hand. Peter sat quietly watching Barbara and the rat. A string of beads belonging to Peter had been left in the crib. Whenever the rat touched a part of the string, he would say "my beads" in a complaining voice, although he made no objections when Barbara touched them. Invited to get down from the chair, he shook his head, fear not yet subsided. Twenty-five minutes elapsed before he was ready to play about freely.

The next day his reactions to the following situations and objects were noted:

Play room and crib. . . . . .Took his toys, got into crib without protest.
White ball rolled in. . . . . .Picked it up and held it.
Fur rug hung over crib. . . . . .Cried until it was removed.
Fur coat hung over crib. . . . . . . .Cried until it was removed.
Cotton. . . . . .Whimpered, withdrew, cried.
Hat with feathers. . . . . .Cried.
White toy rabbit of rough cloth. .Neither negative nor positive reaction.

Wooden doll................Neither negative nor positive reaction.

Training for removal of these fears in Peter was first begun utilizing social factors as discussed on p. 171. There was considerable improvement, but before retraining was completed the child fell ill with scarlet fever and had to go to a hospital for a period of two months. When coming back from the hospital a large barking dog attacked him and the nurse just as they entered a taxicab. Both the nurse and Peter were terribly frightened. Peter lay back in the taxi ill and exhausted. After allowing a few days for recovery he was taken to the laboratory and again tested with animals. *His fear reactions to all the animals had returned in exaggerated form.* We determined then to use another type of procedure—that of *direct unconditioning.* We did not have control over his meals, but we secured permission to give him his mid-afternoon lunch consisting of crackers and a glass of milk. We seated him at a small table in a high chair. The lunch was served in a room about 40 feet long. Just as he began to eat his lunch, the rabbit was displayed in a wire cage of wide mesh. We displayed it on the first day *just far enough away not to disturb his eating.* This point was then marked. The next day the rabbit was brought closer and closer until disturbance was first barely noticed. This place was marked. The third and succeeding days the same routine was maintained. Finally the rabbit could be placed upon the table—then in Peter's lap. Next tolerance changed to positive reaction. Finally he would eat with one hand and play with the rabbit with the other, evidence that his *viscera were retrained along with his hands!*

After having broken down his fear reactions to the rabbit—the animal calling out fear responses of the most exaggerated kind —we were next interested in seeing what his reactions would be to other furry animals and furry objects. *Fear responses to cotton, the fur coat, and feathers* were entirely gone. He looked at them and handled them and then turned to other things. He would even pick up the fur rug and bring it to the experimenter.

The reaction to white rats was greatly improved—it had at least reached the tolerance stage but did not call out any very excited positive manipulations. He would pick up the small tin boxes containing rats and frogs and carry them around the room.

He was then tested in an entirely new animal situation. A gentle mouse which he had not hitherto seen was handed to him together with a tangled mass of earthworms. His reaction was at first partly negative but this gave way in a few minutes to positive response to the worms and undisturbed watching of the mouse.

We suffered here as always in working with home grown fears by not knowing the primary situation upon which the child was conditioned (conditioned reflex of the 1st order). Possibly if we had had information upon this point and had unconditioned him on his primary fear, all of the "transferred" responses would have evaporated at once. Not until we have had more experience with building up a primary fear, noting the transfers and then unconditioning for the primary, will we be working upon sure ground in this interesting field. It is just possible that there may be certain reaction differences (intensity) between the primary conditioned response (1st order), the secondarily conditioned responses (2nd and succeeding orders) and the various transferred responses. If this is true, then we might be able to tell, by presenting widely varying situations to children whose emotional history is unknown, just which one any given child was originally conditioned upon.

The whole field of emotions, when thus experimentally approached, is a very thrilling one, and one which opens up real vistas of practical application in the home and in the school—even in everyday life.

At any rate we have now seen grow up under our eyes the experimental genesis of a fear response and at least one case where the fear response was uprooted by a safe experimental method. If fear can be handled in this way, why not all other forms of emotional organization connected with rage (tantrums) and love? I believe firmly that they can be. In other words, emotional organization is subject to exactly the same laws as other habits, both as to origin, as we have already pointed out, and as to decline.

The use of the method in the case we have sketched had a serious drawback, mainly because we did not have control over all the meals of the child. (By the way, never start an experiment upon a child or infant unless you have full control). Probably if the child had been stroked, petted, and rocked (sexual stimulation, thus leading to retraining of viscera) just as the fear object was presented, unconditioning might have taken place much more rapidly.

Incomplete and unsatisfactory as is this preliminary report upon the work of unconditioning, there are at present few other facts. We must leave the subject of conditioning and unconditioning of emotional reactions until we can work upon a larger number of infants and work with them under better conditions of control.

HOME FACTORS LEADING TO EMOTIONAL CONDITIONING OF CHILDREN

It is conceivable that some day we may be able to bring up the human young through infancy and childhood without their crying or showing fear reactions except when in the presence of the unconditioned stimuli (pain, noxious stimuli, loud sounds) calling out these responses. Since these unconditioned stimuli are rarely present, children ought practically never to cry. And yet look at them—morning, noon, and night they are at it! An infant has an honest right to cry when it has colic, when its diaper pin is sticking into its tender flesh, and to whimper a bit when hungry, when it gets its head in between the slats of the bed, or falls down between the mattress and the side of the bed, or when the cat scratches it, or its bodily tissue is otherwise injured, or when loud sounds and loss of support assail it. But on few other occasions is the cry justifiable. This means that owing to our unsatisfactory training methods in the home, we spoil the emotional makeup of each child as rapidly as the twig can be bent.

WHAT SITUATIONS MAKE CHILDREN CRY

Dr. Jones followed around a group of nine children from the time they first waked up in the morning until they were fast asleep at night. Every cry was noted, every laugh observed. The duration of laughing and crying was noted and the time of day it occurred and, most carefully of all, the general situations calling out these reactions were recorded and the after effects crying and laughing had upon subsequent behavior. Children in the group ranged from 16 months to 3 years of age. These children were tested in the Heckscher Foundation, but they were living there temporarily. They had been brought up in the home. One month after the first set of observations was made another set was undertaken.

The situations calling out cries are listed in the order of the number of cries elicited, as follows:

1. Having to sit on the toilet chair.
2. Having property taken away.
3. Having the face washed.
4. Being left alone in a room.
5. Having the adult leave the room.
6. Working at something which won't pan out.
7. Failure to get adults and other children to play with them, or to look at them and to talk to them.
8. Being dressed.
9. Failure to get adults to pick them up.
10. Being undressed.
11. Being bathed.
12. Having the nose wiped.

These are only twelve of the most usual situations calling out such responses. More than 100 situations called out weeping or whining. Many of the responses to these situations can be looked upon as unconditioned or conditioned rage responses, for example: (1) sitting on the toilet chair, (2) having property taken away, (3) having the face washed, (6) working at something which won't pan out, (10) being undressed, (11) being bathed, (12) having the nose wiped. On the other hand, (5) having the adult leave the room, (7) failure to get adults to play with them, and (9) failure to get adults to pick them up—would seem to belong more in the love conditioned responses approaching somewhat the grief situation where the object or person to whom the attachment is formed is removed or else will not exhibit the customary responses (as where "love" has grown cold). Dr. Jones states that there were a number of cases, too, where fears of both the conditioned and the unconditioned type were responsible for a good deal of crying—for example, when the children were made to stand on the top of the slides, to slide down the slide, to stand on the tables. Possibly (4) and (5) of the above classification may have elements of the fear response in them.

In making a study of this kind, it should be always borne in mind that crying may be due to organic factors, such as sleepiness, hunger, colic and the like. Dr. Jones found that the largest number of cries (probably) due to intraorganic causes occurred between 9 and 11 o'clock in the morning. As a result of this finding, the institution placed its rest hours before lunch instead of after lunch, with two rest periods for the very young children. This considerably lessened the amount of crying and disturbed behavior due to intraorganic factors.

WHAT MAKES CHILDREN LAUGH

The situations which call out laughter and smiling were recorded in the same way. The common causes of laughter are, in order, as follows:

1. Being played with (playfully dressed, tickled).
2. Running, chasing, romping with other children.
3. Playing with toys (a ball was particularly effective).
4. Teasing other children.
5. Watching other children at play.
6. Making attempts which resulted in adjustment (e. g. getting parts of toys or apparatus to fit together or work).
7. Making sounds, more or less musical, at the piano, with a mouth organ, singing, pounding.

In all 85 situations were listed calling out laughter and smiling. *Tickling, playfully dressing, gentle bathing, romping* with other children, *teasing* (but always where there was a chance at a "come-back"—probably a learned response sexually based since the come-back involved being gently handled, pummeled and tickled) were the most frequent situations eliciting laughter. It is hardly possible to attempt to discuss here to what extent these smiling reactions were unconditioned and to what extent conditioned. Attention is called to the fact that depending on the way the situations are manipulated and upon the intraorganic condition of the youngsters, the same stimuli can at one time bring out laughter and at another time bring out crying; for example, although cries predominated in the bathroom when their faces were being washed or when they were being bathed, it was always possible to produce a laugh. On one occasion the introduction of a mouth organ altered the whole tenor of the room, changing distress into laughter. Where the youngsters are just being dressed by the ordinary procedure, that is, being pulled, twisted and turned, crying nearly always results, and where dressing is playfully done, smiles and laughter instead of crying are the responses. Attention should be called to the fact, however, that we can very easily overdo the matter of amusing the child when it is doing the things it has to do. I have seen children who had been spoiled in this way undergo torture when a new nurse was called in who did not or would not yield to their demand to be amused while being bathed, put to bed, dressed or fed.

While our results again are very incomplete, we have gone far enough to show that it is very easy to substitute for a great many of the situations in the home which now call out crying, situations that will call out smiling (and generally laughter) instead, which, in moderation, is unquestionably better so far as concerns the general metabolic state of the organism. Furthermore, when we have gone far enough to learn by continual watching what the sticking points are in the child's environment, we can rebuild his environment and thereby keep an unfavorable organization from developing.

SHOULD WE IMPLANT NEGATIVE RESPONSES IN CHILDREN?

There is a certain amount of sentimentality going the pedagogical rounds in this country to the effect that no negative reactions should ever be forced on the child. I have never been very much in favor of this progaganda. In fact, I believe that certain negative responses should be scientifically implanted as a matter of protection to the organism. I don't see any other way out of it. I think, though, we should make a distinction between conditioned fear responses and mere negative responses. Negative responses conditioned upon the original (unconditioned) fear stimuli always apparently involve vast changes in the viscera—possibly always disruptive to normal metabolism. Conditioned rage responses, while not necessarily negative in character (they include the positive responses in fighting, attack) apparently do the same thing. I have the simple facts in view here which Cannon has brought out, that in fear and rage behavior digestion and absorption are often completely interfered with—food is left in the stomach to ferment and to form a breeding ground for bacteria and to set free toxic products. So there is some justice in the view that fear and rage behavior are in general harmful to the organism (yet the race possibly could not have survived if it had not reacted negatively to loud sounds and loss of support and had not struggled when movement was hampered). Love behavior, on the other hand, seems usually to heighten metabolism. Digestion and absorption apparently take place more rapidly. Questioning of husbands and wives leads to the disclosure of the fact that after normal sexual intercourse hunger contractions begin in the stomach and food is very frequently sought.

But to come back to negative reactions. It is at least an opinion of mine that where negative responses are built into manual behavior (conditioned)—such as withdrawal of hands, legs, body, by the use of faint noxious stimuli, there is little involvement of the viscera. To make myself clear, let me cite a case: I can build in negative behavior to a snake in two ways. Just as I show the snake I can make a terrible noise and cause the child to fall down and cry out completely terror-stricken. Soon the mere sight of the snake will have the same effect. Or I can present the snake several times and each time the infant reaches for it I can tap its fingers with a pencil and gradually establish the negative reaction without shock. I have not tried this with a snake, but I have with a candle. A child can be conditioned by a severe burn with one stimulation, but this involves always a severe reaction. By presenting the candle flame many times and each time letting it just heat the finger enough to produce withdrawal of the hand, a negative conditioned response can be built up without the severe features of shock. Building in negative responses without shock requires time, however.

Civilization is built today upon "don'ts" and taboos of many kinds. Individuals living adjustedly in it must learn to heed them. Since the negative responses must be built in they should be built in as sanely as possible without involving strong emotional reactions. Children and adolescents must not play in the street, run in front of automobiles, play with strange dogs and cats, run up and stand under the feet of horses, point firearms at people, run any chance of catching venereal diseases or having illegitimate children; they must not do thousands of other things that I might mention. I am not saying that all the negative reactions demanded by society are ethically right (and when I say ethically I mean according to the new experimental ethics that will exist some day). I don't know whether many of the taboos now adhered to are ultimately "good" for the organism. I am merely saying that society exists—it is a fact, and if we live under it we must draw back when social customs say draw back, or we must get our adult hands slapped. There is, of course, an ever increasing number of people in the world whose hands are tough and who do many tabooed things and take the social chastisement that inevitably follows. This means of course that social trial and error experimentation is becoming possible—the smoking of women, now tolerated in restaurants and hotels and even in many homes, is a good example. As long as society rules every act through its agencies (such as political systems, church, family), no learning, no trying out of new social responses is possible. In the last 20 years we have seen marked changes in the social status of women, marked weakening of marriage ties, marked diminution in thoroughness of control of political parties (to wit, the overthrow of practically all monarchies), a marked weakening of the church's hold upon genuinely educated people, the lessening of taboos upon sex. The danger, of course, comes now from too rapid lessening of control, too superficial trials of new forms of behavior, and from the acceptance of new methods without sufficient trial.

USE OF CORPORAL PUNISHMENT IN BUILDING IN NEGATIVE RESPONSES

The question of corporal punishment in the bringing up of children at home and at school comes up periodically for discussion. I believe our experiments almost settle the problem. Punishment is a word which ought never to have crept into our language.

Whipping or beating the body is a custom as old as the race.

Even our modern views on the punishment of criminals and children have as their basis the old religious masochistic practices of the church. Punishment in the biblical sense of "an eye for an eye and a tooth for a tooth" honeycombs our whole social and religious life.

Certainly punishment of children is not a scientific method. As parents, teachers and jurists, we are or ought to be interested only in setting up ways of acting in the individual that square with group behavior. You have already grasped the notion that the behaviorist is a strict determinist—*the child or adult has to do what he does do. The only way he can be made to act differently is first to untrain him and then to retrain him.* That both children and adults do things which do not correspond with the standards of behavior set up by the home or by the group, is due to the fact that the home and the group have not sufficiently trained the individual during the formative period. Since the formative period is coextensive with life, social training should be continuous throughout life. It is our own fault, then, that individuals (other than defectives and psychopaths) go "wrong," that is, deviate from set standards of behavior—and by "our own fault" I mean the fault of the parent, the teacher and every other member of the group; we have neglected and are neglecting our opportunities.

But to return to the question of whipping and beating. There is no excuse for whipping or beating!

First, because very often the deviating act occurs many hours before father or mother comes home to engage in the act of chastising. Conditioned responses are not built up by this unscientific procedure. The idea that a child's future bad behavior will be prevented by giving him a licking in the evening for something he did in the morning is ridiculous. Equally ridiculous, from the standpoint of preventing crime, is our legal and judicial method of punishment which allows a crime to be committed in one year and punishment administered a year or two later—if indeed it takes place at all.

Second, whipping is used more often than not to serve as an emotional outlet (sadistic) for parent or teacher.

Third, often when the beating occurs immediately after the act (the only time for it if it is to take place at all), it is not and cannot be regulated according to any scientific dosage. It is either too mild, therefore not a strong enough stimulus to establish the conditioned negative response; or too severe, thus stirring up unnecessarily the whole visceral system of the child; or the deviating act does not occur frequently enough, with attendant punishment, to meet the scientific conditions for setting up a negative response; or, finally, the beating is repeated so frequently that all effect is lost—habituation comes in, leading possibly to the psychopathological condition known as "masochism," a condition in which the individual responds positively (sexually) to noxious stimuli.

How, then, are we to build in the negative responses which I said above it is necessary to build in? I thoroughly believe in rapping a child's fingers when it puts them in its mouth, when it constantly fingers its sex organs, when it reaches up and pulls down glass dishes and trays, or turns on gas cocks or water hydrants, etc., *provided the child is caught in the act and the parent can administer the rap at once in a thoroughly objective way*—just as objectively as the behaviorist administers the faint electric shock when building up a negative or withdrawal response to any given object. Society, both the group and the immediate parents, uses the verbal "don't" to older children in place of the rap. It will of course always have to use "don't" but I hope some time we can so rearrange the environment that fewer and fewer negative reactions will have to be built into both child and adult.

One bad feature in the whole system of the building in of negative responses is the fact that the parent becomes involved in the situation—I mean by that, becomes a part of the punishment system. The child grows up to "hate" the person who has most often to administer the beating—usually the father. I hope some time to try out the experiment of having a table top electrically wired in such a way that if a child reaches for a glass or a delicate vase it will be punished, whereas if it reaches for its toys or other things it is allowed to play with, it can get them without being electrically shocked. *In other words, I should like to make the objects and situations of life build in their own negative reactions.*

PRESENT METHODS OF PUNISHMENT FOR CRIME ARE RELICS OF THE DARK AGES

What we have said about punishment in the rearing of children holds equally well for adults in the field of crime. Since in my opinion only the sick or psychopaths (insane) or untrained (socially untrained) individuals commit crimes, society should be interested in just two things: (1) Seeing that the insane or psychopathic individuals are made well if possible, and if not, placed in well run (non-political) institutions where no harm can come to them and where they can do no harm to other members of the group.[1] In other words, the fate of those individuals should be in medical (psychiatric) hands. The question as to whether the hopelessly insane should be etherized has of course been raised time and time again. There can be no reasons against it except exaggerated sentiment and mediaeval religious mandates. (2) Seeing that the socially untrained individuals, not insane or psychopathological, are placed where they can be trained, sent to school, made to learn, regardless of their age, a trade, made to put on culture, made to become social. Furthermore, during this period they should be placed where they cannot harm other members of the group. Such education and training may take ten to fifteen years or even longer. Failing to put on the training necessary to fit them to enter society again, they should be restrained always, and made to earn their daily bread, in vast manufacturing and agricultural institutions, escape from which is impossible. Naturally, no human

[1] I recently heard Clarence Darrow contribute another thought on crime. He says being brought up in the environment the criminal is brought up in, (he) *can learn no other trade or business* than robbery, or murder.

being—criminal or otherwise—should be deprived of air, sunshine, food, exercise and other physiological factors necessary to optimum living conditions. On the other hand, strenuous work twelve hours per day will hurt no one. Individuals put aside thus for additional training should of course be kept in the hands of the behaviorists.

Naturally such a view does away completely with criminal law (but not with policing). It does away naturally with the criminal lawyer and with legal (criminal) precedent, and with courts for the trial of criminals. Many jurists of note agree substantially with this view. But until all law books are burned in some great upheaval of nature and until all lawyers and jurists suddenly decide to become behaviorists, I never expect to see the present retaliation or punishment theory (a religious theory) of handling the *deviant* give place to a scientific theory based upon what we know of the establishing and breaking down of conditioned emotional responses.

WHAT ARE THE MOST IMPORTANT FORMS OF BUILT IN EMOTIONAL BEHAVIOR?

In additition to the various forms of emotional behavior, both learned and unlearned, that we have discussed in this and in the preceding chapter, there are two other types which interest the behaviorist very greatly. These are *jealousy* and *shame*. So far the behaviorist has had very little opportunity to make any study of them. I believe that both jealousy and shame are built in.

Other forms of emotional behavior, popularly known as sorrow, grief, resentment, anger, reverence, awe, justice, mercy, seem to the behaviorist to be quite simple. He believes them to be vast superstructures built upon the very simple types of unlearned behavior that we have already abundantly discussed.

Jealousy and shame, however, require considerable further study. So far I have not had opportunity to observe the first appearance of shame and its genetic growth. I am inclined to think that shame is in some way connected with the first overt masturbation. The stimulus is the manipulation of the sex organs, the final responses are heightened blood pressure, superficial dilation of the capillaries of the skin known as flushing, among many others. Almost from infancy the child is taught not to masturbate or is punished if it masturbates. Consequently any situation, verbal or otherwise, connected with the touching of the sex organs or reference to the sex organs may condition the blushing and bowing of the head which nearly always take place in masturbation. This, however, is purely speculative.

I have recently made some observations and experiments upon jealousy.

Jealousy: Ask any group of individuals what they mean by jealousy—what the stimulus is that produces it, what the pattern of the response is, and you get only the vaguest, most unserviceable kind of replies. Ask these same individuals what the unlearned (unconditioned) stimulus is that calls out the response; ask them what the unlearned (unconditioned) response pattern is. To both questions you get unscientific answers. Most individuals say, "Oh, jealousy is a pure instinct." If we diagram thus

$$S\dots\dots\dots\dots\dots\dots\dots\dots\dots R$$
$$?\qquad\qquad\qquad\qquad\qquad\qquad ?$$

we have to put a question mark under both stimulus and response.

And yet jealousy is one of the most powerful factors in the organization of present day individuals. It is recognized by the courts as one of the strongest of "motives" leading to action. Robberies and murders are committed because of it; careers are both made and unmade because of it; marital quarrels, separations and divorces are probably more frequently to be traced to it than to any other single cause. Its almost universal permeation through the whole action stream of all individuals has led to the view that it is an inborn instinct. And yet the moment you begin to observe people and try to determine what kinds of situations call out jealous behavior and what the details of that behavior are, you see that the situations are highly complex (social) and that the reactions are all highly organized (learned). This in itself should make us doubt its hereditary origin. Let us watch people for awhile to see if their behavior will not throw light upon the situations and the responses.

WHAT SITUATIONS CALL OUT JEALOUS BEHAVIOR?

In the first place, as we have said, the situation is always a social one—it involves people. What people? *Always the person who calls out our conditioned love responses.* This may be the mother, father, or brother, sister or sweetheart, wife or husband—the object of homosexual attachments also must be admitted to this group. The wife-husband situation is second only to the sweetheart one for calling out violent response. This brief examination helps us somewhat in our understanding of jealousy. The situation is always a substitutive one, that is, conditioned. It involves the person calling out conditioned love responses. This generalization, if true, takes it out of the class of inherited forms of behavior at once.

WHAT ARE THE RESPONSES?

The responses in adults are legion. I have taken notes on a great many cases among both children and adults. To vary our procedure let us take the responses of an adult first. *Case A.* A is a "very jealous husband," married two years to a beautiful young woman only slightly younger. They go out frequently to parties. If his wife (1) dances a little close to her partner, (2) if she sits out a dance to talk to a man and talks in a low tone to him, (3) if in a moment of gaiety she kisses another man in the open light of the room before everyone, (4) if she goes out even with other women to lunch or tea or to shop, (5) if she invites her own group of friends for a party at home—then jealous behavior is exhibited.

Such stimuli bring out the responses (1) refusal to talk or dance with his wife, (2) increased tension of all his muscles, mouth shuts tightly, eyes seem to grow smaller, jaw "hardens." He next withdraws himself from other people in the room. His face becomes flushed, then black. *This behavior may and usually does persist for days after the affair is started. He will talk to no one about the affair. Mediation is impossible.* The jealous state seems to have to run itself down or out. The wife herself by no amount of assurance of love, of innocence, by no system of apology or obeisance can do anything towards hastening recovery. Yet his wife is devoted to him and has never been even in the slightest measure unfaithful, as he himself admits verbally when not in the jealous state. In a person less well bred, less well schooled, it is easy to see that his behavior might become overt—he might blacken his wife's eye, or if there were a real male aggressor, might attack or murder him.

Take the child's jealous behavior next. The first sign of jealousy was noted in child B at about 2 years of age. It shows whenever the mother embraces the father, clings to him, kisses him. At 2½ years of age this child who had never been made the "scapegoat," who had always been allowed to be present and even welcomed into the family love-making, began to attack the father whenever the mother embraced the father. He (1) pulled at his coat, (2) cried out "my mama," (3) pushed his father away and crowded in between them. If the kissing continued, the child's reaction state became very marked and intense. Always in the morning—Sundays especially, when he comes into the bedroom before his parents are up—he is taken up and welcomed and made much of by both. And yet at 2¾ years of age he would say to his father, "You going to office, dada?"—or else give the direct command," You go to office, dada." At three years of age this boy was sent with his infant brother to his grandmother's, in charge of a nurse. He was separated from his mother for one month. During this time his strong attachment for his mother weakened. When the parents visited the child (then 37 months of age) no jealous behavior was exhibited when they made love in front of him. When the parents clung together for a considerable time, to see if jealous behavior would finally occur, he merely ran up and hugged first one and then the other. This test was repeated for four days with the same results.

The father then seeing that the old situation failed to call it out, tried next attacking the mother, striking her on the body and head and shaking her from side to side. She on her part simulated crying, but fought back. The youngster stood this for a few minutes, then started in for his father tooth and nail and would not let up until the fight was over. He cried, kicked, tugged at his father's leg and struck with his hand.

Next the father remained passive while the mother attacked him. She inadvertently punched below the belt, causing the father to double up in no simulated way. Nevertheless, the youngster started his attack on his father again and continued it even after he was *hors de combat*. By this time the youngster was genuinely disturbed and the experiment had to be discontinued. The next day, however, no jealous behavior was exhibited when mother and father embraced.

HOW EARLY DOES THIS FORM OF JEALOUSY AGAINST ONE OR THE OTHER PARENT OCCUR?

To further test the genesis of this type of jealous behavior, a test was made upon an eleven-months-old infant boy. This infant was well nourished and wholly without conditioned fears, yet there was a strong attachment for the mother, but none for the father who often spanked his hand when he attempted to suck his thumb and otherwise broke in upon his quiet by trying various types of experiment. At eleven months he could crawl quickly and for considerable distances.

When father and mother violently embraced, the youngster could not be made to keep his eyes on his parents. Love making between them was nothing in his young life. This was tested again and again. There was no tendency to crawl towards them, much less to crawl in between them. Jealousy was absent.

Next the father and mother attacked one another. The floor was carpeted and the noise of the blows and the low whimper of the mother (or the father in his turn) was not very loud. The fight immediately stopped his crawling about, brought prolonged fixation—always of the mother and never of the father. As it continued, he whimpered and cried out aloud several times but made no effort to enter the fight on either side. The noises, shaking of the floor, and the sight of the parents' faces—which offered the same visual stimulus to him as when he himself got slapped and was made to cry, were sufficiently complex stimuli to call out the observed behavior. His behavior was of the fear type partly visually conditioned. There was apparently no jealousy behavior in this infant, either when its parents made love or when either parent attacked the other.

DOES JEALOUSY APPEAR SUDDENLY WHEN AN ONLY CHILD HAS TO FACE HIS INFANT BROTHER?

Many Freudians insist that the beginning of jealousy behavior very often dates back in the life of the child to the appearance of a brother or a sister. They claim that it starts practically full-blown even though the child in question is a year or less than a year of age. And yet, so far as I know, no Freudian has ever attempted to put his theories to practical experimental test.

During my own observations on the origin of jealousy, I have had one favorable opportunity to observe the behavior of an only child when he received his newborn brother. B, whose jealous behavior directed against his father was cited above, was 2¼ years of age when the event occurred. He had formed a very strong attachment to his mother and to his own regular nurse. He had no organized reactions toward any youngster under a year of age.

The mother had been absent in the hospital for two weeks. B was taken care of by his regular nurse during these two weeks. The day the mother returned, his own nurse kept B busy in his room playing until the conditions for the test were all set. The test was made at noon in a well-lighted sitting room. The mother was sitting nursing the baby, with her breast exposed. B had not seen the mother during the two weeks. In addition to the mother with her infant, there were present a trained nurse new to B, a grandmother, and the father. B was allowed to walk down the steps alone and into the room. Everyone had been instructed to remain absolutely quiet and to make the situation as natural as possible. B walked into the room and up to his mother, leaned on her knee and said, "How do, Mama." He did not attempt to kiss her or hug her. He did not notice the breast, or the baby for 30 seconds. Then he saw the baby. He said, "Little baby." Then he took the baby's hands and gently patted them, rubbed its head and its face and began to say, "That baby, that baby." Then he kissed it without any prompting. He was very gentle and tender in all of his responses. The trained nurse, who was unknown to him, took up the new baby. He reacted against this, at least verbally, saying, "Mama take baby." Thus the baby was reacted to really as a part of the mother situation and the first element of jealousy response was directed against the person who took something away from his mother (hampered his mother's movements). Surely this was as typically an un-Freudian reaction as could be imagined. This was the first sign of a jealousy response. But the response was positive for the infant and not against it—notwithstanding the fact that the brother was usurping his place on his mother's lap.

Then the new baby was taken by its nurse to its room and put to bed. B tagged along, too. When he came back, the father said, "How do you like Jimmie?" And he said, "Like Jimmie—Jimmie sleeping." He did not notice at any time the exposed breast of the mother and really paid very little attention to the mother except when the nurse tried to take the baby away. During the whole setting, he reacted positively to the baby for only a few minutes and then turned to other things.

The following day, B had to give up his own room which contained most of his toys, books, and the like, in preparation for the new baby. He was told that Jimmie had to have his room for a while. *This situation called out only the most eager positive response in helping to push and pull all of his own furniture to the new room.* He slept in the new room that night and every night until the trained nurse left. There was never the slightest sign of resentment or jealousy in his behavior directed against the new baby.

The behavior of these two children was under constant observation for over one year. Never was there the slightest sign of jealousy. At three years of age B was just as kind and considerate to the one-year-old infant as he was on his first introduction. Not even when nurse, mother or father took the infant up and petted it was there any jealousy. Once a new nurse almost succeeded in establishing it by attempting to control the older child by saying: "You are a naughty boy. Jimmie is a nice boy—I love him." For just a few days jealousy threatened, but the discharge of the nurse saved the situation.

Although during these tests there was no brotherly attachment pronounced enough to cause any disturbance of his daily routine, nevertheless if the younger child was around, the older youngster would take the part of the one-year-old if mother or father attempted to chastise the youngster by spanking its hand. The moment the younger infant cried, the three-year-old would actually attack either one or both parents, saying "Jimmie good boy; you mustn't make Jimmie cry."

CAN WE DRAW ANY CONCLUSIONS ABOUT JEALOUSY?

So far our experiments on jealousy are merely preliminary. If any generalization at all can be made, it would seem to take the following form: Jealousy is a bit of behavior whose stimulus is a (conditioned) love stimulus the response to which is rage—but a pattern of rage containing possibly the original visceral components but in addition parts of many habit patterns (fighting, boxing, shooting, talking). We may use this diagram to hold our facts together:

(C) S......................(U&C) R

| Sight (or sound) of loved object being tampered or interfered with. | *Stiffening of whole body,* clenching of hands, reddening and then blackening of face—pronounced breathing, fighting, verbal recrimination, etc. |

Naturally this is reduced only to the barest schematism. The response may take many forms and the stimulus may consist of far more subtle factors than I have noted here, but I believe we are on the right track in trying to formulate jealousy in these terms.

Summary: We have studied several phases of the human being's emotional life. The behaviorist's main contention is that man's emotional life is built up bit by bit by the wear and tear of environment upon him; that hitherto the building-in process has been hit or miss. The various forms of behavior have grown up unscrutinized by society. Some proof, at least, has been offered to show that emotional reactions can be built in in an orderly way—in any way society may specify. In other words, the process of building in emotional reactions is at least partly understood. We are beginning to understand how to tear down such reactions once they have been established. The future development of methods along this latter line interests us all—there are precious few of us who haven't some childish loves, rages or fears that we would like to lose. Such methods will enable us to substitute natural science in our treatment of the emotionally sick in place of the doubtful and passing unscientific method now known as psycho-analysis.

May the behaviorist, though, interject here a word of caution about his own views? All of his conclusions are based now upon too few cases and too few experiments. This will be remedied in the near future. More and more students are at work upon emotional behavior using behavioristic methods. No sane person can ever again use the old introspective method with which James and his immediate followers came so near wrecking this most thrilling part of psychology.

In the next chapter we will take up the steps we use in acquiring our great system of bodily habits, our acts of skill, vocations and the like.

IX. Our Manual Habits

HOW THEY START; HOW WE RETAIN THEM
AND HOW WE DISCARD THEM

I n the last chapter we were impressed by the one-year-old infant's organization. This organization, though, seems to center in the emotional and nutritional behavior patterns. Manual organization—that is, control of arms, legs, and trunk—is distinctly inferior to that displayed by other one-year-old primates.

The year-old monkey (Rhesus) dashes hither and yon, jumping from pillar to post, squealing the adult cry of its parents. It cannot fight with its parents for food, so it resorts to trickery. It gets into a corner, screams, and tears at a stick or watering pan as though some enemy attacked. The parents leave their own food to come to the rescue of the youngster. The youngster stops squealing immediately and dashes to the food trough and steals as much as his food pouches, mouth and paws will hold. On their return the mother or father, or both, may strike, bite or even knock down the youngster, if he has not made good his escape. We are reminded, in watching the year-old monkey, of the behavior of the oversophisticated twelve-year-old newsboy. At one year of age the human infant still gets all of its food at the mother's breast or from the bottle. It still gurgles and coos, saying no words at all or at best only ten or twelve. It moves about by crawling or by standing erect and pulling itself from place to place through the aid of opportunely placed pieces of furniture. Some adult has to fight its battles for it and protect it. It seems to be true, with some exceptions, that the higher we go in the scale of evolution, the more dependent the organism is upon learned behavior.

Notwithstanding the human infant's helplessness he is slowly to emerge into a being the like of which can nowhere be found in the animal kingdom. Greater development in three systems of habit forever differentiates him: (1) The number, delicacy and accuracy of *visceral* or *emotional* habits, which we discussed in the last two chapters; (2) the number, complexity, and fineness of his *laryngeal* or *verbal* habits, which we will discuss in the next chapter; (3) the number and fineness of his *manual habits,* which we will now consider.

The human being has enormous capacity for forming finger, hand, arm, leg and trunk habits. In several of the preceding chapters we have called this whole system the system of manual habits. We must be sure to make the word *manual* include organization in trunk, legs, arms and feet. As was previously brought out the muscular frame work for this organization is largely the striped muscles of the body (p. 60).

THE SHIFTING OF OUR ENVIRONMENT LEADS TO HABIT FORMATION

The reader should be prepared to believe now from what he knows of the human infant and child that it is constantly being stimulated by sights, sounds, contacts, smells and tastes from the outside of its body, and by secretions, absence of secretions, by pressure, lack of pressure, by movements of food along the intestinal tract and by changes in the position of muscles, both striped and unstriped, inside the body. It is, thus, under constant stimulation. Now the human is so built (and so are all other animals) that it must move when these stimuli assail it from within or without. The whole group of visual, auditory, tactual, temperature, smell and taste stimuli (so-called objects of the external world) constitutes what most people think of as environment. This is merely part of man's environment, namely, his external

environment (more or less common to groups). The whole mass
of visceral, temperature, muscular and glandular stimuli, both
conditioned and unconditioned, present inside the body, are just
as truly objects of stimulation as are chairs and tables. They constitute the other part of man's (each man's) environment—his
internal environment, an environment not shared by others. This
part of man's environment is left out usually in all discussions of
the relative influence of environment and heredity. The organism,
being stimulated always as he is by both environments simultaneously, naturally never is responding at any one time just to inside
stimuli or just to the outside stimuli. Under the stimulus of stomach contractions the individual will start to snatch a loaf of bread;
the visual stimulus of the nearby policeman may stay his hand
and lead to the taking up of another notch in his belt. Under
the action of a group of stimuli coming from the sex organs, he
may start to seek a mate, but the flabby condition of his purse may
hold in abeyance conventional courtship and marriage, and verbal
precepts instilled in his youth (laryngeal verbal stimulus) may
check association with a temporary mate.

As long as these powerful stimuli from outside and inside the
body—such as absence of food, absence of sex and absence of customary activity both manual and verbal—assail it, the human organism has to keep responding, keep moving. These stimuli call
out ceaselessly movements of fingers, hands, trunk, legs, arms—
and of the internal motor and glandular organs of response as well.
These movements in the infant have been called "random." They
are naturally not random if one means that they are not caused
like other movements. They are direct responses to stimulation
and are just as orderly as are movements later on in life.

Ceaseless stimulation, ceaseless movement are the order by day
and by night—not even in sleep is the organism unassailable by
stimulation nor is it ever motionless.

One may ask, doesn't the organism ever become adjusted? In

these days of psychologists and psycho-analysts we often hear of "adjustments." We are told that the individual must get adjusted. Sometimes you wonder what these eminent scholars mean. The behaviorist believes that the only adjusted person is a dead person— one from whom no response can be called out to any stimulus. *The facts seem to show that when the individual by responding (by learned or unlearned reactions, or both in combination) to stimulus A, changes his environment in such a way that he next has to react to stimulus B, then one of two things takes place: Stimulus B may actually remove stimulus A; or, by reacting to stimulus B, he may so change his environment that he passes out of the range of stimulus A. In the first case A is annihilated or "downed"; in the second case A ceases to be an effective stimulus in the new environment.* Does this sound complicated? Let us take an example. Hunger contractions begin in the stomach (stimulus A). The individual begins to move about. He reaches an environment where food is plentiful—in other words, he goes to the pantry and eats (stimulus B). The hunger contractions (stimulus A) stop immediately. This represents adjustment, you will say. To be sure he is no longer stimulated by food, *but after having eaten, other stimuli, non-food stimuli, immediately become effective and lead to other reactions—thus proving my contention that the organism is not and cannot be "adjusted" for longer than a period corresponding almost to a mathematical point.* Let me illustrate the second case— where the reaction of an individual to stimulus A leads to such an alteration of the environment that stimulus A is no longer effective. Individual X is lying on the bed trying to get to sleep. The arc light on the street shines through a crack in the shade. He wriggles around a bit. It still strikes his eye. He wriggles about some more. Again it strikes the eye. He puts his head under the covers. There the stuffiness and the heat soon make him put his head out. Again the insistent light strikes him. Then he gets up and does the one sensible thing—he pins a heavy piece of paper over the break in the shade. This response to A leads him into a new environment which no longer contains A as a stimulus. The two cases are thus on analysis not very different. The individual gets rid of the stimulus! But he gets rid only of that stimulus! Some other one can now effectively and successfully assail him. What the psychologists mean by maladjustment usually is that two stimuli with opposed action tendencies keep the organism from getting out of range of the inciting stimulus. The term "adjustment" however is convenient and we may still use it provided we mean by it the momentary point where the individual by his action has quieted a stimulus or has gotten out of its range. Let us mean by "adjustment," then, something similar to the end of a trial in learning—where the animal gets food, sex or water, or becomes oriented away from a stimulus that produces negative reaction.

Our illustrations so far show cases where the individual possesses an organization adequate to "meet the situation." This means merely that he has had to form habits of such a type that he can either blot out stimulus A or move in such a way that he can get out of its effective range. He reaches that happy state through no flowery path. *He has to form habits to effect it.* He has *learned* to go to the pantry when he is hungry. Not so the one-year-old—he can only cry. The adult has *learned* to get up and pin a piece of paper over the crack in the shade when the light strikes his eye. The three-year-old can only call aloud to his mother to shut out the light.

This is the keynote of the formation of all our habits. Some stimulus in the outside environment or in the inside environment (please remember that the so-called "absence" of a stimulus is also a perfectly good stimulus) sets the individual moving. He may move in many ways, do many hundreds of things, before he blots out stimulus A or moves himself beyond its range. If, when he gets into the same situation again, he can accomplish the one or the other of these results more rapidly and with fewer movements, then we say he has *learned* or *has formed a habit.*

WATCHING THE STEPS IN HABIT FORMATION

To understand the formation of basal habits, we must again observe the human infant. Take a baby brought up on the bottle.
When he is three months of age, slowly present the bottle of milk.
When it is close to him, almost within reaching distance, you will
find that his body begins to wriggle and squirm, his hands, feet
and arms become slightly active, his eyes fixate, his mouth moves,
he cries, but he does not extend his arms towards the bottle. At the
end of the test always give him his bottle immediately. Repeat the
procedure the next day. Notice that all of the bodily movements
are a bit more pronounced. As this routine is repeated daily,
movements of the whole body become still more perceptible but
the arms are levers built to permit wide excursive movements.
The trunk, the legs and the feet, while they are levers, are levers of
a different kind—powerful ones but with slight range of movement. The chance of the arms and the hands striking or touching
the bottle before the rest of the body is great. This is why our habits of manipulation are formed with the arms, hands and fingers,
and not with the feet, legs and toes. If the infant loses its arms,
or has never possessed them, these habits form with the feet.

Once the bottle, or, better for our immediate purposes, some
other food object, like a piece of candy or a lump of sugar, is
touched, the hand closes over it (unlearned grasping). It is then
carried to the mouth (part of a habit system previously learned).
In 30 days, by giving the baby 10 or 12 trials of this kind each
day, *the habit of reaching for a small object and carrying it to the
mouth becomes nearly perfect*. Note at this point that the reaction
to the milk bottle or lump of sugar is a conditioned visual response. The infant has become conditioned through having been
fed with the bottle, so that even in this simple experiment we are
starting with a certain amount of organization which has been
going on for a considerable time. If we wanted him to reach for a
pencil or some other object not connected with food, we would

have to start farther back and condition him to the pencil before that stimulus would call out a response. Note, too, that the stimulus of the bottle calls out a more and more complicated reaction: first just squirming, then more and more active movements of the whole body but most active movements of arms, hands and fingers, as I have pointed out before. In other words, the reaction is becoming changed, organized or, as we sometimes say, integrated. Possibly it is better to speak of the reaction as becoming more and more highly integrated (newer and newer elements becoming conditioned in such a way that they come together and function as a new or more complicated response).

Note, finally, that as the arm, hand and finger movements are perfected—that is, as the response becomes more highly organized —movements not related to the business in hand, such as in this instance those of the trunk, legs and feet, die away. In its perfected form, reaching takes place with perfect efficiency; movements not demanded in the act do not appear. Reaching is the child's basal primary manual habit. Very soon it grows more complex. He not only reaches and grasps but he learns to let the object drop at times. Again, he reaches not only for an object held out in front of him, but for objects to the right or left of him. Finally he learns to turn and twist and pull at his objects—to pull the top from a box, to take the cork from a bottle, to stick the end of his rattle into a box, to close and open the lid of the box. This whole complicated group of habits starting with reaching we call *manipulation*. Any one who thinks that manipulation is an instinct should work daily with a baby from the 120th day to the 200th day. The baby learns to manipulate objects and even its own bodily parts literally by the sweat of its brow.

I do not want to mislead any one into thinking that habits of manipulation involve only arm, hand and finger movements. It is easily understood from all that has gone before that any movement such as reaching for an object brings about an adjustment of practically every muscle of the body—and let us include

the viscera here as well. In other words, every movement accurately executed involves a response of the whole body in each and
in every part. This is what we mean by a total reaction. This is
what we mean by perfect integration. Movements of the shoulder,
the arm, the elbow, the wrist, the palm, the fingers, the trunk, the
legs, the feet, yes, even breathing and circulation, all have to take
place according to a certain order. This order must be beautifully
timed and the amount of energy in each muscular group must
be just right before any fine act of skill, such as hitting the bull's
eye with the rifle or making a perfect shot at billiards, can take
place.

With these early basal habits of reaching and manipulation
established, the infant begins his mastery of the world.[1] The steps

[1] Gesell and Thompson rather doubt the importance of early training in manual
activities (*Genetic Psychology Monographs*, Vol. VI, 1929). They emphasize maturation
(growth factors) rather than training in the early behavior patterns put on by infants.
They used the method of "co-twin control" to arrive at these results. One of the
(identical) twins, C, was allowed to mature without training. The other, T, was
subjected to training. For example, a typical experiment: twin T was subjected to training
in climbing stairs for a period of six weeks at the age of 46 weeks. Twin C was
deprived of all training in these reactions. At the age of 52 weeks, twin T after six
weeks' training climbed the staircase in 26 seconds. Twin C, without any training at
53 weeks climbed the staircase unaided in 45 seconds. After two weeks of training,
twin C climbed the staircase in 10 seconds. "The climbing performance of twin C
at 55 weeks was far superior to the climbing performance of twin T at 52 weeks,
even though twin T had been trained seven weeks earlier and three times longer. The
maturity advantage of three weeks of age must account for this superiority." Other
experiments of these authors lead them to the same conclusion.
    The behaviorists find it hard to accept such conclusions if the authors mean to imply,
as they seem to, that conditioning is of relatively slight effect in hastening the formation
of different behavior patterns in infancy. The behaviorist would be the first to admit
that muscular growth and strength (I confess I am not quite sure what these authors
mean by "maturation") in any complicated activity are undoubtedly factors in behavior. We would never attempt to teach a 52-week-old baby to drive an automobile
nor to run a foot race. One would like to point out here though that the method of
conditioning described in these experiments was quite amateurish in character. It is
evident too through the experiments that twin C and twin T were different in their
behavior patterns. Surely even the neophyte in conditioning would have used first T
and then C as control in different but similar experiments. The conclusion that training
on simple sensory motor responses around the age of 46 to 56 weeks is relatively
without effect in comparison with maturation is rather startling to one sophisticated
in infant conditioning. Any one who had the opportunity to observe the gymnastic

from fashioning his implements of clay and mud to fashioning them from tempered steel; from bridging a stream by crudely felling a tree to bridging a part of the ocean with steel and concrete; from building houses of rough grass and clay to building the sky-scraper of concrete and steel, are largely but illustrations of the growth of manual habits.

EXAMPLE OF THE GROWTH OF A HABIT

To make the whole process a little more concrete, let us put in front of the three-year-old child, whose habits of manipulation are well established, a problem box—a box that can be opened only after a certain thing has been done; for example, he has to press inward a small wooden button. Before we hand it to him, we show him the open box containing several small pieces of candy and then we close it and tell him that if he opens it he may have a piece of candy. This situation is new to him. None of his previously formed manipulation habits will completely and instantly work in this situation. None of his unlearned reactions will help him very much. What does he do? That depends upon his previous organization. If well organized by previous handling of toys, he goes at the problem at once—(1) he picks the box up, (2) he pounds it on the floor, (3) he drags it round and round, (4) he pushes it up against the base-board, (5) he turns it over, (6) he strikes it with his fist. In other words, he does everything he has learned to do in the past in similar situations. He displays his whole repertoire of acts—brings all of his previously acquired organization to bear upon the new problem. Let us suppose that he has 50 learned and unlearned separate responses at his command. At one time or another during his first attempt to open the box, let us assume that he displays, as he will, nearly all of them before he

behavior of Professor Horace Kallen's first born at the age of 52 weeks would need no further proof that training is of extreme importance in differentiating motor behavior at any time during the first year of infancy. It is to be hoped that Prof. Kallen will some day publish his results.

pushes the button hard enough to release the catch. The time the whole process takes, we will say, is about twenty minutes. When he opens it, we give him his bit of candy, close up the box and hand it to him again. The next time he makes fewer movements; the third time fewer still. In 10 trials or less he can open the box without making a useless movement and he can open it in two seconds.

Why is the time cut down, and why do movements not necessary to the solution gradually drop out of the series? This has been a hard problem to solve because no one has ever simplified the problem enough really to bring experimental technique to bear upon it. I have tried to explain on what we may call a *frequency* and *recency* basis, why the one movement finally persists whereas all the rest die away. I think I can make clear to you what we mean. Let us designate each of the separate acts of the three-year-old by a number. We will designate the final act—pressing the button which opens the box—number 50. Then on the first trial all of the 50 acts will occur (and many may appear more than once), let us say, in chance order:

47, 21, 3, 7, 14, 16, 19, 38, 28, 2, etc. 50
On the second trial:
18, 6, 9, 16, 47, 19, 23, 27, etc. 50
On the third trial:
17, 11, 29, 66, 71, 18, etc. 50
On the ninth trial:
14, 18, etc. 50
On the tenth trial and all succeeding trials:
50

In other words, number 50 tends to come earlier and earlier in the series and by doing so there is less and less opportunity for other movements to appear. Why? On our premise we can see that response number 50 is the only one that occurred on each and every trial; that is, the environment in the shape of the person conducting the test arranges the series in such a way that 50 has to be the end of the series—the infant then gets food; the box is closed and is handed to him again. Act number 50 is therefore the one most frequently repeated—more frequently, that is, than any of the other 49 acts.

Again, since act number 50 is always the last response in the previous trial, there is some reason for believing that it will appear sooner in the series of acts on the next succeeding trial. This is what is called the factor of *recency*. The recency and frequency factors as explanations of the formation of habit have been criticized by some writers—among others: Professor Joseph Peterson, of George Peabody College, Nashville, Tennessee, and Bertrand Russell.[1] No experimental test, that I consider crucial at any rate, has ever been made in this very important field. Only a few psychologists have been interested in the problem. Most of the psychologists, it is to be regretted, have even failed to see that there is a problem. They believe habit formation is implanted by kind fairies. For example, Thorndike speaks of pleasure stamping in the successful movement and displeasure stamping out the unsuccessful movements. Most of the psychologists talk, too, quite volubly about the formation of new pathways in the brain, as though there were a group of tiny servants of Vulcan there who run through the nervous system with hammer and chisel digging new trenches and deepening old ones.

I am not sure that the problem when phrased in this way is a soluble one. I feel that there must come some simpler way of envisaging the whole process of habit formation or else it may remain insoluble. Since the advent of the conditioned reflex hypothesis in psychology with all of the simplifications (and I am often fearful that it may be an over-simplification!) I have had my own

[1] Still more recently Clark Hull has given an interesting analysis of the factors entering into the learning of simple acts (*Psychol. Rv. No. 3, May, 1930*).

laryngeal processes stimulated to work upon this problem from another angle.

The relationship, theoretically, between the simplest cases of the conditioned responses we have studied and the more complicated, integrated, spaced and timed habit responses we are considering, seems to me to be quite simple. It is the relationship apparently of part to whole—that is, the conditioned reflex is the unit out of which the whole habit is formed. In other words, when a complicated habit is completely analyzed, each unit of the habit is a conditioned reflex. Let us go back a moment to the type of conditioned reflex we have already considered in previous chapters:

S................................ R

Electrical Contact (Noxious)	Movement of the foot
When conditioned, the	
visual stimulus of circle	Calls out same movement of foot

This is a simple type of conditioned response. Now by hypothesis every complicated habit is made up of just such units. Suppose in place of conditioning a subject to withdraw his foot when a visual stimulus of a circle is shown, we condition him to turn, say, one step to the right. When he turns to the right he faces a visual stimulus of a square. To this stimulus he is conditioned to walk forward five steps. He then faces a triangle. To this stimulus he is conditioned to move two steps to the right. This puts him face to face with a cube. In response to this he has to step up three steps instead of turning to right or left. You can see from this simple illustration that one can lead him all around the room and back to the starting point. We do this by arranging a series of visual stimuli to each of which we condition him so that he must move in a certain way—that is, turn to the right, to the left, move upward, downward, forward or backward, put his right hand up, stretch out his left hand, and the like. Now suppose each time we begin experimenting upon him, we run him through the whole series from the beginning. Isn't this a description (after the whole system has been turned over to kinaesthesis—see p. 219) of just what happens when the rat or the human learns, say, a complicated maze? Does not every alley, bypath or turn in the maze represent a unit in the whole process of learning the maze? Isn't typewriting, piano playing and every other special act of skill resolvable or analyzable into just such a set of units? Of course in real life, in establishing separate conditioned reflexes making up the whole habit, we sometimes use food or we pet the child to condition it when the right response is made; we may cuff it or otherwise punish it for a wrong response or allow it to run itself down into blind alleys, bringing on partial fatigue (which probably is an equivalent of punishment).

And why are these units timed and spaced as they are? There is no order or sequence as such in the world we live in—except in a few such things as the sun, moon and the stars. The answer is: *society,* or the *accident of environment arranges the series.* By *society* is meant the men and women constituting it who have set up complicated patterns of response that must be literally followed. Words have a certain number of letters and they follow one another in a definite sequence established by Mr. Johnson or Mr. Webster or some other early lexicographer. The holes of the golf course must be played in a certain sequence, pool balls must be shot into certain pockets. By *accident of environment* we mean, for instance, the simple fact that if you are to go from your own home to the old swimming hole you must (1) go to the right of a certain hill, (2) cross a small stream, (3) pass through a grove of pine trees, (4) follow down the left bank of a dry stream until you (5) get to the cow pasture, (6) then from behind a clump of large willow trees (7) you have come to your desired haven. Each of the numbers represents a visual stimulus that must be reacted to, at least during the learning stages.

You may say "Yes" to all this, "but what of it? Is the explanation of the formation of a conditioned reflex any simpler than that of *habit?*" The answer is: Even though we cannot "explain" a conditioned reflex, we have by analysis reduced to simpler terms a complicated process which we have neither been able to solve nor, apparently, to begin experimentation upon. I believe we can now turn our formulation over to the physiologist or to the physiological chemist for solution.

The problem we leave with him is:

Stimulus X will not now call out reaction R; stimulus Y will call out reaction R (unconditioned reflex); but when stimulus X is presented first and then Y (which does call out R) is presented shortly thereafter, X will (in time) call out R. In other words, stimulus X becomes substitutable for Y.[1]

The physiologist may come back at once with some such explanation as this: "You are wrong in your assumption about X not stimulating the organism. X does stimulate the whole organism and consequently does faintly arouse reaction R, only not strongly enough to appear as an overt response. Y does call out R overtly because the organism is biologically built to respond overtly with R when stimulated by Y (unconditioned response). But after Y has called out R, resistance or inertia in this whole sensory motor segment is lessened to such an extent that X, which only faintly called out R, will now call out R overtly." Certainly if the physiologist attempts to explain the various phenomena underlying conditioned responses at the present time, he will have

---

[1] This is not an exaggeration. I have seen a conditioned response firmly set up in a child by one contact with a hot radiator, a conditioned response which has been retained for two years without further training. If we should keep our old habit terminology, we should have in this example a habit formed by a single trial. There can be then in this case no "stamping in of the successful movement" and no "stamping out of the unsuccessful movements."

to couch his explanations in terms of resistance in the nervous system, interference, summation, inhibition, reinforcement, facilitation, all or none law, because these are the phenomena he works with; but they are very complicated phenomena, far too complicated for us even to attempt to describe them. Until he has reduced them to electrical and chemical processes I am afraid he cannot help us very much.

Fortunately we can continue our work in behavior without awaiting the true explanation of these biological phenomena couched in physico-chemical terms.

SOME DETAILS OF THE LEARNING CURVE

Below (fig. 16) is the curve showing the records of 19 rats in learning the complicated Hampton Court maze (modified). The horizontal line shows the number of trials the rats were given.

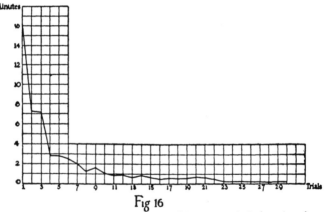

Fig 16

This curve shows the progress 19 white rats made in learning the complicated Hampton Court Maze.   The vertical line shows the number of minutes required to get to the food.   The horizontal line shows the number of trials given.   Thus, on the first trial an average of 16 minutes was required; on the thirtieth trial approximately 20 seconds. Note that improvement at first was very rapid and then went on more and more slowly.

Each rat was tested separately. Each point on the vertical line shows the average number of minutes it took the rats to reach the food on the various trials. Note that the first trial required on the average over 16 minutes. During this time the rat was running around the maze, into blind alleys, running back to the starting point, starting for the food again, biting at the wires around him, scratching himself, smelling this spot and that on the floor. Finally he got to the food. He was allowed only a bite. Again he was put back into the maze. The taste of the food made him almost frantic in his activity. He dashed about more rapidly. The average time for the group on the second trial is only a little over 7 minutes; on the fourth trial not quite 3 minutes; from this point on to the 23rd trial the improvement is very gradual. Then improvement seems to cease (with this method of training). Whether or not they have reached the physiological limit of training, cannot be determined from this curve. Less frequent practise than five trials per day might create a new situation which would bring about improvement. Partial starvation might bring about improvement. Many other factors may be operative in bringing it about (see page 213).

This animal curve of learning illustrates the details of learning possibly better than one taken from the human field because most of the curves showing the learning of humans contain many complications. When we work with rats we can keep the stimulus fairly constant. The rat has to run that maze five times or he does not get his full quota of food. At the end of his fifth and last trial for the day he can eat his fill. The human being becomes bored while learning. Other things stimulate him. The internal environment is complicated; internal speech (thought), for example, may always be a disturbing factor. Social and economic factors may enter. His learning curves often show so-called resting places or plateaus in the learning process. These are periods where no improvement seems to be taking place, where the curve remains horizontal instead of constantly dropping.

How to get individuals off these plateaus and to start improving
again is one of the problems both in business and in the laboratory.
The offering of so-called incentives, such as increases in salaries,
bonuses, participation in profits, increased responsibilities, has
been tried in business, resulting in rapid improvement at first, followed usually by another plateau. Sometimes the trouble is a
family situation—a sick wife or child, or the individual may be
jealous of his wife. Sometimes it is economic—the individual may
have as much money as he needs to get along in his group; there
is no stimulus to improvement. Usually when increased demands
are made upon him, improvement begins again. He may get married and beget a child, he may move to another more expensive
city. No cure-all method for bringing improvement can be found.

It seems to be a human failing to stop improving at the lowest
economic level that enables an individual to get along in his group.
People are lazy. Few want to work; the sentiment of the times is
all against it. The least work and the sloppiest you can get by on
is the present order of the day in most industries. The worker, be
he executive, foreman or manual laborer, often rationalizes it to
himself in this way: "I am not working for myself; why should I
slave for a corporation and let some one else get all the profits of
my work?" The individual loses sight of the fact that the improvement in skill and the general organization that come in work
habits are his own. They are personal possessions in which no one
else can share. The formation of early work habits in youth, of
working longer hours than others, of practising more intensively
than others, is probably the most reasonable explanation we have
today not only for success in any line, but even for genius. The
only geniuses I have ever met have been thoroughly hard working
fellows.

WHAT FACTORS INFLUENCE THE FORMATION OF MANUAL HABITS?

The factors influencing the formation of manual habits (and
verbal as well) have never been worked out in a wholly satisfac-

tory manner. The results of experiments are conflicting and there is considerable variation even in theory. The problems themselves are interesting, however. Let us raise some of them and give examples of the types of work now going on to solve them.

(1) *The effect of age on habit formation:* We know very little about the effect of age upon habit formation in the human. There seems to be a curious resistance to working at the problem. We know the difference between an old rat's way and a young rat's way of learning the maze. We have charted the difference in the number of steps they take, in the length of time they consume on each successive trial and in the final time of running errorless trials. A rat apparently never grows too old to learn the maze. There is very little difference in the number of trials required by the young rats and by the old rats to learn the maze. The old rats do less scampering about; they are slower in their explorations. Their final running time—that is, the minimal time in which they can run the maze after it is learned—is considerably longer than that of the young animals.

We have no similar series of facts on humans. It is obvious that humans stop learning too soon. Something ought to be done to disturb the average householder once in a while and force him to learn something new; but we have no control over him. In the case of the animal, we have complete control over food, water, sex and other factors in its environment. Only an earthquake, a flood or some other catastrophe can put the average adult individual back into a situation where he has to learn something new. The stock market break in 1929 is a good illustration of a sudden change of situation. What effect it has had cannot yet be stated in full, certainly it changed the buying habits of a wide group. Luxuries were dispensed with. Motor car orders were canceled. Jewelry was not bought. People did not have the money. Many individuals who had not worked in all the years of the Coolidge boom went back to work. Our inability to control the stimuli to learning explains, too, why there are so few good experiments upon human learning.

The psychologists know that the stimulus cannot be kept constant or the same in different laboratories. Most of the work on learning has, therefore, been incidental—classroom devices, doctors' dissertations, and the like. We have no real facilities for doing the complicated work which should be done on human learning. Some day we ought to have great laboratories where squads can be kept at work. Their food, water, sex and shelter could then be kept under very definite control—this all by way of proof of the fact that there is no real evidence that the human ever needs to quit learning. If the situation is urgent enough, the man of 60, 70 and, yes, even 80 can learn. James was right when he said most people do not learn after 30, but there is no reason for it except that most people after 30 have explored the mysteries of sex and get their food and water without speeding up or having to do anything unusual in order to obtain them. Poor as they are in their vocation, they can still live.

(2) *Distribution of practise:* Considerable work has been done both in the manual field and in the verbal field on the effect of variously distributing practise in learning.

Shall we give our rat learning the maze five trials per day, three trials per day, one trial per day or one trial every other day? If we take different groups of animals and train each group in a different way, we find, strange to say, that the less frequently the practise is given within certain limits, the more efficient is each unit of practise. In other words, if each of the groups gets only a total of 50 trials, the longer the interval between the various 50 practise periods the better the results (Dr. J. L. Ulrich). Dr. K. S. Lashley found the same thing to be true for humans learning to shoot the English long bow. Others working upon typewriting and upon other acts of skill have also confirmed this general principle.

Rosalie Rayner Watson (Psychological Laboratory, Johns Hopkins University) in her unpublished dissertation, presents some interesting results bearing on several phases of the learning process. All of her work was upon the learning of adults to throw a small steel-pointed dart with feathered shaft at a target. The target was a piece of cork matting 8 x 8 feet tacked vertically upon a frame. In the center of the target was a two-inch white paper bull's eye. The subjects threw the darts from a distance of 20 feet. The first problem she undertook to study was the effect of continuous practise upon learning—in other words, what would happen if individuals threw darts at the rate of one every two minutes for 24 hours? The curve below (fig. 17) shows what actually happened. Ten persons took part in the experiment. Each shot

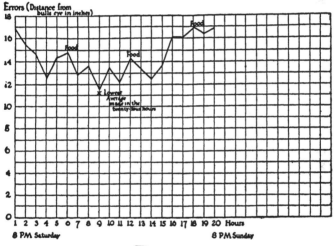

Fig 17

This curve shows what happens when 10 subjects throw darts at a target every two minutes for 20 hours. The vertical line shows the error—that is the distance the shot was from the center of the target. The horizontal line gives the record by hours. Note that progress for the first 4 hours was rapid, then accuracy fell off a little until food was taken; then follows another period of 3 hours' progress. Learning was fairly steady and uniform up to the 9th hour. After that apparently no further improvement was made.

in turn once every two minutes beginning at 8 P. M. Saturday evening and ending at 8 P. M. Sunday evening. The last four hours
were used for testing the effects of drugs so that only 20 hours are
shown on the chart. The moment each individual shot was made,
the distance in inches of the dart from the center of the bull's eye
was measured. Each point on the curve is thus an average of approximately 300 shots. Food was taken at six-hour intervals. Eating was not allowed to interfere with or to interrupt the work—
the individuals eating between shots. A regular cold meal was
served. If the individual usually took coffee or tea, he was allowed to take it in this experiment. It can be seen that the average
distance from the center of the bull's eye of the first hour's shooting was nearly 17 inches. Improvement was rapid for the first
four hours, then the shooting became less efficient during the
next two hours. Food at the end of the sixth hour seemed to bring
a certain improvement which continued to the end of the ninth
hour. After that, efficiency was gradually lost. At the end of the
twentieth hour the group was shooting no better than at the beginning of the experiment. Learning apparently had been either
obscured or lost—whether obscured or lost the experimenter has
not yet determined.

Just why widely distributed practise does bring better results
only can be guessed at with the facts we now have at hand. We
have no real explanation. It should be made clear though, that if
our object were to teach individuals to shoot the long bow so as to
have warriors as soon as possible, we should crowd them with
practise as long as practise produced any improvement at all. Concentrated practise is wasteful from the standpoint of the number
of trials required for learning, but sometimes our practical needs
demand that we adopt this wasteful method.

The main moral to be drawn from these experiments is that even
though we have little time at our disposal, still if we use that little
time in concentrated practise, even over widely spaced time intervals, we can get astonishingly good results.

(3) *Exercise of acquired functions:* After practising a given act for a sufficient time, the learning curve becomes horizontal. No further improvement comes (unless new factors are introduced). Let us call all such well learned habits, *functions.* Suppose one is exercising one of these functions day in and day out—for example, typewriting which one has been doing for ten years, or doing piece-work of one kind or another in a factory. Does one do the job faster in the morning, towards noon, after lunch, or just before quitting time? Does one do it better on Monday, Wednesday or Friday? Better in spring, summer, fall or winter? All of these problems have been worked upon but the results do not agree.

The whole subject of the course of diurnal efficiency, to single out just one of the problems, is in quite a muddle. In order to throw some light upon this problem, Rosalie Rayner Watson, whose work we cited above, took nine subjects whose learning curves on dart throwing had been thoroughly practised (daily for more than 2 months) and allowed them to throw darts from 8 A. M. to 8 P. M. Her results (Table 1) show that efficiency in this function and under the conditions of this experiment does not vary during the whole of the 12 hours.

In this experiment there was considerable rivalry among the participants and the stimulating value of the situation was kept high throughout the 12 hours. Where there is variation—that is, where efficiency itself declines at one time of day or another—it is probably due to such things as hunger contractions, slight torpidity after lunch and various other easily explainable factors. We cannot take time to discuss them now. The facts have not been brought out clearly enough yet.

(4) *Effects of Drugs upon the Exercise of a Function:* In a similar way the effect of drugs upon the efficiency of given functions has many times been tested. The effects of cocaine, strychnine, alcohol, caffeine, of starvation, cold, heat, oxygen hunger, of castration (upon animals), of administration of thyroxin, adrenalin,

TABLE I SHOWING DIURNAL COURSE OF EFFICIENCY IN A PRACTISED FUNCTION

(*Figures are given in inches from center of bull's eye.*)

	B	Gich	Gre	H	L	Ray	Rich	G	W	Av.
8–9 AM—Av. end of 1st hr.	6.3	10.3	12.5	11.5	10.2	10.4	7.0	11.8	5.6	10.7
9–10 AM—Av. end of 2nd hr.	7.2	9.5	11.1	9.9	9.2	11.6	6.9	11.4	6.9	9.3
10–11 AM—Av. end of 3rd hr.	7.0	10.2	11.6	11.7	8.3	12.1	8.3	9.8	5.9	9.4
11–12 AM—Av. end of 4th hr.	8.8	9.7	9.6	10.9	8.9	12.3	7.2	11.7	6.3	9.5
12 Noon–1 PM—Av. end of 5th hr.	10.0	9.7	9.7	12.7	11.3	8.4	8.4	12.5	5.1	8.7
1–2 PM—Av. end of 6th hr.	7.6	11.6	9.5	10.9	10.0	11.0	7.7	12.5	5.5	9.5
2–3 PM—Av. end of 7th hr.	8.8	10.0	10.6	11.4	8.8	10.8	6.2	13.0	5.3	9.4
3–4 PM—Av. end of 8th hr.	6.9	9.8	9.6	12.2	10.0	10.4	5.5	12.1	5.6	9.1
4–5 PM–Av. end of 9th hr.	7.6	13.3	12.5	9.8	8.7	10.2	5.7	11.0	4.9	9.3
5–6 PM—Av. end of 10th hr.	9.2	12.3	11.4	9.9	11.0	8.9	5.6	11.7	5.2	9.5
6–7 PM—Av. end of 11th hr.	7.1	11.3	9.3	16.7	10.3	9.8	5.5	11.8	7.4	9.9
7–8 PM—Av. end of 12th hr.	8.8	....	10.4	15.6	9.3	10.0	7.0	11.0	5.5	9.7

testicular extracts and the like, have all been tested. It requires a monographic treatment to do all this work justice. In general though, when the function has been practised for a long time, as was true for example, in my own work on dart throwing (see record on "W" in Table 1), it is surprising how little effect drugs have upon the score. On different days I took double doses of strychnine and of cocaine; on another day I drank 50 c.c. of rye whisky every two hours for approximately six hours; none of these had the slightest effect upon the score. (The score when drugs were used is not shown in the above table.) Results obtained upon other individuals possibly would have been different. Such results might not have held true in my own case if some other function had been under the test. Of course, when such drugs as strychnine and cocaine are taken in unduly large quantities, they must necessarily affect all motor coördination.

THE FINAL STAGE IN THE FORMATION OF MANY HABITS

After a habit has been set up by reacting to visual, auditory, tactual and other stimuli, such as we have described above, an additional factor enters in. As we exercise the habit continually, the actual visual, auditory, olfactory and tactual stimuli become of less and less importance. When habits are thoroughly ingrained, we can execute many of them blindfolded and with our ears and noses plugged up and our skin covered with cloth. In other words, visual, auditory, olfactory and tactual stimuli no longer have to be placed at turning points. What has happened? A second stage of conditioning has taken place. In the early stages of the learning process, each time the visual stimulus is given us we make a muscular response (primarily with our striped muscles) to that visual stimulus. In a very short time the muscular response itself can serve as a stimulus to set off the next motor response in order, and then the next motor response can set off the succeeding motor response, so that thereafter complicated mazes can be run, complicated acts of various kinds can be accomplished without the presence of visual, auditory, olfactory and tactual stimuli. *The muscular stimuli coming from the movements of the muscles themselves are all we need to keep our manual responses occurring in proper sequence.* To understand this process thoroughly, the reader should recall what was said about the muscles being not only responding organs but sense organs as well (p. 66). We can diagram this double conditioning as follows:

After the individual is conditioned to respond to the sight of the circle thus:

(C) S .... (C) R	
(1st order) Visual (circle)	Two steps to right (or any other
Then	muscular response called for by
(after further conditioning)	habit series)
Movement of muscle itself	Can call out the identical response.

This is often called a kinaesthetic or "muscular" habit. Our internal language habits (thought) are very good examples of such habits. There seems to be a strong tendency for all of our habits to reach this second stage which we may call kinaesthetic. This process represents no mysterious vitalistic energy-saving function on the part of the organism. It is exactly what you would expect from the law of the formation of conditioned reflexes.

HAS THE BEHAVIORIST ANY MEMORY?

The behaviorist since he never uses the term "memory," is under no compulsion to attempt to define it. So many individuals getting their first orientation in behaviorism seem to be troubled by the omission of the term that it seems best to use some illustrations and analogies here to show why we do not need the term to account for our observed facts.

Let us start illustrations with an animal lower in the scale than the human—with the white rat, for example. I have in front of me the record of a rat's learning of the maze. It took this particular rat 40 minutes, on his first trip, to get to the food in the center of the maze. He made almost every error possible to make in the maze—that is, he retraced his steps many times and ran into all the blind alleys again and again. On his 7th trial he got to the food in 4 minutes and made only 8 errors. On his 20th trial he reached the food in 2 minutes and made only 6 errors. In his 30th trip he reached the food in 10 seconds and made no errors. On his 35th trip and on practically every trip thereafter for 150 trips, he reached the food in about 6 seconds and made no errors. From the 35th trip on, he ran the maze like a beautiful machine. No further work in the maze improved his record. Learning was complete. He had reached his limit in speed.

Suppose we keep the rat away from the maze for six months. Does he have any memory of it? Let us not speculate. Let us try him out. We arrange everything as it was on his last trip. To our astonishment we find that he gets to the food in just 2 minutes and makes only 6 errors. *In other words, the habit of running the maze was largely retained.* A part of the organization was gone, but even at the end of 6 months without practise his initial relearning record was as good as was the record of his 20th trial in the original learning series.

Let us next look at the record of a Rhesus monkey learning to open a complicated problem box. It took him 20 minutes to open it the first time. On the 20th trial, 20 days later, it took him only 2 seconds to open it. We gave him no further practise for 6 months, then we tried him again. He opened it in 4 seconds with barely a fumble.

Are things different with the human child? The year-old child crawls to his father, gurgles and coos and pulls at his legs. He will come to his father if a dozen people are in the room. Now send him off for two months and surround him with other people. Try him again with his father. He no longer crawls (or walks) to his father but goes to the person who fed and cared for him during the two months interval (much to the chagrin of the father if it happens to be his first born and only boy). His habit of reacting positively to his father has been lost.

Let us take the three-year-old boy and let him learn to ride his scooter and tricycle until they are skillfully handled. Put them away for six months and test him again. He dashes off on either with little loss in skill.

Finally, take a youth of twenty and let him learn to play golf. Keep a record of his slow, laborious progress in mastering the game. In two years, with twice weekly practise, he will get his score down to 80 or to an occasional 78 on an 18-hole course. Take him away from golf for three years and try him again. He will probably make a 95 on his first round. In two weeks he will again be making his 80.

Putting all of our various facts together, we find that after a manual act has been learned and then put aside for a definite period of disuse or no practise—some loss in the efficiency of the habit occurs, but usually (except for the baby in our illustration, for instance) the loss is not total. If the period of disuse is long enough, a total loss can occur in any habit. The amount of loss in a given habit varies in different individuals. Again, the same individual will show a different rate of loss for different types of habit.

It is astonishing how little loss there is in most of our manual habits during relatively long periods of disuse: e. g. swimming, boxing, shooting, skating, dancing, golf and the like. If a poor shot or an inexpert golfer tells you that he was good five years ago but that lack of practise has made him poor, don't believe him; he never was good! In general, if we keep a record of an individual's learning and compare it with his relearning record, we can always measure accurately the loss during any given period of disuse.

But to come back to the question of our lack of need for the term "memory" in psychology: the behaviorist if he were speaking scientifically, would never say, "Does James remember how to ride his bicycle after all these years of no practise?" He would say, rather, "How accurately can James ride his bicycle now that he hasn't touched it in five years?" He doesn't ask James to introspect and tell him. He proceeds to give James his bicycle and then to measure the time for riding six blocks, to record the number of falls, and the like. At the end of the test he will say, "James rides his bicycle after five years of no practise 75% as well as he rode it five years ago." In other words, to find out how much has been retained and how much has been lost, the behaviorist has only to put the individual into the old situation, after a period of no practise, and watch what happens. If James in the above situation rode no better than he did the first day he got his bicycle, the behaviorist would say, "James has lost the habit of riding a bicycle."

This applies to every form of organization the human being puts on. It is surprising how well even the simple conditioned reflexes are retained by both humans and lower animals. In the laboratory I have been able to reëstablish a conditioned reflex to a bell (R = withdrawal of finger) after only one punishment with the electric current, following a year of no practise. G. V. Anrep speaks of a similar retention in the case of his dog after a year of no practise (tonal stimulus with a conditioned salivary response).

So, instead of using the term memory, the behaviorist speaks of how much skill has been retained and how much has been lost in a period of no practise. Our objection to the term memory is that it is shot through with all kinds of philosophical and subjective connotations.

This treatment of memory is not complete because we have not yet discussed word and language habits. The next chapter concerns itself with the formation of our verbal habits.

X. Talking and Thinking

WHICH, WHEN RIGHTLY UNDERSTOOD, GO FAR IN
BREAKING DOWN THE FICTION THAT THERE IS
ANY SUCH THING AS "MENTAL" LIFE

INTRODUCTION: In the last chapter we brought out the fact that the man, although born more helpless than almost any other mammal, very quickly learns to outstrip other animals by reason of the manual habits he acquires. He can never learn how to run fast enough to win in a foot race with a greyhound or a deer, he can never learn how to compete in sheer strength with a horse or an elephant, yet he masters all of them. He does it by learning how to construct and how to use *manual devices*. First he learns to use a club and then to throw stones—later he learns to use the sling so that he can throw stones with greater force. Then he constructs sharp stone instruments. Next he fashions and learns to use the bow and arrow with which he can conquer even the fleetest animal; then he learns how to start a fire. Next he learns how to make bronze and iron knives, then the cross bow and finally firearms. His mastery of the world is made complete.

But with all the delicacy of his manipulative skill, man is not the exclusive possessor of acquired manual dexterity. The elephant can be trained to assist in loading and unloading heavy trucks of lumber. Even the lower types of monkeys can be trained to manipulate delicate latches, pull strings, and the like. The chimpanzee learns to ride the bicycle with grace, to weave his way on it in and out among a dozen bottles standing in a row without touching one; to uncork and drink from a bottle, smoke a pipe, light a cigarette, to lock and unlock doors and to do many hundreds of other things.

In this chapter we take up a great field of learned activities which the brute cannot even enter, much less compete in. This is the field of *language habits*—habits which when exercised implicitly behind the closed doors of the lips we call *thinking*.[1]

WHAT IS LANGUAGE?

Language as we ordinarily understand it, in spite of its complexities, is in the beginning a very simple type of behavior. It is really a manipulative habit. Down in the throat at the level of the Adam's apple we have a simple little instrument called the *larynx* or "voice box." It is a tube made up largely of cartilage across which two very simple membranes are stretched (membranous glottis), the edges of which form the vocal cords. Instead of manipulating this quite primitive instrument with our hands, we manipulate it with its attached muscles as we expel the air from our lungs. When you think of it, try to think of some simple reed instrument which we hold between our lips and blow air through. We tighten the vocal cords, change the width of the opening between them much as we tune the strings of a violin by turning the pegs. The air is expelled from the lungs through the opening between the vocal cords. This causes them to vibrate and to give out a sound. We call this the voice. But as we make this sound another group of muscles changes the shape of the throat, still another set changes the position of the tongue, another the position of the teeth, and still another the position of the lips. The mouth cavity above the larynx and the visceral cavities below constantly alter in size and in shape so as to change the volume of the sound, the character of the sound (timbre), and the pitch

---

[1] We will defer until later the question whether the man who cannot talk, cannot think. When we have made our elementary presentation complete, you will find that man both talks and thinks with his whole body—just as he does everything else with his whole body. We will discuss this more completely in the next chapter.

of the sound. All of these responses are called into action the first time the baby cries. They are called into action again when he makes his unlearned preword sounds such as "da" or "ma." The picture is then not very different from the one we saw in studying the movements of hands and fingers, is it?

EARLY VOCAL SOUNDS

It will be remembered from the last chapter that in order to begin to build in manipulative habits one has to have something to start on, namely, the unlearned movements of fingers, hands, toes and the like. In language we have something similar to start on, *namely, the unlearned vocal sounds the infant makes at birth and afterwards.* From the first moment such sounds as "a," "u," "nah," "wah," "wuh" appear, then later "la," "ah," "ba," "ahgoo," "ma," "da." Mrs. Blanton from her experience in a nursery of 25 babies during the first month of infancy says, "Of interest was the variety of animal cries simulated in the nursery. The "pot-rack" of the guinea fowl, the cry of the goat, the whine of the young pig, and the wail of the wild cat, each has a close imitation."

BEGINNING OF WORD ORGANIZATION

In studying manual activity we found that the habit of reaching begins about the 120th day; that by the 150th day, under proper training, it is fairly well developed. The first true vocal habit starts at a much later age and develops more slowly. In some children we find no verbal habits of the conventional kind even at 18 months of age. In some we find quite a few at the end of the first year.

My wife and I attempted to form a simple verbal habit in a very young infant. The experiments were carried out upon B., the infant whose jealous behavior we discussed on p. 189. He was born November 21st, 1921. Up to the end of the 5th month he showed merely the repertoire of almost every other child of that age. The cooing sounds, "ah goo" and variations of "a" and "ah" were quite pronounced. We began on the 12th of May to tie this sound up to the bottle (this infant was bottle-fed from the end of the second month). Our method was as follows: We gave him the bottle and allowed him to nurse for a moment, then we took it away and held it in front of him. He began to kick and squirm and reach for it. We next gave the stimulus sound "da" aloud. We repeated this procedure once per day for three weeks. When he began to whimper and whine we always gave him the bottle. On June 5th, 1922, he said the word "dada" when we gave the stimulus word and held the bottle in front of him. The bottle was immediately given him. This procedure was repeated three times with success on that occasion—each time we gave the stimulus word. Then we took the bottle away five successive times and without our giving the stimulus word he said "dada" for the bottle. At one of the trials he kept on saying "dada," "dada," "dada," several times without our giving the stimulus word. Thereafter for several weeks it was as easy to touch off this response as to call out any other bodily reflex. The verbal response was confined almost exclusively to this one stimulus. On a few occasions he said it when his rabbit was held in front of him but not when other things were shown him.

It was very interesting to note that on June 23rd he got his mouth set on other types of sound, such as "booboo" and "bla-bla" and "googoo" (newly appearing unlearned sounds). On this occasion he could not reset for "dada." He would splutter out these other sounds valiantly and in a string but never once got out "dada." On the following day "dada" appeared again without the slightest difficulty. On July 1st the "dada" sound was changed suddenly without any stimulus word being given to "dad-en" with the old "dada" appearing once in awhile. I think it is quite probable that if we had been willing to break up the infant's strict feeding habits and had watched for the verbal occasions on which he himself made the sound "dada" and had given him the bottle immediately, on each such occasion, then he would have formed this habit much earlier and much more quickly. I think it is quite debatable whether our speaking aloud the stimulus word "dada" had the slightest effect in calling out this response on the favorable occasion it did appear when we started to feed him. In other words, I doubt if there was any verbal imitation at this early age. Later on, of course, such so-called verbal imitation does appear but most of it is more a matter of our imitating the child than the child imitating us. Once these sound responses have been conditioned, naturally the whole of language may be looked upon as being "imitative" since socially the spoken word of one individual is the stimulus touching off the same or another verbal response in another individual.

Thus at the end of 6½ months we established a conditioned vocal response corresponding roughly, let us say, to the reaching habit which is fairly well perfected at the end of the 150th day.

THE FURTHER DEVELOPMENT OF LANGUAGE

After conditioned word responses have become partly established, phrase and sentence habits begin to form. Naturally single word conditioning does not stop. All types of word, phrase and sentence habits thus develop simultaneously.

When B., whose word conditioning we have just considered, had 52 words at his command [1] we noticed the first putting together of two words. This occurred on August 13th, 1923, at the age of 1 year, 7 months, 25 days. For a month prior to that date we had

---

[1] The full list of his words is as follows: Ta-ta (thank you), Blea (please), Mama, Da, Roe (Rose), No-No (Nora—disappeared when maid left), Yea (yes), No, Bow-Wow, Melow (miow), Anna, Gigon (Dickey), Doan (Joan), Bèbè (baby), Ja (Jack), Puddy (pretty), Co-Co (bird), Archa (Archer), Tick (stick), Tone (stone), Dir (dirt), Sha (shame), Toa (toast), Cra-ca (Cracker), Chee (cheese), Nanny (candy), Abba (Albert), Bleu (blue), More, Moe (water), Boa (boat), Go-Go (wheelbarrow), Awri (all right), Te-te (pee-pee), Shan (sand), Sha-Sha (Sara), La-La (lady), Gir (girl), Maa (man), Choo-Choo (train), Ball, Baa (Box or bottle), Haa (hot), Co (cold), Sow (soap), Plower (flower), How-do (how do you do—new Aug. 14), Boo (book), Shee (see), Hello, Bye-Bye, Shoe.

been setting a verbal pattern of two words for some time, such as "hello, mama," "hello, dada," without results. On this day his mother said, "Say good-bye to daddy." She set the pattern "good-bye da." He repeated after her, "bye"—then hesitation and five seconds later came the word, "da." This brought upon him a shower of petting, verbal commendation and the like. Later in the day he said with the same long interval between the two sounds, "bye —bow wow." On August 15th, two days later, we got him to say "hello—mama," "hello—Rose," "ta-ta—Rose," "ta-ta—mama" ("ta-ta" means "thank you"). In each case the two word stimulus had to be given before the response could be called out. He also said, "blea—mama" for the first time. Never up to this time could we get the two word response without giving the two word stimulus. On August 24th he put two words together without any verbal stimulus from the parents, for example, he pointed to his father's shoe and said "shoe—da," and pointing to his mother's shoe, "shoe—ma." Then the next four days he used all of the above two word responses at one time or another without any pattern being set, and some additional ones for which a two word pattern had never been set, such as the following: "tee-tee bow-wow (dog urinates), "bébé go-go" (when a little neighbor took his cart), "mama toa," "how-do shoes," "haa mama," "awri mama." Often when put back into his room for his sleep or his midday nap, he ran over these words and combinations again and again aloud in his room—an observation which has considerable importance in the behaviorist's theory of thinking as we shall see later.

From this time on development in the two-word stage took place rapidly. The three-word stage was somewhat slow in coming, as was talking in sentences corresponding to the ordinary adult social patterns. No new facts, however, seemed to come to light during these stages.

At three years of age this child had a remarkable command of language, although nothing was done to force it. At one year of age he had only 12 words which is about the average number for one-year-olds. At 18 months B., with his 52 words was distinctly behind the average, a condition which often occurs when a child is constantly attended by a nurse who waits upon it hand and foot—and in this case a French woman who used scarcely a larger number of English words than the child used. I mention these facts to bring out the point that many factors play a rôle in the speed at which word, phrase and sentence habits form.

WORDS ARE BUT SUBSTITUTES FOR OBJECTS AND SITUATIONS

You can see from this example of the formation of single and double word habits that the process is entirely analogous to that of the establishment of simple conditioned motor reflexes such as the withdrawal of the hand upon the presentation of an auditory or visual stimulus. We may again employ our old familiar formula

$$S \dots\dots\dots\dots\dots\dots R$$

Some intraorganic stimulus	Dada
When conditioned—	
then	"
Sight of bottle	

The unconditioned or unlearned stimulus is some change in the muscular and glandular tissues of the throat, chest and mouth regions (of course changes in this region in turn may have been brought about by stimulation from the stomach or from the external environment). The unlearned response is the vocal utterance we call "dada"—in other words here, as in manual activity, we have the unlearned and unconditioned responses to start building upon. *We watch our chances and build upon these.* Word conditioning in this early stage is pretty harum-scarum because we know so little about the fundamental stimuli calling out the repertoire of unlearned vocal responses. Indeed we know more about the stimuli calling out the unlearned responses in animals than we do in babies. We know how to make a frog croak by rubbing a certain spot on its body. We can make a dog bark, or a monkey give out a certain sound. We do not know how to "press that button" on his body, be it inside or out, which will make a baby say "da," "glub," "boo-boo" or "aw." If we did, we could build in words and phrases and sentences at an early date and very, very rapidly. In the case of the human young we just have to watch for a sound which is nearest some conventional word and try to tie it up to the object (make it substitutible for the object) that calls out that word in the adult. In other words, we begin to attempt to bring him into verbal conformity with his group at even this early age. Sometimes we have to condition syllable by syllable in order to get a complete word, that is, in a long word there may be a dozen separate conditioned responses. A long word would thus correspond to the picture we drew on p. 207 of the learning of the maze. But even so, it is my belief that in the unlearned sounds made by the infant we have all the units of response which when later brought together (by conditioning) are the words of our dictionaries. Thus all the sounds that the distinguished, eloquent and facile lecturer makes in his impassioned address are but his unlearned infantile sounds put together by patient conditioning in infancy, childhood and youth.

One thing seems quite obvious in the formation of verbal habits and that is that conditioned reflexes of the second, third and succeeding orders are formed with very great rapidity. It is quite obvious in the child of three that the word "mama" is called out (1) by the sight of the mother, (2) by the photograph of the mother, (3) by the sound of her voice, (4) by the sound of her footsteps, (5) by the sight of the printed English word "mother," (6) by the sight of the written English word "mother," (7) by the sight of the printed French word *mère,* (8) by the sight of the written French word *mère,* and by several other stimuli such as the visual stimulus of her hat, her clothes, her shoes. While these substitute stimuli are being set up, the response "mama" itself becomes elaborated. Sometimes he screams it at the top of his voice, sometimes he speaks it in an ordinary conversational tone, sometimes in a whining tone, sometimes down deep in his throat, sometimes softly, sometimes harshly. Set verbal patterns for him to imitate and he can say "mama" in many different ways. This means that the response "mama" is made with dozens and possibly even with hundreds of different muscular sets.

In other words, in bringing children up in our own verbal footsteps we verbally condition them as we were conditioned both as to the words themselves (English, French, German) and as to their pronunciation and inflexion. We can spot a southern child by the way it says "store" or "door" and by several phrases such as "you-all," "may I carry you home," by a certain softness and a certain slowness in speech. We can spot a Chicago child by the way it says one word, "water." We can spot the East Side newsboy of New York by the harshness of his high pitched voice, and by the types of words he uses. We not only learn our parents' language—we learn their tricks of language as well. These differences between north and south, east and west, between the Latin or Oriental and the Negro or the Saxon are not due to differences in throat formation or in the numbers and types of the elementary unlearned infantile response units. Many northern mothers and fathers went south in "carpet bagging" times and their children learned to speak Southern and not New England English. Certainly children of French parents put on perfect English when brought to this country and reared by English people.

It is difficult to learn to speak a foreign language without accent if we start to learn that language late in life, for the very same reason that a 40-year-old blacksmith can never learn toe dancing. Habitual types of response rob the organism of its muscular flexibility—they tend to shape the actual structures of the body. A person always despondent, always with drooping facial muscles, tends to take on that facial set that we characterize as gloomy, despondent, kill-joy. Another important factor comes in at this point, too. The larynx begins to change structurally in adolescence. It actually becomes less flexible, less capable of being shaped to utter new sounds.

As the child grows up, then, it establishes a conditioned word response for every object and situation in its external environment. Society in the form of parent and teacher and other members of the social group arranges this. But strange as it may seem at first sight, it does not have to be word conditioned to many, many objects in its internal environment—to changes in the viscera themselves—because parents and the other members of the social group haven't any words for them. Visceral happenings are at present largely unverbalized even in the human race. The significance of this as an explanation for the so-called "unconscious" we shall bring out in the next chapter.

THE BODILY ECONOMY OF HAVING WORD SUBSTITUTES FOR OBJECTS

The fact that every object and situation in the external environment is *named* is of vast importance. Words not only can and do call out other words, phrases and sentences, but when the human being is properly organized they can call out all of his manual activity. The words function in the matter of calling out responses exactly as did the objects for which the words serve as substitutes. Wasn't it Dean Swift who had one of his characters who couldn't or wouldn't speak carry around in a bag all the objects of common use so that instead of having to say words to influence the behavior of others, he pulled out the actual object from his bag and showed it? The world would be in this situation today if we did not have this *equivalence for reaction* between objects and words. You get something of the helpless state humanity would be in unless you had this *equivalence* in your own household when you by chance employ a Roumanian nurse, a German cook and a French butler and you yourself speak only English.

Think what it means in the economy of time and ability to call out coöperation from groups to have word substitutes for objects common to all members.

Soon the human has a verbal substitute within himself theoretically for every object in the world. *Thereafter he carries the world around with him by means of this organization.* And he can manipulate this word world in the privacy of his room or when he lies down on his bed in the dark. Many of our discoveries come largely through this ability to manipulate a world of objects not actually present to our senses. We carry this world around with us as actual bodily organization, in the muscular and glandular organization of our throat, chest (including, of course, the sense organs in the muscles and the nervous system). That organization is ready to function day and night whenever the appropriate stimulus is given. What is this appropriate stimulus?

THE FINAL STAGE IN OUR WORD ORGANIZATION (KINAESTHETIC)

It is clear now that word habits are built up like manual habits. You will recall from p. 219 that once a series of responses (manual habits) is organized around a series of objects, we can run through the whole series of responses without having the original series of objects present. In other words, when you are first learning to pick out the air of "Yankee Doodle" on the piano with one finger from the printed score, you first look at the score and see note G, then you strike it; then you see note A and strike it; then note B and strike it. Your notes are a series of visual stimuli, your responses are organized according to this series. But when you have practised a short time, some one can remove the score and you can go right on. You can even go to the piano at night, if some one asks you to (in this case the spoken word of a friend is the initial stimulus that starts the process going) and hammer it out without a falter. You know how to explain this—you know that the first *muscular response* you make—the first key you strike in beginning to play the melody, *substitutes for the visual stimulus of the second note.* Muscular stimuli (kinaesthetic) now serve in place of visual stimuli and the whole process goes on as smoothly as before.

Now exactly the same thing happens in word behavior. Suppose you read from your little book (your mother usually sets an auditory pattern), "Now—I—lay—me—down—to—sleep." The sight of "now" brings the saying of "now" (response 1), the sight of "I," response of saying "I" (response 2) and so on throughout the series. Soon the mere saying of "now" becomes the motor (kinaesthetic) stimulus for saying "I." This explains why we can shut off the world of stimuli and talk glibly about sights and sounds in distant places or about things that happened years ago. A chance word from a bystander, or a question of a friend, or even the sights and sounds in front of you may touch off this old verbal organization. But one may ask is this not "memory"?

"MEMORY," OR THE RETENTION OF VERBAL HABITS

What the man on the street ordinarily means by an exhibition of memory is what occurs in some such situation as this: An old friend comes to see him, after many years' absence. The moment he sees this friend, he says: "Upon my life! Addison Sims of Seattle! I haven't seen you since the World's Fair in Chicago. Do you remember the gay parties we used to have in the old Windermere Hotel? Do you remember the Midway? Do you remember——," *ad infinitum.* The psychology of this process is so simple that it seems almost an insult to your intelligence to discuss it, and yet a good many of the behaviorists' kindly critics have said that behaviorism cannot adequately explain memory. Let us see if this is a fact.

When the man on the street originally made the acquaintance of Mr. Sims, he saw him and was told his name at the same time. Possibly he did not see him again until a week or two later. He had to be re-introduced. Again, when he saw Mr. Sims he heard his name. Then, shortly afterwards, the two men became friends and saw one another every day and became really acquainted—that is, formed verbal and manual habits towards one another and towards the same or similar situations. In other words, the man on the street became completely organized to react in many habit ways to Mr. Addison Sims. Finally, just the sight of the man, even after months of absence, would call out not only the old verbal habits, but many other types of bodily and visceral responses.[1]

Now, when Mr. Sims came into the room, the man on the street might have rushed to him and showed every evidence of "memory," but when he got to him he might have stumbled over his name. If so, he would have had to fall back on the old alibi, "Your face is familiar but I can't quite get back your name." What happens here is that the old manual and visceral organizations have persisted (handshaking, noisy welcome, slapping on the shoulder), but the verbal organization is partially if not wholly gone. One overt repetition of the verbal stimulus (the sound of the name) would reëstablish the whole of the old habit.

But Mr. Sims may have stayed away so long, or our original acquaintance with him (period of practise) may have been so slight that, after an absence of ten years, the whole organization may have been lost—manual, visceral and verbal (all three are necessary to a complete reaction). In your terminology, you would have completely "forgotten" Mr. Addison Sims.

In the course of our lives we are daily being organized in this way by the people we meet, by the books we read and study, and by the events that happen to us. Sometimes the organization is incidental and casual; sometimes it is drilled into us by teachers, as in the case of the multiplication tables, facts of history, stanzas of

---

[1] Indeed you don't need even the visual (or other sense organ) stimulus of Mr. Sims to start verbal processes ("memory") going about that gentleman. Some one may, in the course of a business conversation, ask you about the type of people living in Seattle. This may start off a whole chain of verbal organization about the names of people living there. Almost inevitably Mr. Sims' name will come up in its turn.

poetry and the like. In learning, sometimes the organization is predominantly manual, sometimes largely verbal (e. g. the multiplication tables), sometimes largely visceral; usually it is a combination of all three. This organization is constantly renewed and strengthened, as long as the stimulus is present daily (or frequently); but when the stimulus has been long removed (period of no practise), the organization disintegrates (retention becomes imperfect). When, after absence, the stimulus is presented once more, the responses involving the old manual habits appear along with the name (laryngeal habits) and the smiling, laughter (visceral habits), and the response is complete—"memory" is intact. Any part of this total organization may be totally or partially absent. What James means, behavioristically, when he says that a feeling of warmth and intimacy clings around true memory, is that there has been a retention of the visceral organization as well as of the laryngeal and manual organizations.

By "memory," then, we mean nothing except the fact that when we meet a stimulus again after an absence, we do the old habitual thing (say the old words and show the old visceral—emotional—behavior) that we learned to do when we were in the presence of that stimulus in the first place.

WHAT IS THINKING?

Before trying to understand the behaviorists' theory of thinking, won't the reader please pick up any introspective psychological text and read the chapter on thinking? Won't he then try to digest some of the pabulum the philosophers have offered us on this all-important function? I have tried to understand it. I had to give it up. I believe the reader will give it up too. But until he has read their explanations, don't quarrel with the behaviorist for weaknesses in his presentation. His own theory is quite simple. The only difficulty about it lies in our previous organization. We begin to resist it, to show negative reactions, the moment we hear about it. We have been trained both at our mother's knee and in psychological laboratories to say that thinking is something peculiarly uncorporeal, something very intangible, very evanescent, something peculiarly mental. To the behaviorist this resistance is due to the reluctance of the psychologists to give up the teaching of religion in their psychology. Thinking, on account of the concealed nature of the musculature with which it is done, has always been inaccessible to unaided observation and to direct experimentation. And there is always a strong inclination to attach a mystery to something one can't see. As new scientific facts are discovered we have fewer and fewer phenomena which cannot be observed, hence fewer and fewer pegs upon which to hang folk-lore. The behaviorist advances a natural science theory about thinking which makes it just as simple, and just as much a part of biological processes, as tennis playing.

THE BEHAVIORIST'S VIEW OF THOUGHT

The behaviorist advances the view that *what the psychologists have hitherto called thought is in short nothing but talking to ourselves.* The evidence for this view is admittedly largely theoretical but it is the one theory so far advanced which explains thought in terms of natural science. I wish here expressly to affirm that in developing this view I have never believed that the *laryngeal movement* (see page 225) as such played the predominating rôle in thought. I admit that in my former presentations I have, in order to gain pedagogical simplicity, expressed myself in ways which can be so interpreted. We have all had the proofs before us time and again that the larynx can be removed without completely destroying a person's ability to think. Removal of the larynx does destroy articulate speech but it does not destroy whispered speech. Whispered speech (without articulation) depends upon muscular responses of the cheek, tongue, throat and chest—organization which, to be sure, has been built up with the use of the larynx,

but which remains ready to function after the larynx has been removed. Any one who has read my various presentations knows
that I have tried everywhere to emphasize the enormous complexity of the musculature in the throat and chest. To claim that a
mass of cartilage such as that composing the larynx is responsible
for thought (internal speech) is like saying that the bone and
cartilage that make up the elbow joint form the chief organ with
which one plays tennis.

My theory does hold that the muscular habits learned in overt
speech are responsible for implicit or internal speech (thought).
It holds, too, that there are hundreds of muscular combinations
with which one can say either aloud or to himself almost any word,
so rich and so flexible is language organization and so varied are
our overt speech habits. A good imitator, we know, can say the
same phrases in dozens of different ways, in a bass voice, in a tenor
voice, in a mezzo, in a soprano, in a loud whisper, in a soft whisper, as an English cockney would say them, as a broken-English-
speaking Frenchman would say them, as a Southerner would say
them, as a child. The number and variety of habits we form in the
speaking of almost every word is thus well-nigh legion. We use
speech, from infancy on, a thousand times to using our hands
once. From this circumstance there grows up a complexity of organization which even the psychologist seemingly cannot grasp.
Again, after our overt speech habits are formed, we are constantly talking to ourselves (thought). New combinations occur,
new complexities arise, new substitutions take place—for example,
where the shrug of the shoulders or the movement of any other
bodily part becomes substituted for a word. Soon *any, and every*
bodily response *may become a word substitute* (see p. 233).

The alternative sometimes advanced to this theory is that so-
called central processes may take place in the brain so faintly that
no neural impulse passes out over the motor nerve to the muscle,
hence no response takes place in the muscles and glands. Even
Lashley and his students, on account of their strong interest in the

nervous system, seem to hold this view. Recently Agnes M. Thorson [1] has found that tongue movements are not universally present in internal speech. This, even if true, can have no bearing upon the present view. The tongue, while bearing very delicate receptors, is on the muscular side a bulk organ for rolling our food around. It plays a part in internal speech to be sure, but probably about the same part that the fist of the jazz cornet player plays when he thrusts it into the horn to modify the sound.

SOME POSITIVE EVIDENCE FOR THE BEHAVIORIST'S VIEW

(1) Our main line of evidence comes from watching the child's behavior. The child talks incessantly when alone. At three he even plans the day *aloud,* as my own ear placed outside the key hole of the nursery door has very often confirmed. Soon society in the form of nurse and parents steps in. "Don't talk aloud—daddy and mother are not always talking to themselves." Soon the overt speech dies down to whispered speech and a good lip reader can still read what the child thinks of the world and of himself. Some individuals never even make this concession to society. When alone they talk aloud to themselves. A still larger number never go beyond even the whispering stage when alone. Watch people reading on the street car; peep through the key hole sometime when individuals not too highly socialized are just sitting and thinking. But the great majority of people pass on to the third stage under the influence of social pressure constantly exerted. "Quit whisper-

[1] The Relation of Tongue Movements to Internal Speech, *Journal of Experimental Psychology,* 1925. Her experiments are very inconclusive. Tongue movements were recorded by a compound system of delicate levers. Her setup could probably be depended upon for positive results, but the method was too inexact to serve as a basis for negative conclusions. No instrument less sensitive than the string galvanometer can be depended upon for negative results. Her saying that because she could find by the use of this method no correlation between tongue movements and internal speech therefore "this leaves only the hypothesis that the activities are intra-neural,' and do not necessarily involve complete motor expression at each stage of the process," is in need of modification.

ing to yourself," and "Can't you even read without moving your lips?" and the like are constant mandates. Soon the process is forced to take place behind the lips. Behind these walls you can call the biggest bully the worst name you can think of without even smiling. You can tell the female bore how terrible she really is and the next moment smile and overtly pay her a verbal compliment.

(2) I have collected considerable evidence that those deaf and dumb individuals who when talking use manual movements instead of words, use the same manual responses they employ in talking, in their own thinking. But even here society forces minimal movements so that evidence of overt responses is often hard to obtain. To Dr. W. I. Thomas I am indebted for the following observation: Dr. Samuel Gridley Howe, Superintendent of the Perkins Institute and Massachusetts Asylum for the Blind, taught the deaf, dumb and blind Laura Bridgman a hand and finger language. He states (in one of the annual reports of the Institute) *that even in her dreams Laura talked to herself using the finger language with great rapidity.*

Possibly it always will be difficult to obtain an overwhelming mass of positive evidence for this view. The processes are faint and other processes such as swallowing, breathing, circulation, are always going on and they will probably always obscure the more delicate internal speech activities. But there is no other theory at present advanced which is tenable—no other view in line with the known facts of physiology.

This throws all the burden of proof on any contrary hypothesis, such as that advanced by the imagists and by the psychological irradiationists. Naturally we are all interested in facts. If when they are obtained they make the present theory untenable, the behaviorist will give it up cheerfully. But the whole physiological conception of motor activity—that motor activity follows sensory stimulation—will have to be given up along with it.

WHEN AND HOW WE THINK

Before trying to answer the question "When do we think?" let me put a question to the reader. When do you act with your hands, legs, trunk? You answer rightly, "Whenever action with hands and legs and trunk will help me escape from a situation to which I am not adjusted." The example I used on p. 199 was walking to the ice-box and eating when stomach contractions became intense; or pasting a piece of paper over a hole in the window shade to shut out the light. I would like to ask one other question, too. When do we *overtly* act with the laryngeal muscles—in other words, when do we talk and whisper aloud? The answer is: Whenever a situation demands it—whenever overt action with the voice will help us out of a situation which we cannot get out of otherwise. For example: I get upon a platform to lecture; I won't get my fifty dollars unless the words are forthcoming. I have broken through the ice and am in the water; I cannot get out unless I call aloud for help. Again, somebody asks me a question; politeness bids me return a civil answer.

This all seems fairly clear. Now let us go back to the original question—when do we think? And please bear in mind that thinking with us is subvocal talking. We think whenever by the subvocal use of our language organization we can escape from a situation to which we are not adjusted. Thousands of examples of such situations confront us almost daily. I give a somewhat dramatic one. R's employer called him in one day and said, "I think you would become a much more stable member of this organization if you would get married. Will you do it? I want you to answer me one way or the other before you leave this room, because you either have to get married or I am going to fire you." R cannot talk aloud to himself. He would tell too much about his private affairs. If he did, he would probably get fired anyway! Manual action will not help him out. *He has to think it out and having thought it out he must speak aloud "yes" or "no"*—make the final overt response in a whole series of subvocal reactions. Not all situations which must be met by subvocal language responses are quite so severe or so dramatic. Daily you are asked such questions as, "Can you lunch with me next Thursday?"—"Would it be possible for you take a trip to Chicago next week?"—"Could you lend me one hundred dollars until the first of the month?"—and the like.

In accordance with our theory of thinking we would like to suggest certain definitions and propositions.

The term "thinking" should cover all word behavior of whatever kind that goes on subvocally. If we use this formulation, are people who talk to themselves or whisper to themselves thinking? By definition this would not be thinking in the strict sense. We would have to say in such cases: He talks out his verbal problems aloud to himself or he whispers them aloud to himself. This does not mean that thinking is really different from the process of talking or whispering aloud to oneself. But since most people do really think according to the strict definition of the term, how many obviously different kinds of thinking must we assume in order to account for all the facts that we know about thinking— which facts we arrive at by watching the end result of thinking? And by end result we mean the final overtly spoken word (con- clusion) of the individual, or the manual action that he performs after the process of thinking comes to an end. We believe that all forms of thinking can be brought under the following heads:

(1) The subvocal use of words which have been already com- pletely habitized. For example, suppose I ask the question. "What is the last word in the little prayer 'Now I lay me down to sleep'?" If the question has not been asked before, you merely run it off to yourself and then respond overtly with the word "take." No learn- ing whatsoever is involved in thinking of this kind. You run through the old verbal habit just the way the accomplished musi- cian runs through a familiar selection, or a child says a well mem- orized multiplication table aloud. *You are merely exercising im- plicitly a verbal function you have already acquired.*

(2) Thinking of a slightly different type goes on where fairly well organized implicit verbal processes are initiated by the situation or stimulus but are not so well or so recently exercised that they can function without some learning or relearning occurring. I can make this clear also by an example. Very few of us can give off-hand the result of subvocally multiplying 333 by 33, yet all of us are familiar with subvocal arithmetic. No new process of procedure is demanded, and with a few inefficient verbal movements (verbal fumbling) you can arrive at the correct answer. The organization for carrying out this operation is all there but it is a little rusty. It has to be practiced before the operation can proceed smoothly. A few weeks of intense practice of multiplying three place numbers by two place numbers will enable you to give perfect answers almost immediately. We have in this type of thinking something similar to what we have in many manual activities. Nearly everybody knows how to shuffle and deal cards. At the end of a long summer vacation we get pretty adept at it. If we happen to go a year or two without playing bridge and then take up the cards to shuffle and deal, the operation is a little rusty, must be practised for a few days before we become adept again. Similarly in this kind of thinking, we are exercising a verbal function implicitly which we never completely acquired, or acquired so long ago that there has been some loss in retention.

(3) There is still another kind of thinking. Historically it has been called constructive thinking, planning, and the like. It always involves the same amount of learning that any first trial involves. The situation is new, or practically new to us—that is, it is as new as any situation can be to us. Before examining a case of a new thinking situation, let us react to a new manual situation. I first blindfold you and then hand you a mechanical puzzle consisting of three rings joined together. The problem is to get the three rings to come apart. No amount of thinking or "reasoning" or even talking aloud or whispering to yourself will bring the solution. You pull at the rings, turn them this way and that; finally in one

combination of positions of the rings they suddenly slip apart. Such a situation corresponds to one trial—the first one in a regular learning experiment.

In a similar way we are often placed in new situations which we can react to only by *thinking*. Consider an example.

A friend comes to you and tells you that he is forming a new business. He asks you to leave your present splendid position and come into the new business as an equal partner. He is a responsible person; he has good financial backing. He makes the offer attractive. He urges the larger ultimate profits you will make. He enlarges upon the fact that you will be your own boss. He has to leave at once to see other people interested in the venture. He asks you to call him up and give him an answer in an hour. Will you think? Yes, you will, and you'll walk the floor too, and you will pull your hair, and you may even sweat and you will smoke. Follow out the process step by step: Your whole body is as busy as though you were cracking rock—but your laryngeal mechanisms are setting the pace—they are dominant.

The most interesting point in this kind of thinking is the fact that after such new thinking situations have been met or solved once, we usually do not have to face them again exactly in the same form. *Only the first trial of the learning process takes place.* But many of our manual situations are like this too. Suppose I start out to drive my car to Washington. I do not know much about the insides of a car. The car stops—something is wrong. I work and work and finally get it going. Fifty miles farther on something goes wrong again. Again I meet the situation. In real life we go from one difficult situation to another, but each situation is a little different from all the others (except where we are acquiring definite functions like typewriting or other acts of skill). We cannot plot the curves of our escapes from these situations as we can plot learning curves in the laboratory. Our daily thinking activity goes on in exactly the same way. Complicated verbal situations usually have to be thought out but once.

What evidence has the behaviorist that the complicated thinking such as we have just described goes on in terms of internal
speech? We gain some data when we ask our subjects to *think
aloud* in words. Their behavior is quite similar psychologically
to the behavior of the rat in the maze. The rat starts out from
the entrance point slowly; on the straightaways he runs rapidly;
he blunders into blind alleys and often goes back to the starting point, instead of going on toward the food; after getting
back to the starting point, he turns and again starts toward the
food. Now put a question to your human subject. Ask him to
tell you what a certain object is to be used for (it must be new
and strange to him, and complicated) and ask him to figure it
out aloud. See if he does not wander about into every possible
verbal blind alley, get lost, come back and ask you to start
him off again, or to show him the object or to tell him again
all you propose to tell him about it, until finally he arrives at
the solution or else gives it up (the equivalent of the rat's giving up the problem of the maze and lying down in it and going
to sleep).

I am sure when you have tried this out for yourself you will
be convinced that you have an accurate story of how your subject
worked his problem out by word behavior. If then, you grant
that *you have the whole story of thinking when he thinks aloud,
why make a mystery out of it when he thinks to himself?*

But how does the subject know when to stop thinking, when
he has solved his problem? One may argue that the rat "knows"
when it has solved its problem because it gets the food which
makes the hunger contractions die down. How does a man know
when a verbal problem is solved? The answer is equally simple.
Why in the example I cited on page 199 did our individual not
keep pasting pieces of paper over the hole in the shade when he
had shut out the light? Because the *light was no longer present
as a stimulus to keep him moving.* Just so in thinking situations; as long as there are elements in the situation (verbal) that

keep stimulating the individual to further internal speech, the process keeps going. When he reaches a *verbal conclusion,* there is no further stimulus to thinking (equivalent of getting food). But the verbal conclusion, the Q. E. D., may not be reached at one sitting—he may get tired or bored. He goes to sleep and tackles it again the next day—if it has to be tackled.

How the "new" comes into being: One natural question often raised is: How do we ever get new verbal creations such as a poem or a brilliant essay? *The answer is that we get them by manipulating words, shifting them about until a new pattern is hit upon.* Since we are never twice in the same general situation when we begin to think, the word patterns will always be different. The elements are all old, that is, the words that present themselves are just our standard vocabulary—it is only the arrangement that is different. Why can't those of us, who are not literary, write a poem or an essay? We can use all the words the literary man uses. The answer is, it is not our trade, we do not deal in words, our word manipulation is poor; the literary man's is good. He has manipulated words under the influence of emotional and practical situations of one kind or another, as we have manipulated the keys of the typewriter or a group of statistics, or wood, brass and lead. It may help us to go to manual behavior again here. How does Patou build a new gown? Has he any "picture in his mind" of what the gown is to look like when it is finished? He has not, or he would not waste his time making it up; he would make a rough sketch of it or he would tell his assistant how to make it. In starting upon his work of creation, remember that his organization about gowns is enormous. Everything in the mode is at his finger tips, as is everything that has been done in the past. He calls his model in, picks up a new piece of silk, throws it around her; he pulls it in here, he pulls it out there, makes it tight or loose at the waist, high or low, he makes the skirt short or long. He manipulates the material until it takes on the semblance of a dress. *He has to react to it as a new creation before manipulation stops.* Nothing exactly like it has ever been made before. His emotional reactions are aroused one way or another by the finished product. He may rip it off and start over again. On the other hand, he may smile and say, "Voilà, parfait!" In this case the model looks at herself in the mirror and smiles and says, "Merci, monsieur." The other assistants say, "Magnifique!" Behold, a Patou model has come into being! But suppose a rival couturier happens to be present and Patou hears him in an aside say, "Very pretty, but is it not a little like the one he made three years ago? Is it that Patou grows a little stale? Is he not becoming too old to keep up with this rapidly shifting world of fashion?" One can believe that Patou would tear off the creation and trample it under foot. In this case manipulation would start again. Not until the new creation aroused admiration and commendation, both his own (an emotional reaction either verbalized or unverbalized) and others', would manipulation be complete (the equivalent of the rat's finding food).

The painter plies his trade in the same way, nor can the poet boast of any other method. Perhaps the latter has just read Keats, perhaps he is just back from a moonlight walk in the garden, perchance his beautiful fiancée has hinted just a little strongly that he has never sung her charms in sufficiently impassioned phrases. He goes to his room, the situation is set for him, the only way he can escape it is to do something and the only thing he can do is to manipulate words. The touch of the pencil starts the verbal activity just as the whistle of the referee at the football games releases a group of fighting, struggling men. Naturally words expressive of the romantic situation he is in soon flow—being in that situation he could not compose a funeral dirge nor a humorous poem. Again the situation he is in is slightly different from any other he was ever in before and therefore the pattern of his word creation will also be slightly new.

One of the chief criticisms directed against the behaviorist's view of thinking is that it gives no account of meaning. May I point out that the logic of the critic here is poor? The behaviorist's theory must be judged on its own premises. The premises of the behaviorist contain no propositions about meaning. It is an historical word borrowed from philosophy and introspective psychology. It has no scientific connotation. But let us turn to those philosophical psychologists who use the term *meaning*. Can we make sense out of what they say?

Let me paraphrase their words—the *meaning* of the fragrant, yellow orange in front of me is an idea, but if at any time there happens to be an idea in my mind instead of a perception, the meaning of that idea is another idea, and so on *ad infinitum*. Mrs. Eddy, even in her most ingenious verbal moments, could have constructed nothing more fitting to tantalize the earnest seeker after knowledge than the current explanations of meaning.

Here is the story as I see it, since the behaviorist in order to protect himself must give some kind of account of it. Let us take a simple case. Let us take the object "fire."

(1) I am burnt by it at three years of age. For some time thereafter I run away from it. By a kindly process of unconditioning, my family gets me over the complete negative response. Then new conditioning takes place.

(2) I learn to approach the fire after coming in from the cold.

(3) I learn to cook my fish and game upon it on my first hunting trip.

(4) I learn that I can melt lead in it and that if I heat my iron red hot I can fashion it to suit my needs.

During the course of many years I become conditioned in a hundred ways to fire. In other words, depending upon the situation I am now in and the series of situations leading up to the present one, I may do one of a hundred things in the presence of fire. As a matter of fact *I do but one at a time. Which one? The one which my previous organization and my present physiological state call forth.* I am hungry; the fire makes me start to cook bacon and fry eggs. On another occasion I go to the brook and get water to put out the fire after I am through camping. On another, I run down the street yelling "Fire!" I chase to the telephone and send for the fire department. On still another occasion when a forest fire hedges me about, I jump into the lake. On a cold day I stand in front of the fire and toast my whole body. Again, under the influence of some propagandist of murder, I pick up a burning brand and set fire to a whole village. *If you are willing to agree that "meaning" is just a way of saying that out of all the ways the individual has of reacting to this object, at any one time he reacts in only one of these ways, then I find no quarrel with meaning.* While I have chosen my illustrations in the manual field, the same procedure holds good in the verbal field. In other words, when we understand the genesis of all forms of an individual's behavior, know the varieties of his organization, can arrange or manipulate the various situations that will call out one or another form of his organization, then we no longer need such a term as meaning. Meaning is just one way of telling what the individual is doing.

So the behaviorist can turn the tables upon his critics. They cannot give any explanation of meaning. He can, but he does not believe the word is needed or that it is useful except as a literary expression.[1]

In this preliminary sketch of the function of language in our total organization, there are doubtless many things not yet made

[1] Many of the introspectionists' terms should be similarly turned back upon them. For example, attention. The behaviorist, if he felt inclined, could "explain" attention and define it and use it, but he doesn't need the word. The introspectionist, even James, has to define it in terms of vitalism as an active process that selects this or that from other happenings. Such terms, of course, only slowly die out. Until they are dead some one will always be criticizing the behavioristic explanation for inadequacy.

clear. In the next chapter we will take up two of the most difficult points not yet discussed. They are (1) What is the relation
between verbal behavior and manual and visceral behavior?
(2) Do we have to think always in terms of words?

XI. Do We Always Think In Words?

OR DOES OUR WHOLE BODY DO THE THINKING?

Introduction: The casual reader might gather the impression from reading the last two chapters that *manual, language* and even *visceral* habits are developed independently and even at different times. Such is not the case. *When an individual reacts to an object or situation, his whole body reacts.* For us this means that manual organization, language organization (after it begins) and visceral organization all function together—each and every time the body reacts. There are some exceptions to this, of course, but let us not trouble with them at the present time. These three forms of organization could not function together in mutually supplementary (and often in substitutive) ways unless we put on these organizations simultaneously as parts of one complete and integral function.

If this seems a bit difficult, possibly an illustration will clear it up. Watch two individuals walking through the woods. Suddenly a snake crawls out into their path, coils and sends forth a faint rattle. Both spring back, turn pale, the hair on their heads stiffens, their mouths fly open, respiration is checked. Suddenly one cries, "Snake," the other cries, "Rattler." Both cry, "Kill it." One runs for a large stick, the other for a rock. While they are wrestling implements from the wayside, the snake starts for the brush. One calls out, "There he goes to the right under that little scrub pine." Is there any doubt in your minds that this coiled rattler produced a profound reaction in each individual?

Is there any doubt that language, manual and visceral organizations functioned simultaneously?

SIMULTANEOUS ACQUISITION OF ALL THREE GROUPS OF HABITS

It certainly requires little argument to convince those interested in genetic psychology, that our hands, larynx and viscera learn together and later function together. Under the influence of social demands, the young, developing human who has well entered into his world of speech has to put on his verbal and visceral habits simultaneously with his manual habits. The only exception is the silent soul who grows up in an isolated community around parents too stern to talk to him. In his case speech habits lag behind the other two sets. Possibly it is more nearly accurate to say that verbal, manual and laryngeal activities become organized together as parts of the total habit system we

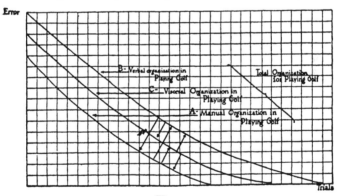

Fig 18

Rough sketch showing what goes on in learning to play golf. Our hands (and arms, trunk, legs and feet), our larynx and our viscera all learn at the same time how to play golf.

A—shows the curve of manual organization
B—the verbal organization
C—the visceral organization

form around each object and situation in the world we live in. We may illustrate this by a simple sketch.

This rough sketch gives an indication of the kind of organization that goes on when we learn to play golf. The three separate but not independent habit systems are shown developing together—the arrows indicate that they are mutually interdependent: (A) represents manual organization in playing golf —the use of feet, legs, trunk, arms, hands and fingers; (B) represents language—overt, whispering, subvocal, such as the names of the holes, the clubs, types of shots, the various lies, how the shot should be played, the types of faults we make in playing, repetition of the admonition of the professional who is teaching us, and the like; (C) represents the curve of visceral organization—circulation changes occur during, before and after each shot is made, the stomach glands change their rhythm, the elimination apparatus is probably slowed down or else speeded up, all of the viscera must share in the training. In chapter IV I spoke about the great mass of unstriped muscular tissue present all over the body. It is the main mass composing the stomach, heart, lungs, diaphragm, blood vessels, glands, excretory organs, and sex organs. I spoke there of the evidence that is slowly accumulating to show that the movements of these muscular and glandular organs soon become conditioned. I need only to enumerate our facts again. Eliminative functions become conditioned at an early age. The glands of the mouth and stomach and possibly many others likewise soon become set in habit moulds. The pupils of the eyes, breathing, and circulation all show the effects of habit formation. Now these so-called autonomic processes do not become conditioned for no reason at all. They actually play a rôle in acts of skill. Who can shoot accurately or drive a golf ball well if eliminative functions are threatening—with a full bladder—with gas pressure, if the sweat glands are not functioning, or are functioning too intensely with a mouth dry—if digestion is upset—if yawning takes place just as a shot is being made—if internal sex stimuli are insistent? All of these must fall into line when accurate acts of skill are taking place. They are just as dangerous to efficiency as instability and trembling in the striped muscles of our arms and legs, or as sore and hide-bound muscles of arms and fingers.

I will assume, then, that training of the viscera, even in acts of motor skill, is just as important as training of hands and fingers. Language is an equally important element in total bodily organization.[1]

Oftentimes, indeed, it is more important. The business man must talk golfing, hunting, fishing even if he cannot exhibit much proficiency in them. He can always refuse to go golfing, hunting or fishing when his lack of manual skill is not equal to his verbal performance, but he cannot refuse to talk about the technical points of these avocations and stay in the athletic group.

Soon we verbally react, overtly or covertly *first* to nearly all situations (so-called "dominance" of verbal reactions)—then the manual and visceral reactions follow in the order and to the extent to which they are conditioned. In other words we, as sophisticated adults, behave as though verbal conditionings were of the primary order and the manual and visceral of the secondary order.[2]

Watch the golfer as he makes a bad shot; ask him what he did wrong. If you are a lip reader you can in many cases read his words without asking him any questions. "I stood too close to the ball. I've got to learn to stand back. I bent my legs; I didn't follow through." Watch him address the ball for his next shot. He says to himself, "Stand back a little," and he

[1] A fact which, if it had been grasped by the introspectionists, would have saved them from considerable perturbation. For example, when they call themselves parallelists on the first page and use interaction all through the rest of their text; when they try to make "consciousness" do something—correct an error in a habit—or fix the happy accidental movement when a new habit is being formed by the trial and error process.

[2] See K. S. Lashley's article, *Psychol. Rev., 1923.*

steps back; "Don't put your left foot so far forward or you will slice"; immediately the foot is brought inward. The verbal organization, in addition to its usefulness in getting notice in the club house, *is on the field an intimate part of the total organization called into action when learning to play golf.*

The behaviorist believes that the verbal process whenever it is present is always an actual functioning part of every act of skill.

If this view, that we verbalize our manual acts, is accepted, it gives us a new way of looking at "memory" which we discussed in the last chapter. You can see that *"memory" is really the functioning of the verbal part of a total habit.* Once we have verbalized a bodily habit we can always talk about it. If we couldn't talk about golf, the only way we could prove or exhibit our organization in it (our "memory" of it) would be to go to the golf field and play it out hole by hole. But the situation for touching off our verbal organization on golf occurs a thousand times more frequently than does the actual situation touching off our organization for playing golf (simultaneous presence of links, leisure, clubs, golf balls, companions, clothes, plus bodily and verbal set—"I am going to play golf now"). What is popularly meant by "memory" is, then, *the running through or exhibition of the verbal part of a total bodily organization.* The manual part of this organization is not being called out—if the manual part were called out, we'd say "he is doing it" instead of "he is remembering it." In the diagram on page 253 it is clear that if one other part—the manual ("A" in our diagram)—of the total organization should become operative under appropriate stimulation (of the golf field), the individual's organized manual response with the club would be just as good a demonstration of "memory" as the verbal talk about golf.

Now let us attempt to make the whole process of bodily integration involving all these factors clear by a series of diagrams. Let us first diagram hand response to visual stimuli. In these diagrams we are not picturing the nervous system but units of bodily organization involving receptors, conductors, effectors, with all their subsidiaries.

Environment, presenting as it does its objects always in a series (because man is a moving animal), forces a certain 1—2—3 order in our manual organization as Fig. 19 shows.

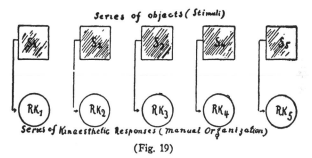

(Fig. 19)

Sketch to show how manual habits form. S1, S2, S3, are objects (for example, the separate notes of a musical score). RK1, RK2, are the separate manual responses made to each separate note. This shows that when one sees note G (S1) one strikes Key G (RK1).

In this diagram S1, S2, represent visual stimuli—for example, the notes of a melody one is playing with one finger on the piano. RK1, RK2, RK3, represent respectively the responses to the visual stimuli S1, S2, S3.

But after the notes have been played a considerable number of times (habit formed), only the initial note (S1) is necessary to call out the total organization. The change in the diagrammatic illustration is now as follows:

RK1, RK2, RK3, RK4 and RK5, while they are still responses as in the first case, when the notes could be seen, now become substitutible for the visual stimulus of the notes in the order in which they were learned; that is, the moment they cease being *responses* (or during the process) they become kinaesthetic stimuli for the next response. This is the old standard habit diagram I promised in the last chapter to present.

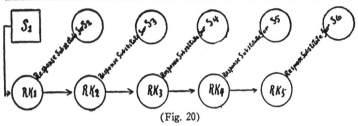

(Fig. 20)

Fig. 20 shows what happens when one has learned to play a simple melody. S1—the first note (G)—is shown, then the score is taken away. But one goes on playing. Why? Because as soon as one saw the first note G and struck Key G on the piano, that movement (RK1) became the stimulus for the next movement (RK2). In other words, the first response one made became a substitute stimulus for the second object.

This diagram has, of course, been used many times before. What is not often incorporated in it—and this is the central topic in this chapter—is the fact that the environment simultaneously organizes the other two sets of processes—viz., those connected with *words* and those connected with the *viscera*. Let us change our diagram to show the facts. In the diagram below S1 and S2 remain the objects; RK1 stands for the kinaesthetic

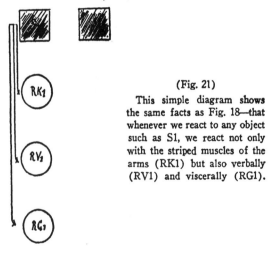

(Fig. 21)

This simple diagram shows the same facts as Fig. 18—that whenever we react to any object such as S1, we react not only with the striped muscles of the arms (RK1) but also verbally (RV1) and viscerally (RG1).

organization with respect to the object; RV1 the verbal organization; and RG1 the visceral organization respectively. I would like to point out here that just as RK1 becomes a motor substitute stimulus for the object S2, just so do RV1 and RG1 become laryngeal and visceral substitutes respectively for S2.

Every complex bodily response then must involve manual, verbal and visceral organizations. In acquiring skill in language, the segments of the body undergoing the most active training or organization are the mouth, neck, throat and chest; in acquiring muscular skill, the most active segments are the trunk, legs, arms, hands and fingers; in acquiring emotional organization, the visceral segments are most active. In later everyday performance we can describe the relative rôle each plays in any act of the whole body by saying that in chopping wood, for example, manual organization is most in evidence; in lecturing, the verbal; in grieving, sorrowing, loving, the visceral.

SOME EXCEPTIONS TO THE GENERAL RULE

There are at least two things in the way of accepting the above generalization as a complete expression of the facts. Some bodily organization seems to go on without the formation of corresponding verbal habits, viz.,

(1) *All organization put on in infancy;*
(2) *All organization put on throughout life where visceral segments are dominant.*

Let us look at each of these separately for a moment.

ORGANIZATION IN INFANCY

The recent work on infants, with which you are now so familiar, seems to show that an almost unbelievable amount of organization goes on in infants too young to talk. This shows itself not only in the overt organization of arms and legs and trunk, but equally well in the visceral field, as shown in the

conditioned fears, rages, loves (taking the form of strong attachments to mother or nurses), tantrums, negative reactions to
people, and the like.

Our observation shows that the infant cannot before thirty
months of age parallel each unit manual habit with a corresponding word habit. Today in front of me is a child two and one-
fourth years of age. He can speak, under appropriate stimulation
of object or situation, possibly five hundred words, but sentence
formation is of the level of "Rose take Billy bye-bye," "Put Billy's
coat on." He is still at the age of incessant repetition of words
and sentences. When the nurse brings him in, the father says:
"What did you see, Billy?" and he says: "What did you see?"
In contrast, this same infant learned to manipulate at two years
of age a rather large, pedalled "kiddy car," to propel it, guide it,
mount it, coast down hill, drag it up inclines and along the side-
walk, and to fly down. He reacted against help, would fall off
without crying, mount and start over again. The *only verbal*
parallel is, "Billy ride kiddy car." There is no verbal organization which you can call out relating to turning the bar to the
left or right when he turns to left or right; about pedalling
being harder uphill than down; pointing out that the greater
the incline the more rapid his speed. Yet overt, manual responses
are perfect, even after weeks and months of no practice. This
example from hundreds of others shows that the manual habits
of two-and-one-half-year-and-under infants are unverbalized. The
only way you can show "memory" or organization in such cases
is to put the child in the situation where he can exhibit that
bodily organization. Contrast this with the three-and-a-half to
four-year-old who goes walking, to a party or to a movie, or
who takes a railway trip, and talks you blind, deaf and dumb
about it. This conception helps us, I believe, in removing a lot
of mystery in psychology, for example, it throws most of Freud's
psychology out of court (but not his *facts* nor his *therapy*).

The Freudians, as is well known, claim that the childhood

memories are lost because childhood is an age where free, spon-
taneous actions bringing "pleasure" come under the ban of the
social; society punishes and a painful repression into the "unconscious" takes place. They claim further that these childhood
memories are lost until the analyst gives the mystical phrase
which opens the cave where the memories are stored. The unsatisfactory ground for this assumption is now apparent. *The
child had never verbalized these acts.*

I have become totally skeptical of any so-called adult "memory"
antedating certainly the two-and-one-half-year childhood period.
My skepticism comes too from observation of children and not
through any presuppositions. Recently I tested out a hungry two-
and-one-fourth-year-old baby with a nursing bottle filled with
milk. The test in detail follows:

TEST ON MEMORY FOR BOTTLE

Baby B, 2 years, 3 months of age.

At 12:30 noon, the baby's meal time, his regular nurse picked
him up and said: "Dinner, Billy," laid him flat on his back in
the crib as was her usual custom when he formerly was fed
from the bottle. She handed him the warmed bottle just as she
had one and one-fourth years before.

The baby took the bottle in both hands, then began to manipulate the nipple with his finger, then began to cry because
"dinner" with him at noon, at this age, consisted of meat and
vegetables. When told to "Take his milk," he put the nipple to
his mouth and got a taste of milk and began to *chew the nipple.
Nursing could not be called out.* He called to his mother and
cried and handed her the bottle and raised himself to a sitting
posture. He pushed the bottle toward the mother, then toward
the father, with both hands. He was then let down to the floor
and good humor was restored.

He was told "Jimmie drinks from bottle" (his infant brother).
Then he took the bottle, put it in his mouth and walked off,

chewing the nipple as he went. *Nursing had disappeared through disuse. It had been "forgotten."* [1] (This act when practiced can continue indefinitely. I have records of children who nursed at the breast until they were over three years of age.)

Billy nursed at the mother's breast only during the first month and was then put wholly on the bottle. At the end of nine months he was weaned from the bottle and made to drink from a silver mug. Until he was one year of age he drank his morning orange juice from a nursing bottle. He never saw a nursing bottle from that day until the day of the test.

Before the test took place every effort was made to stir up a verbal memory of some kind, but unavailingly. He was asked, "Didn't you used to drink from a bottle when you were little?" Then he was told that he used to drink from a bottle. Then he was asked, "Can't Billy drink from a bottle?" His behavior throughout was exactly that of reacting to a strange new object, of being forced to react to it when his whole body was ready to react to his regular food.

The test shows that not only was there around this once all-important infant act no verbal organization that could be tapped, but that even the manual organization (including of course sucking) was gone.

Thus infancy, where the process of "repression" is supposed to bury so many unconscious treasures which come to light under the prestidigitation of the analyst, turns out to be a wholly natural kind of state. Bodily habits form normally, both habits of avoidance and approach, and habits of manipulation; but the bodily habits *lack verbal correlates because the infant puts them on at a later age.*

I believe the whole of Freud's "unconscious" can be adequately cared for along the lines I have indicated. The Freudians have

---

[1] On the same date he was similarly given an opportunity to nurse from the breast. He could not be made to take the nipple into his mouth and soon began to struggle at being held in the lap in the nursing position.

no positive evidence to offer in controversion, at least they have offered none. I find no actual observation in their literature of the day-by-day life of the infant. Hug-Hellmuth's volume on infant psychology might just as well have been written without any infant being present, so inaccurate and *non*-scientific are its observations and assumptions.

UNVERBALIZED ORGANIZATION WHERE VISCERAL SEGMENTS INITIATE THE TOTAL REACTIONS

It has been demonstrated that conditioned visceral or emotional responses are constantly forming from infancy on; that these conditioned responses are "transferred" to a variety of situations; and that they persist for long periods of time, possibly throughout life. And yet we cannot talk about visceral organization.

One reason for this is of course social. Society makes no demands upon us, or few at any rate, to talk about unstriped muscular and glandular habits. When conditioned salivary reflexes are established in childhood, the child is never told about them; no demand is made upon man to verbalize elimination habits, habits connected with the slowing or speeding of the sexual orgasm. Few men and fewer women have paralleled their sex organization with words.

Again, what child has ever verbally organized its incestuous attachments? Not one. Nor has there been any "repression" because society was not and is not organized to place youthful incestuous attachments under the ban (quite the contrary). Some time ago one of our most distinguished pediatricians, in condemning the idea of an experimental nursery, said, "Infants need a mother's love; they should be danced at her knee, petted and made much of." To tell a mother who is breeding habits of dependence in her child by letting it always play under her eye, who always feeds it herself (creating thereby a situation where a violent tantrum will occur if any one else ever has to feed it), that she is laying up trouble for the child when it has to break its nest habits, is to arouse a storm of protest.

Only a slight study of this field convinces the psychological geneticist that a large part of our visceral organization goes on from infancy to old age without corresponding verbalization. Even an adequate list of names for visceral objects and situations is absent and there is no social mechanism for the word-conditioning of the developing subject. A little of it is verbalized. This comes about when the acts of belching, elimination, releasing of gas, masturbation, and the like are exhibited in the presence of elders. The psychological process of verbal conditioning takes the form of, "You must not let your *stomach growl* in company." "Run outside or cough to cover it up." "Say 'excuse me' when you do that in company." While many similar examples of verbalization in the visceral realm occur, verbalization is the exception, not the rule. To help hold all this together, let me give a short summary:

1. An enormous number of manual habits are formed, especially during infancy, without corresponding verbal habits.

2. A still larger amount of visceral organization (organization in unstriped muscles and glandular components) is constantly forming without verbal organization, not only during infancy but also throughout life.

3. The assumption seems to be reasonably grounded that this unverbalized organization makes up the Freudian's "unconscious." (Another possible source of the so-called "unconscious" in line with natural science might be found in cases where for one reason or another the verbal organization is blocked, e. g., where there is simultaneously present a stimulus to say the girl's name in a love affair and one to remain silent. In such cases only the visceral organization appears, such as incoherent sounds, blushing and the like.) It likewise makes up possibly the introspectionist's "affective processes."

4. The genetic rule, when the proper age is reached, is to put on simultaneously word, manual and visceral organizations.

5. Once the verbalization of the manual begins, word organization soon becomes "dominant" because man has to solve his problems verbally. The word stimulus can thereafter call out any organized response in the organism, or modify any activity already going on. For example, "I must start to build that bookcase now," or "I am shooting too high; I must aim lower."

6. That aspect of "memory," which is supposed by the introspectionist to be difficult for the behaviorist to cope with, is merely the calling out of the verbal parallels of habits earlier put on. Memory in the behaviorist's sense is any exhibition of manual, verbal or visceral organization put on prior to the time of the test.

I believe that when subjective psychologists have given verbalization its due place in the whole process of bodily organization they will be ready to admit that "being conscious" is merely a popular or literary phrase descriptive of the act of *naming our universe of objects both inside and outside,* and that "introspecting" is a much narrower popular phrase descriptive of the more awkward act of *naming tissue changes that are taking place,* i. e., movements of muscles, tendons, glandular secretions, respiration, circulation and the like. They must be looked upon solely as literary forms of expression.

CAN WE THINK WITHOUT WORDS?

One of the stumbling blocks in the way of the complete acceptance of the behaviorist's theory of thought is the implied assumption that we think only in words, that is, in terms of verbal motor contractions. My answer has been: Yes, or in *conditioned word substitutes,* such as the shrug of the shoulders or other bodily response, found in the eyelids, the muscles of the eye or even in the retina (I assume of course that "images," those ghostlike "memory" pictures of objects not present to the senses, have been given up in psychology!). These conditioned substitutes represent the abridging and short-circuiting process that goes on in all original learning.

I am inclined now to bring out some points I neglected in my paper before the International Congress for Psychology and Philosophy. I should like to say here emphatically that *whenever the individual is thinking, the whole of his bodily organization is at work (implicitly)*—even though the final solution shall be a spoken, written or subvocally expressed verbal formulation. In other words, from the moment the thinking problem is set for the individual (by the situation he is in) activity is aroused that may lead finally to adjustment. Sometimes the activity goes on in terms of (1) implicit manual organization; more frequently in terms of (2) implicit verbal organization; sometimes

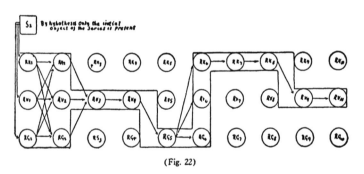

(Fig. 22)

This diagram shows the behaviorist's theory of thinking. Sometimes we think by using manual, verbal and visceral organizations simultaneously. Sometimes only the verbal, sometimes only the visceral and at other times only the manual. In the diagram the organization taking part in the whole thinking process is enclosed between the two continuous solid lines.

The diagram shows clearly that thinking involves all three sets of our organized reaction systems.

in terms of (3) implicit (or even overt) visceral organization. If (1) or (3) dominates, thinking takes place *without words*.

The diagram I show on page 266 is only an elaboration of Fig. 21. It makes clear my present convictions about thinking. In this diagram I take it for granted that the body has been simultaneously organized to respond to a series of objects, manually, verbally and viscerally (Fig. 18). I take it for granted further that one of the objects, the initial one, S1, is at hand and that it starts the body to work on its problem of thinking. The object actually present may be a person asking the individual a question (take the question I asked in the last chapter—"Will X leave his present job to become Y's partner?"). By hypothesis the world is shut off from him and he has to *think* his problem out.

Please note that RK1 can arouse RK2, RV2, RG2; whereas RV1 can call out RK2, RV2, RG2; and RG1 can call out RK2, RV2 or RG2; and that all of them can serve respectively as kinaesthetic, laryngeal or visceral substitutes for S2, the next real object in the series of objects originally producing the organization. Note that, in accordance with the diagram, thinking activity may go on for a considerable time without words. If at any step in the process the RV organization does not appear, thinking goes on without words.

It seems reasonable to suppose that thinking at successive moments of time may be kinaesthetic, verbal or emotional. When kinaesthetic organization becomes blocked or is lacking, then the verbal processes function; if both are blocked, the emotional organization becomes dominant. By hypotheses, however, the final response or adjustment, if one is reached, must be verbal (subvocal). It is convenient to call this final verbal act a *judgment*.

This line of argument shows how one's total organization is brought into the process of thinking. It shows clearly that manual and visceral organizations are operative in thinking even when no verbal processes are present—*it shows that we could still think in some sort of way even if we had no words!*

We thus think and plan with the whole body. But since, as I pointed out above, word organization is, when present, probably usually dominant over visceral and manual organization, we can say that *"thinking"* is largely *subvocal talking*—provided we hasten to explain that it can occur without words.

This chapter has helped us to put various bits of the human being's organization, hitherto studied part by part, together again. We had to dissect man for pedagogical purposes. In the next and final chapter, on personality, we shall try to put man completely together and look at him as a complicated, going, organic machine.

XII. Personality

PRESENTING THE THESIS THAT OUR PERSONALITY IS
BUT THE OUTGROWTH OF THE HABITS WE FORM

WHAT does the behaviorist mean by personality? In this chapter let us try to think of man as an assembled organic machine ready to run. We mean nothing very difficult by this. Take four wheels with tires, axles, differentials, gas engine, body; put them together and we have an automobile of a sort. *The automobile is good for certain kinds of duties.* Depending upon its make-up, we use it for one kind of job or another. If it is a Ford, it is good for going to market, for running errands and for driving over the roughest roads and in the most difficult kinds of weather. If it is a Rolls Royce, it is good for pleasure riding, calling on people who are just a little above us in the social scheme, impressing upon those poorer than ourselves that we are persons of wealth. In a similar way this man, this organic animal, this John Doe, who so far as parts are concerned is made up of head, arms, hands, trunk, legs, feet, toes and nervous, muscular and glandular systems, who has no education and is too old to get it, is good for certain jobs. He is as strong as a mule, can work at manual labor all day long. He is too stupid to lie, too bovine to laugh or play. He will work all right as a "white wing," as a digger of ditches or as a chopper of wood. Individual William Wilkins, having the same bodily parts but who is good looking, educated, sophisticated, accustomed to good society, travelled, is good for work in many situations—as a diplomat, a politician or a real estate salesman.

He, however, was a liar from infancy and could never be trusted in a responsible place. He is too selfish to be placed over other people. He would leave his work in the middle of any afternoon for golf or a bridge game.

Whence come these differences in the machine? In the case of man, all healthy individuals, as we saw in our discussion of Instincts, start out *equal*. Quite similar words appear in our far-famed Declaration of Independence. The signers of that document were nearer right than one might expect, considering their dense ignorance of psychology. They would have been strictly accurate had the clause *"at birth"* been inserted after the word equal. It is what happens to individuals after birth that makes one a hewer of wood and a drawer of water, another a diplomat, a thief, a successful business man or a far-famed scientist. What our advocates of freedom in 1776 took no account of is the fact that the Deity himself could not equalize 40-year-old individuals who have had such different environmental trainings as the American people have had.

In studying the personality of an individual—what he is good for, what he isn't good for and what isn't good for him—we must observe him as he carries out his daily complex activities; not just at this moment or that, but week in and week out, year in and year out, under stress, under temptation, under affluence and under poverty. In other words, in order to write up the personality, the "shop ticket," for an individual, we must call him in and put him through all the possible tests in the shop before we are in a position to know what kind of person—what kind of organic machine—he is.

What do we mean by putting the individual through his various paces in the world we live in? Well, I have in mind the answers to such questions as these: What kind of work habits has John Doe? What kind of husband does he make? What kind of father? How does he behave toward his subordinates? His superiors? How does he behave toward his partners or equals in whatever group he works? Is he really a man of principle or is he a psalm-singing, sanctimonious individual on Sunday and a grasping, close-fisted, unscrupulous business man on Monday? Is he pleasantly well-bred, or is he over-courteous, with accent and mannerisms dependent on the college he grew up in, or the last country he visited? Does he make a faithful friend to friends in need? Will he work hard? Is he cheerful? Does he keep his troubles to himself?

The behaviorist naturally is not interested in his morals, except as a scientist; in fact he doesn't care what kind of man he is. He must study any individual, though, whenever society calls for analysis. As a scientific man the behaviorist would like to be able to give answers not only to such questions as we have raised, but to all other questions which could be asked about John Doe. It is a part of the behaviorist's scientific job to be able to state what the human machine is good for and to render serviceable predictions about its future capacities whenever society needs such information.

ANALYSIS OF PERSONALITY

In order that there may be no vagueness about the behaviorist's use of "personality," let me say more concretely what I mean by the term. Do you remember the diagram on page 138? There I talked about the development of the activity stream. I pointed out that at birth and at different intervals thereafter unlearned beginnings of behavior are always present. I pointed out also that most of these unlearned activities begin to become conditioned a few hours after birth. *From that time on each such unit of unlearned behavior develops into an ever expanding system.* In the chart I gave there we could draw in only a few lines to indicate what happens.

Suppose now that this chart of the activity stream be made complex enough to show the history of every bit of organization the individual has had from infancy to the age of 24. Just assume, for purposes of argument, that the habit curve for everything that you can possibly do had been plotted out by a behaviorist who had studied you under experimental conditions throughout the whole of your life up to the age of 24. *Now it is obvious that if at the age of 24 he took a cross section of your activity, he would be able to catalogue everything that you can do.* He would find that many of these separate activities are related—grew up around the same object such as the family, the church, tennis, shoemaking, and so on. Let us stop and look at any habit system chosen at random, such as shoemaking for example.

Shoemaking, in the old days, meant first the rearing of cattle, then slaughtering them, then taking the hides to the tan yard. In the tan-yard vats were dug in the ground, filled with water and some caustic substance for removing the hair from the hides. Next the hides were dyed or stained with tannic acid made from grinding up the bark of oak trees and mixing it with water. This is called tanning the leather. After the hides were tanned, they were washed and put through a process of drying and treating. Lasts had to be made for the customers' shoes, leather had to be cut up and shaped over the lasts. Soles had to be sewed on. It is needless to enumerate every operation that had to be gone through before a finished pair of shoes could result. On my grandfather's place there was a man who knew every detail of every one of these operations and actually performed them. I should call all of the acts connected with shoemaking (of course the group of acts differs considerably from one decade to another because of the specialization going on in labor) the *shoemaking habit system*. You can easily understand that if we broke that system up into the separate activities we should need something like a thousand divisions on a chart just to describe shoemaking organization. And to make our chart complete and serviceable in helping us to predict something about the future behavior of an individual's shoemaking activities, we should have to show the age at which each of these habits began to form and their history from that time up to the present time. This whole study would give us the life history of that individual's shoemaking habits.

Now let us turn to another complex system of habits. In talking about the personality of an individual we often hear the phrase, "He is a deeply religious man." What does that mean? It means that the individual goes to church on Sunday, that he reads the Bible daily, that he says grace at the table, that he sees to it that his wife and children go with him to church, that he tries to convert his neighbor into becoming a religious man and that he engages in many hundreds of other activities all of which are called parts of a modern Christian's religion. Let us put all of these separate activities together and call them the *religious habit system* of the individual. Now each of these separate activities making up this system has a dating back in the individual's past and a history from that point to the age of 24 where we are taking the cross section. For example, he learned the little prayer, "Now I lay me down to sleep," at 2½. This habit was put away at 6 and the Lord's Prayer took its place. Later on, if he entered the Episcopal faith, he read the printed prayers. If a Baptist, Methodist or Presbyterian, he made up his own prayers. At 18 years of age, having certain organization in public speaking, he began to "lead" in prayer meeting. At 4 years of age, he began to look at pictures in the Bible and to have the Bible stories read to him and told to him. He began to go to Sunday School at this time and to memorize certain biblical passages. Soon he was able to read the Bible through and to memorize whole books of it. Again it is far too complex a task for us to attempt to take each of the strands of this religious organization and to trace out its beginning and its genetic history.

So far we have discussed in detail only two of these systems, but the cross section at 24 years of age would show many thousands of such systems. You are already familiar with many of them, such as the marital habit system, the parental system, the public speaking system, the thought system of the profound thinker, the eating system, the fear system, the love system, the rage system. All of these are broad general classifications, of course, and should be split up into very much smaller systems, but even these divisions will serve to give you a conception of the kinds of facts we are trying to present. Let us draw a diagram to help us hold all of these facts together (Fig. 23).

This survey of human activity leads us to an objective formulation of personality. *Personality is the sum of activities that can be discovered by actual observation of behavior over a long enough time to give reliable information. In other words, personality is but the end product of our habit systems. Our procedure in studying personality is the making and plotting of a cross section of the activity stream.* Among these activities, however, there are dominant systems in the manual field (occupational), in the laryngeal field (great talker, *raconteur*, silent thinker), and in the visceral field (afraid of people, shy, given to outbursts, having to be petted, and in general what we call emotional). These dominating systems are obvious, easy to observe, and they serve as the basis for most of the rapid judgments we make about the personalities of individuals. It is upon the basis of these few dominant systems that we classify personalities.

This reduction of personality to things which can be seen and observed objectively possibly will not square very well with the sentimental attachments most people have for the word personality. It would fit much more easily into your present organization if I did not define the word personality and merely characterized people by saying, "He has a commanding personality," "She has an appealing and charming personality," "He has a most disagreeable personality." But what does one mean by a commanding personality? Isn't it generally that the individual speaks in an authoritative kind of way, that he has a rather large physique and that he is a little taller than the average?

Another factor that does not come out in the activity chart is this—*personality judgments* usually are not based purely on the life chart of the individual whose personality is being studied. If the person studying the personality of another were free from slants and if accurate allowance could be made for the effects of

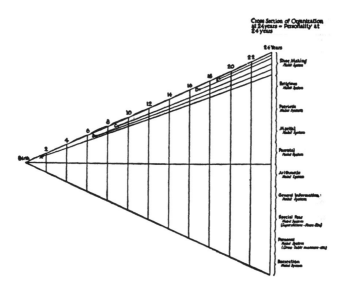

Fig. 23. Rough diagram to illustrate what the behaviorist means by "personality" and to show how it develops. In examining this diagram refer also to the diagram illustrating the stream of activity on page 138. The central thought in the diagram is that personality is made up of dominant habit systems (only a few of these are shown in the 24-year-old cross section—there are really many hundreds).

All the other habit systems—for instance, the religious, the patriotic, etc.—should have similar lines extending backward into the adolescence, youth and infancy of the individual in order to make them complete. For the sake of clearness, we have omitted them.

his own past habit systems, he would be able to make an objective study. But none of us has this kind of freedom. We are all dominated by our past and our judgments of other people are always clouded by difficulties in our own personality. Let us look a moment further at a "dominating personality." Under the present system of rearing children the father is usually reacted to as though he were a large, powerful man, a kind of superhuman brute who must be obeyed instantly or punishment will be either threatened or applied. Hence the adult is easily liable, when an individual possessing these characteristics comes into the room, to fall under his "spell." This means nothing more to the behaviorist than an expression of the fact that people who act like our father still have the power to make us behave like a child. It would not be difficult to pick out any of these cherished convictions about personality and show it up in its true light.

In presenting personality in this way, it should become clear now that the *situation we are in dominates us always and releases one or another of these all-powerful habit systems*. For example, the ringing of the Angelus stops the reapers in the field, breaks in on their manual systems and throws them for the time being under the dominance of their religious habit systems. In general, we are what the situation calls for—a respectable person before our preacher and our parents, a hero in front of the ladies, a teetotaler in one group, a bibulous good fellow in another.

One other thing the activity chart fails to show—and one which is of the very greatest importance. In developing so many hundreds and thousands of habit systems it is almost inevitable that these systems must conflict at one time or another. Thus it comes about that one stimulus may call out, or partially call out, two opposed types of action in the same muscular and glandular group. Inaction, fumbling, trembling, may result. In certain cases there are apparently almost permanent conflicts, conflicts of such extent and of such magnitude that a psychopathological individual results. I shall develop this farther on.

In a perfectly integrated (!) individual the following events happen: As soon as a situation begins to call for the dominance of a certain habit system, the whole body begins to unlock: the tensions in every set of striped and unstriped muscles not to be used in the immediately forthcoming action are released so as to free all of the striped and unstriped muscles and glands of the body for the habit system now needed. Only the one habit system, the operation of which is called for, can work at the maximum efficiency. The whole individual thus becomes "expressed," his whole personality is "engrossed," in the act he is doing.

This way of looking at the dominance of habit systems removes from the psychology of the behaviorist any need of the term *attention*. *Attention is merely then synonymous with the complete dominance of any one habit system,* be that a verbal habit system, a manual habit system or a visceral one. *"Distraction* of attention," on the other hand, is merely an expression of the fact that the situation does not immediately lead to dominance of any one habit system, but first to one and then to the other. The individual starts to do one thing but falls under the partial dominance of another stimulus which partially frees another habit system. This leads to a conflict in the use of certain muscle groups. A fumbling of speech may result, a fumbling with the hands or the body may result, or an insufficient amount of energy may be released for use of the muscle groups. Some examples are these: just as you are taking the high jump your schoolboy friend derides you; when you are preparing to take your swing in golf somebody speaks; when you are deeply engaged in thinking out a problem the water begins to drip in the bathroom: action is interfered with or even fails altogether. Illustrations of the attempted double and triple (and sometimes multiple) dominance of habit systems are very numerous. For these reasons the behaviorist feels that the term "attention" has no application in psychology and is just another confession of our inability to think clearly, and to keep mystery out of psychological terms. We like to keep mystery in so we can use it on a rainy day—when we are ill or low or particularly dissatisfied with what we are getting out of this existence of ours.

HOW TO STUDY PERSONALITY

In youth personality changes rapidly: Naturally if personality is but a cross section at any given age of the complete organization of an individual, you can see that this cross section must change at least slightly every day—but not too rapidly for us to get a fair picture from time to time. Personality changes most rapidly in youth when habit patterns are forming, maturing and changing. Between 15 and 18 a female changes from a child to a woman. At 15 she is but the playmate of boys and girls of her own age. At 18 she becomes a sex object to every man. After 30 personality changes very slowly owing to the fact, as we brought out in our study of habit formation, that by that time most individuals, unless constantly stimulated by a new environment, are pretty well settled into a humdrum way of living. Habit patterns become set. If you have an adequate picture of the average individual at 30 you will have it with few changes for the rest of that individual's life—as most lives are lived. A quacking, gossiping, neighbor-spying, disaster-enjoying woman of 30 will be, unless a miracle happens, the same at 40 and still the same at 60.

DIFFERENT WAYS OF STUDYING PERSONALITY

Most people pass their judgments on the personalities of their associates without ever having made a real study of the individual. In our rapidly shifting life we often have to make these rapid judgments. But we get into a habit of making superficial estimates and we often do people a serious injury as a result. Sometimes we pride ourselves on being able to make rapid diagnoses of personalities. We pride ourselves on knowing at first sight whether we are going to like a person or not and on never changing our judgments. This means all too often that the person under this superficial kind of observation does some one or two things which do not square with our own particular slants and bents, hence our judgments are not real conclusions about personality at all but are really an exposé of our own particular pet aversions which must never be run afoul of. The real observer of personality tries to keep himself out of the picture and to observe the other individual in an objective way.

Assuming that we are all careful observers of personality, that we are pretty free from sensitive spots ourselves and are really seeking to get a true estimate of the personality of any given individual, what shall we do to gain this information? Here are a few ways of going about our quest:

(1) By studying the educational chart of the individual; (2) by studying the individual's achievement chart; (3) by using psychological tests; (4) by studying the spare time and recreation record of the individual; (5) by studying the emotional make-up of the individual under the practical situations of daily living. *There is no rapid way of studying the behavior or psychological make-up of individuals.* There are various psychological fakers in the field who believe there are such shortcuts but their methods are unproductive of any satisfactory results.

Let us take up these various ways of studying personality. In no sense do I claim that the behaviorist has any definite scientific system for studying personality. He goes about the study in a practical, commonsense, observational way.

(1) *Studying the educational chart of the individual:* Considerable information can be gathered about the personality of an individual by charting his educational career. Did he finish his grade school, or did he drop out at 12 years of age? Why did he drop out? Economic pressure? Was it to seek adventure? Did he finish high school? Did he continue to the bitter end of college and graduate? It speaks well for his work habits, if not for his intelligence, if he

did stick it out. Going through college today is like going through with a foot race—you must finish if you start. I somehow need to be convinced that a man's work habits are an asset to him if when he comes up for a position I find that his chart shows that he started college and then dropped out. I look upon college as a place to grow up in—a place for breaking nest habits; as a place for learning how to make oneself friendly; for acquiring a certain *savoir faire;* as a place for learning how to keep one's clothes pressed and one's person looking neat; as a place in which to learn how to be polite in a lady's or a gentleman's presence—in a word a place in which to find how to use leisure and to find culture. Finally it should be a place where the student can learn respect for thinking and *possibly even learn how to think.* If it fails in these respects, college is a failure indeed. The manual and verbal habits put on there are rarely carried through life. I spent four years in undergraduate work. During all those years I "took" Greek and Latin. Today I couldn't write the Greek alphabet or read Xenophon's *Anabasis* to save my life. I couldn't read a page of Virgil or even Caesar's *Commentaries* if food, sex and shelter depended upon it. I studied history faithfully and I couldn't name ten presidents or give ten important dates in history. I couldn't summarize the Declaration of Independence or tell what the Mexican War was about.

And yet with all the fault we have to find with colleges, college bred men in business (just as they were in war) are uniformly more successful, receive fewer hard knocks, than the non-college men, and are generally more likable persons. There are many exceptions to this rule, however, and the lack of a college education does not always mean that the individual is a boor, or that he is lacking in the equipment for a successful life.

(2) *Studying the achievement chart of the individual:* In my opinion, one of the most important elements in the judging of personality, character and ability, is the history of the individual's yearly achievements. We can measure this objectively by charting

the length of time the individual stayed in his various positions and the yearly increases he received in his earnings. The boy or man who has changed his job twenty times at 30 without definite improvement at each change, will probably change it twenty times more before he is 45. If I owned a flourishing commercial business I should not want to employ a man for a responsible position at the age of 30 who had not earned or was not earning at least $5000 per year. I should confidently expect such a man to be earning still more at the age of 40. No hard and fast rule can be drawn—there are exceptions. But certainly yearly increase in responsibilities and yearly increase in salary are important factors in the progress of an individual.

In a similar way, if the individual is a writer, we should want to draw a curve of the prices he gets for his stories year by year. If from our leading magazines he receives the same average price per word for his stories at 30 that he received when he was 24, the chances are he is a hack writer and will never be anything but that. In the literary and artistic fields, as well as that of business, we must judge men and women from the point of view of achievement, measured by whatever standards you will, if you wish to be able to predict just how good an organic machine each is and just how well that machine will run in the future.[1]

[1] Bertrand Russell in commenting upon this attempt to measure literary and artistic production in terms of dollar value says:

"Applying this criterion to Buddha, Christ, and Mahomet, to Milton and Blake, we see that it involves an interesting readjustment in our estimates of the values of personalities. In addition to points already noted, there are two ethical maxims implicit in this passage. One is that excellence must be easily measureable, the other that it must consist in conformity to law. These are both natural consequences of the attempt to deduce ethics from a system based upon physics. For my part, the ethic suggested by the above passage from Dr. Watson is not one that I can accept. I cannot believe that virtue is proportional to income, nor yet that it is wicked to have difficulty in conforming to the herd. Doubtless my views on these matters are biased, since I am poor and a crank; but although I recognize this fact, they remain my views none the less." (*Sceptical Essays.*, 1928 p. 96)

I think there is a good deal of truth in what Mr. Russell says. It is too bad that monetary standards are dominant today. I venture to say though that all of us who write, paint or sing, charge all that the traffic will bear and that the rates we actually

(3) *Psychological tests as a method of studying personality:* Psychology, since the work of Münsterberg began in this country, is at the present time reaping just such a harvest as one might expect. It has made too many extravagant claims—that it can save industry seventy millions a year and that it should be the bright and guiding star in the selection of employees and in the placement and promotion of employees after entering office or factory. These claims have been made by some of our leading psychologists. Business organizations of today have become leery of these claims, partly because the psychologists have been too ambitious and have tried to walk before they learned to crawl, and partly because business houses have not been willing to wait until the psychologist could develop his methods for the particular business he was studying. Business firms have been at fault, too, not only because of unwillingness to wait for results which are necessarily slow in coming, but because they have not been willing to expend money on psychological work. They are willing to wait indefinitely for the results of the work of the chemists and the physicists, but they expect the psychologist to come in and, by some legerdemain and by some offhand pronunciamento, to settle the problems of industry which business men have been unable to settle by other means during the whole course of the existence of industry. I have in mind here, naturally, selection of personnel, placement and advancement of personnel after it has been chosen, efficiency of the worker, and finally happiness and contentment of the worker—using these last two terms as they are popularly used. Certainly, in all these, personality in our sense is the chief factor.

Psychology has made some progress in taking cross sections of vocational organization. We can test, quickly, a man's arithmetical ability, his general range of information, whether or not he knows Latin or Greek, whether or not a woman can take 60 words of

charge for our services have steadily increased during the past ten years, even though advancing years give no proof that our productions have improved. Our market has expanded—our services are more in demand. We charge more and we receive more. In other words, our productions are sold like any other commodity.

shorthand a minute, whether or not she can write a hundred words a minute for 40 minutes with relatively few errors and type-write with even impression, and whether or not an individual can drive an automobile over a tortuous course without striking stakes or other automobiles. Many other different vocational tests are in the process of being perfected.[1]

But it must be remembered always that vocational tests show only sheer ability to accomplish such and such things in a given time and with a given number of errors. But sheer ability to do certain things tells us little about the *systematic work habits* of the individual. Suppose he is efficient when actually hungry or in need of shelter—is he efficient after feeding and housing? Has he so many personal affairs to attend to that watching the clock becomes one of his liabilities? This is true of many individuals. For them, nine o'clock comes too early and five o'clock too late. Once I had to write a little brief on the chief factors in judging men for jobs. I wrote that if I had to select an individual on the basis of any one characteristic, I should choose *work habits*—actual love of work, willingness to take an overload of work, to work longer than actual specified hours and to clean the chips up after the work is done. These things, I find, have to be drilled into the individual pretty early or he will never get them. No psychological test so far devised will bring out the strength or weakness of the individual in these particulars.

(4) *Studying the spare time and recreation record of individuals:* Every individual must have some form of recreation. With some, recreation is found in reading, with others in games, with others in sports. Still others find it in sex, in alcohol, in fast driving; others in being with their families; and then there is the rare group quite often mentioned in the newspapers, which finds recreation in work—but, like the report of Mark Twain's death, these statements are often "grossly exaggerated."

[1] H. M. Johnson has sounded a timely note of warning on the value of all psychological tests—"Science and Sorcery in Mental Tests," the *Forum*, December, 1929.

I believe that sports and recreation are quite revealing. We can look upon certain sports as distinct assets, others as liabilities. The speed mania leads to accidents; the sex mania into many and difficult complications; alcohol mania into organic disturbance, unfitness for work and finally into actual disease.

Outdoor activity leads to physical fitness, to keenness in competition, to steadiness in coördination. I always feel more favorably disposed in going over the record of a man, if I find that he has one form of outdoor recreation in which he excels, be it golf, tennis, canoeing, fishing, hunting, boxing or track.

I search almost as eagerly for proficiency in indoor activities, such as cards, chess, dancing, singing and the playing of musical instruments. I believe that it is difficult for a man or woman to acquire proficiency in a recreational activity and not at the same time have ability along bread-earning, vocational lines. Then again, it is difficult for a man to achieve proficiency in sports who is not friendly and who cannot get along well with people. So let us admit, tentatively at any rate, that sports and recreations are probably indicative of personality, and that the individual's record along sport and recreational lines is worth studying.

(5) *Studying the emotional make-up of the individual under practical conditions:* The study of all the factors so far considered, such as the educational achievements of the individual, his work achievements and what he does in his spare time, does not give the whole personality story. An individual might be successful in all his work habits, both manual and verbal, and still he might be a terrible bore, unwelcome at dinner, unwelcome at golf or in travelling; he might be mean, niggardly, unfriendly, overbearing in his way of treating other people—in general, a terrible person to live with or near. I mean by this that certain people are inadequately developed along emotional lines. *They are emotional failures.* Observation helps us to gauge this. If we do not quite have the courage to invite this person to our home or to visit him in his, and thus get into a position to observe him for ourselves, we can

find out how many friends he has and how long those friendships have endured. One can almost state positively that if he has no large circle of friends and no friends of long standing, he will be a difficult person to be near always—no matter how well he may do his work. Success on the emotional side is never a safe guide, however, as to whether a man will succeed in business or in professional work. How often have we heard the expression "He is God's worst fool but even God likes him"? The record of work habits and achievement always must be read along with the emotional chart.

In judging personalities, we find it much more difficult to get any cross section of habits about lying, and about honesty and other so-called moral virtues. There is no way of finding these things out except by looking into the history of the individual and checking up rather closely on his life. This, however, can be done only by carrying out an extensive observation among his friends and by observing his behavior for a considerable length of time. If people would write honest letters about other people, our judgments of the emotional make-up of an individual could be much more safely formed. But most of us are too cowardly to write honest letters, hence letters of recommendation are rarely worth the paper they are written upon. I doubt that we shall ever be able to reach valuable judgments on the emotional phases of personality —such as the individual's ability to get along with others, whether he works well under a heavy load or under a slight load, whether he works better alone or in a crowd, whether he is slovenly in his work habits, whether he keeps up with his work or merely conceals the things he hasn't done, whether he works better under encouragement or under the lash—unless we provide a preliminary school where the individual actually can be kept under close observation for a definite period of time. Granting that the individual has considerable so-called intellectual ability (and by that we mean nothing more than considerable manual and verbal organization), he often *falls down in his various jobs in life largely through lack of visceral organization—that is, lack of well balanced emotional training.* You probably could understand this better if I used your terms—such as, the individual is *"sensitive," "touchy," "crusty," "vindictive," "overbearing," "seclusive," "exclusive," "cocky," "takes criticism unkindly,"* and the like. To bring out these emotional factors, the individual must be placed under certain situations, as we saw in our study of the infants. They are really unorganized, infantile types of reaction—carry-overs from infancy. Such situations, in the ordinary course of a week's or a month's work, may present themselves infrequently, hence the individual must be watched for a considerable time. I think that business houses are more or less convinced of this and that they are prepared to give longer preliminary training than formerly and to accept the relatively large labor turn-over that such a system involves.

ARE THERE ANY SHORTCUTS IN THE STUDY OF PERSONALITY?

Can we learn anything about personality by "interviewing" the subject? We can learn something about an individual in a personal interview. Personal interviews, however, should be rather extended, and more than one interview should be given and more than one person should interview the applicant. During an interview many little things are apparent which a close observer may note and profit by. The voice of the person under observation, his gestures, his gait, his personal appearance—all of these I think are significant. You can tell in a moment whether the individual is or is not a cultivated individual, whether or not he has good manners. One individual will come in for an interview and will keep his hat on his head and his cigar in his mouth; another will be so scared that he cannot even talk; still another will be so boastful that you want to escape his presence immediately.

Then there are many little things about a person's clothes that will show whether or not he has neat and cleanly personal habits. If he wears a soiled collar, if his hands are soiled above the wrist, we have pretty good evidence that he is an unpleasant and un-clean person. But personal interviews tell us nothing about work habits and nothing about the honesty of the individual, nothing about the steadfastness of his principles and little about his ability. Here again, we have to fall back upon a study of the life history of the individual.

Why is it, then, that office managers and the public generally believe that they can read personalities? Probably the main reason is that it flatters them to think that they can. It gives them a certain standing in the circle in which they move. The reason they get away with it is that they cannot be checked up. If you wish to pick out an individual from a group applying for, say, a job as office boy, or for any other kind of job which does not require ability of a specialized kind, such as that of typewriting or stenography (where checking is possible), the chances are fifty-fifty or better that you will pick him out right if you pick him blindfolded. Our standards of efficiency are not very high and hence every office is crowded with individuals able just to hold their jobs but who could not hold them if work were better standardized. If, however, the office manager is really keen, as many are, and engages the ap-plicants in conversation, puts them up against certain verbal ques-tions of a searching kind and carefully notes their answers, there are signs which are helpful to him. But at best the selection of per-sonnel today is little better than a hit or miss affair. This is the reason the psychological faker gets along so easily.

SOME OF THE WEAKNESSES OF OUR ADULT PERSONALITY

Human nature has so many weaknesses in it that it is difficult to make a start in pointing out the chief failures. Indeed, as one ob-serves human life more and more closely, one comes to the point of view that what often seems to be strength is but one of the in-dividual's chief points of weakness. Let us look at weaknesses in personality under a few such headings as (1) our inferiorities, (2) our susceptibility to flattery, (3) our constant strife to become kings and queens, and finally (4) the carrying over of our childhood heritages.

(1) *Our inferiorities:* I need to discuss very little today the steps by which we "organize" our inferiorities into systems. The psychoanalysts have done this for us. We would phrase what happens in scientific terms, however. Most of us have groups of reactions developed which do cover up, conceal and hide our inferiorities. Shyness is one form, silence is another, outbursts of temper are another, advanced stands on moral or social questions are other very common forms. The most selfish of individuals has a well organized verbal scheme which hides his selfishness from the uninitiated —the most "impure" of individuals often talks loudest of purity. The person who is often most easily a prey to temptation proclaims most loudly the rules and regulations upon which he bases his standards of ethics and conduct. Poor fellow, he is so weak he needs them to bolster himself up. Again, one of the outstanding examples is the fellow who, all but impotent, boasts loudest of his sex powers.

We likewise organize habit systems that serve the purpose of concealing our physical inferiorities. The little short man often talks loudly, dresses "loudly," wears high-heeled shoes, is "cocky" and forward. In order to be seen at all he must act in an unusual way. Women try to balance one thing off against another. Their faces may not be beautiful, but their forms are exquisite; their arms may be clumsy, but their legs are objects of admiration by discriminating artists. Nothing in their anatomy may be supreme —then they fall back upon style. When too fat to be stylish, they have wonderful cars to ride in, beautiful jewels, well appointed homes.

Somehow most human beings can't permanently face inferiority —nor are the analysts any exception. A great many of my friends are analysts. They can still be made angry when their theories are attacked or if some one challenges their superior powers as analysts. Who would have them different? All I ask from anybody when he has to boast or to play up the good side a little is that he display a sense of humor—admit, at least by a sign, that it is as necessary for him to do this once in a while as it is for the baby to have its milk bottle. Indeed, the origin of these so-called "compensations" is infantile. We teach the child that he is "smart," smarter than the neighbor's child. We pet him, make much of him. The analysts call this expression of the "ego." Not at all—it is merely an organized habit system built in at the mother's knee. The parent's own inferiorities start it. No matter how "dumb" her own child is, when the neighbor comes in she must find something in her little Reginald or Heloise that the neighbor's child does not possess. If her child's feet are large, maybe her hands are small and shapely. All the child hears from her beloved parents are praises for her good parts and no mention of her poor ones. *The individual thus forms a verbal organization about her assets—can talk about them—but she never learns to talk about her liabilities.*

(2) *Our susceptibility to flattery:* Observation of personality in male and female shows some weak spots in all our armor. If I had to give you just one weapon for piercing the armor of most individuals, that weapon would be *flattery*. Flattery has become an art, however. Only the well schooled and the graduates in the art should attempt to use it. I have already brought out for you the fact that most individuals have a group of dominating habit systems. It may be their religious habit systems, their moral habit systems, their vocational habit systems, their artistic habit systems, or others. If the individual is constantly flattered on his achievements in these directions, the chances are good that the person trying to approach him will have success. Sometimes a five-minute conversation will give the key-note of this dominating organization. The anti-smoker, the strict prohibitionist, the efficiency bug, the money king, the speed and sex mania organizations show up very quickly in conversation. Much observation has shown me that almost invariably when the skillful stranger makes the acquaintance of these individuals and approaches them on their

weak side, their verdict is, "He is a remarkable fellow, agreeable, charming, quite intelligent. I think we ought to have him around again."

Often the vulnerable point in character is what the Freudians call an avoidance mechanism. For example, A does not like to hurt anybody's feelings. Rather than do it, he yields not only his dollars but his principles. He will burden himself with the cares of other individuals and carry their woes around with him because he is too chicken-hearted to stand up and tell them what he thinks.

I doubt very seriously whether any man or woman is invulnerable on any commandment, on any code of honesty, on any life-long settled conviction. I think the time was when invulnerability was a more nearly possible thing. Today conventions are so universally overstepped, religious mandates so often transgressed, business honesty and integrity so often a matter of legal decision, that all of us are vulnerable if and when approached long enough and hard enough and subtly enough on our weak side. This does not mean that you or I would rob a bank today, commit murder or rape, take undue advantage of our neighbor; yet almost invariably we do many so-called unethical things, given certain conditions. It often happens in business and in the professions that as long as a man ahead of you is helpful and useful to you, you are meticulous in giving him his due. He can do no wrong. You back him up, support him on every occasion. But when you reach him, when you begin to share the throne with him, you, without ever verbalizing it, somehow find your ear more attuned to faults. A strong visceral toning appears when you hear things not quite to his credit! Then again, when you pass him, you begin to wonder if your former rival cannot be replaced by a less expensive man. You rationalize this on the grounds of economy, thus killing two birds with one stone, strengthening your balance-sheet and making your own throne more secure against the possible recrudescence of a former rival.

I have no venom to display here against human nature. I am just trying to show that our way of acting in certain situations is almost automatic. Some of us know these kinds of weaknesses in ourselves and we are constantly on the watch for them. Others are not quite so well analyzed. They call it being human and forgive themselves on such grounds. Here is where I think psychology can be most helpful in every phase of human relationship. The old biblical saying which I shall paraphrase: First take out the beam from your own eye that you may see the mote in your fellow man's eye, is a far more psychologically convincing maxim than the Golden Rule, or even Kant's "Universal." We know all too little about "Do unto others as you would that they should do unto you." Most of us are pathological in certain directions; the other fellow is pathological in different directions. If you tried to do unto him as you would like to be done by, you would very often get into difficulties, sometimes of the most pronounced kinds! Again, take Kant's universal, "Act by a maxim fit to become universal." With this ever-changing psychological world no maxim is fit to become universal. A maxim which would have worked in the Garden of Eden, would never have worked in the time of Caesar, nor would it work any better in 1930. But every man can watch his own way of acting and he will often be surprised when he comes to face the real stimuli that touch off his actions. Susceptibility to flattery, selfishness, avoiding difficult situations, unwillingness to show or to confess weakness, inadequacy or lack of knowledge, jealousy, fear of rivals, fear of being made the scapegoat, hurling criticism upon others to escape it oneself—make up an almost unbelievable part of our natures. The individual when he really faces himself is often almost (if not quite) overcome by what is revealed—infantile behavior, unethical standards, smothered over by the thinnest veneer of rationalization. Nakedness of "soul" can be faced only by the truly brave.

(3) *Our constant strife to become kings and queens:* As the result of our training at the hands of our parents, of the books we

read and of the biographies of those around us, every man deems
it his inalienable right to become a king and every woman a
queen. All history breeds this in. Kings and queens are petted and
made much of; kings and queens have things done for them;
they get more food and better food; they get better shelter, more
artistic shelter; they get more sex and greater aesthetic values in
sex. It is in childhood that most of these things come to us. This
is one reason why it is so hard to give up our childhood and, as a
matter of fact, as I shall show you later on, we rarely do completely
give it up. We try to carry over into everyday adult life the dominance we have put over on our parents in our childhood. The labor
leader who says, "Down with the capitalists and up with labor,"
is just as anxious as any of us to be king. The capitalist who says,
"Down with labor," is just as eager either to become king or
else to stay king. No one can object to this kind of strife. It is a
part of life. There always has been and there always (until the
behaviorists bring up all the children!) will be this kind of
struggle for dominance. Every man ought to be a king and every
woman a queen. Each must learn, however, that his domain is
restricted. The objectionable people in the world are those who
want to be kings and queens but who will allow no one else to be
regal.

(4) INFANT CARRY-OVERS THE GENERAL CAUSE OF UNHEALTHY PERSONALITIES

The weaknesses in our personalities which we have just considered are but examples of the general fact that we carry over
many organized habit systems from our infancy and early youth
into our adult life. Most of these systems, as I pointed out on
page 259, are of the unverbalized types—verbal correlates and
substitutes are lacking. The individual cannot talk about them,
he would deny that he has carried over his infantile behavior,

yet the appropriate situation brings out its expression. These carry-overs are the most serious handicaps to a healthy personality.

One of the systems we carry over is that of strong attachments (positive conditionings) for one or more individuals in the home —mother, father, brother, sister—or some adult who played an important rôle in our upbringing. Too faithful attachments to objects, places, localities are often serious. The general name to apply to all such carry-overs is *nest habits*. The South especially develops them—"My family does so and so," "No Smith was ever conquered," "The Joneses never forget an insult." Families belonging to the nobility have bred in them the same kind of systems. These habits are consolidated into family mottoes and coats of arms. Since marriage nearly always means the bringing of a stranger into the group, serious difficulties often arise before the stranger is accepted even by the wife or husband. This is one reason why there are so many blood feuds. Thus, owing to the fact that your father and mother bred these habits into you, and your father and mother had them similarly bred into them, we get infantilism as a kind of perpetual social inheritance. In a somewhat less insistent way *racial* habit systems are also bred into people.

But we are interested in the growth of the individual, mainly. Let us return to him. Suppose by the time you are 3 years of age your fond and doting mother has got you into the following ways of behaving. She waits on you hand and foot. You are an angel child and anything you do or say is perfectly wonderful. Your father must not correct you. Your nurse is always wrong if she scolds you. Three years later you start to school. You are a problem child all through. Soon you play hookey; your mother backs you up. You steal and lie repeatedly, and your teacher sends you home and closes the school to you. Your mother gets a tutor—but a tutor over whom she has the control. He educates you. You are "finished off" by travel. One meets everywhere people of this kind.

They cannot break their nest habits—they can never "make a go of it" when the home quits petting them. When youth is gone they fall back on chronic invalidism.

We should shed our childish habits yearly as the snake sheds its skin—not all at once like the snake, but gradually as the new situations caused by growth demand it. At three years of age the normal child has a well-organized 3-year-old personality—a system of habits that works well for that age. But as he progresses towards 4, some of the 3-year-old habits must give way—baby talk has to be given up, personal habits have to change. At 4 the wetting of the bed, thumb-sucking, shyness at meeting strangers, failure to talk fluently will not be so lightly overlooked. Exhibitionism has to give way; the child is taught not to burst into a room and start a conversation regardless of whether others are talking. He must begin to dress himself, to take his bath unaided, to get up at night and go to the toilet if necessary, and to do thousands of other actions not expected of the 3-year-old.

If only our home life were constructed so that 3-year habits could give way to 4-year habits without the infantile carry-over! But this cannot and never will happen until parents have fewer carry-overs from their own infancy—until they learn how to rear children.

Let me give one or two illustrations of how these carry-overs influence our adult lives. Owing to a mother's too tender love, marriage is difficult or impossible for the son—the mother objects to every choice made by the son. He finally marries and a family row occurs. This is temporarily patched up. Son and daughter-in-law, after a few days, come to live with the parents. Then the fat is in the fire. Then the son has two wives, his mother and his bride. This youth has to be remade—forced to lose this unnatural, but by him unnoted, mother conditioning.

Again, a girl attached from infancy to her father, lives on until the age of 24 and does not marry. She finally marries. Because she has, of course, never had sexual relations with her father, she will not have them with her husband. If she is forced to she breaks down. She may commit suicide or become insane to escape.

May I express the thought here if from morning till night the average adult could chart in detail his verbal, manual and visceral behavior which is released by infantile carry-overs, he would be not only astonished but even fearful of his future. Our "feelings are hurt," we "grow angry," we "become exasperated," we "handed some one a good one," we "got in a good lick at some one"; the man over you is "stupid," "ignorant," you quarreled, you "blew up," you got sick, you had a headache, you had to show off before your subordinate, you were sulky, moody, abstracted all day. Your work did not go well, you fumbled your work, spoiled your material. You were cruel to those below you, you were "conceited"— one of the almost inevitable forms of display. "Conceit," which all too often mars personality, is but a confession of the grossest kind of ignorance. A person who is wise always has such a vista of things he knows nothing about in front of him that he grows more and more humble as his wisdom increases. Conceit comes from infant spoiling. Humility and inadequacies are similarly carry-overs and are bred in usually by an "inferior" or inadequate father or mother. Slants of the parents in these directions account so well for the so-called "dispositional" factors in families (I mean the slants that can be seen through several generations) that I cannot see why we have to fall back upon inheritance to account for them.

WHAT IS A "SICK" PERSONALITY?

There is no more confusing field today, so far as use of terms goes, than that of Psychopathology. Physicians know little of behaviorism. Hence you find in psychopathology the terms of the old introspective psychology or the demonological terminology of the Freudians. I once hoped to live long enough to train a man thoroughly in behaviorism before he went into medicine and later into psychopathology, but so far I haven't succeeded. The

behaviorist who is a layman from a medical standpoint cannot
drain this swamp and the physician who is not a behaviorist cannot do it. Hence the concepts of "mental disease" and of the "unconscious" with all of their confusions still flourish. The main
difficulty with the physician working in these fields is that he is
unversed in the history of philosophy and even in *physics*. To the
majority of psychopathologists and analysts, *consciousness* is a real
"force"—something that can *do something, something that can
start up a physiological process, or check, inhibit or down one already going on*. No one unless he ignores physics and the history
of philosophy could hold this view. No psychologist today would
like to be classed as believing in *interaction* (I think some of them
do!) of which this is an expression. Until you can get the physician
who deals with behavior to face the physical fact that the only
way you can get a billiard ball on the table in front of you to start
moving—to go from a state of rest to a state of motion—is to strike
it with a cue or to get another ball already in motion to strike it
(or else have some other moving body hit it)—until you can get
him to face the fact that if the ball is already in motion you cannot
make it change its rate of motion or its direction unless you do
one of these same things—you will never get a scientific viewpoint
about psychopathological behavior. The psychopathologists—most
of them—*believe today that "conscious" processes can start the
physiological ball rolling and then change its direction*. Much as I
have maligned the introspectionists, they are not quite so naïve in
their concepts. Even James long ago expressed the view (although
he did not stick to it in "will" and in "attention") that the only
way you could "down" or change a bodily process was to start
some other bodily process going. *If "mind" acts on body, then all
physical laws are invalid*. This physical and metaphysical naïveté
of the psychopathologist and analyst comes out in such expressions
as "This conscious process inhibited this or that form of behavior";
"the unconscious desire keeps him from doing so and so." Much of
the confusion we have today dates back to Freud. His adherents

cannot see this. Most of them through having to undergo analysis at his hands (either first, second, or third hand) have formed a strong positive "father" organization. They have been unwilling to have their "father" spoken of in criticism. This unwillingness to accept criticism and to find progress through it has brought the crumbling at the top of what started out to be one of the most significant movements in modern times. I venture to predict that 20 years from now an analyst using Freudian concepts and Freudian terminology will be placed upon the same plane as a phrenologist. *And yet analysis based upon behavioristic principles is here to stay and is a necessary profession in society—to be placed upon a par with internal medicine and surgery.* By analysis I mean studying the cross section of personality in some such way as I have outlined it. This will be the equivalent of diagnosis. Combined with this will go *unconditioning* and then *conditioning.* These will constitute the *curative* side. Analysis as such has no virtue— no curative value. New habits, verbal, manual and visceral, of such and such kinds, will be the prescriptions the psychopathologist will write.

ARE THERE SUCH THINGS AS MENTAL DISEASES?

I know that all of this more or less vague discussion about the analyst and the physician raises some definite questions which may be phrased as follows: Isn't there such a thing as a mental disease? If so, what is it like and how do you cure it?

As long as there is the misconception going the rounds that there is such a thing as the mental, I suppose there will be mental diseases, mental symptoms and mental cures. I view the whole matter other-wise. I can only roughly outline my own viewpoint. Sickness of personality, or behavior illnesses, behavior disturbances, habit con-flicts, are terms which I should like to use in place of mental dis-turbances, mental diseases and the like. In many of the so-called psychopathological disorders ("functional psychoses," "functional neuroses,") there are no organic disturbances of sufficient gravity to account for personality disturbance. There may be no infections, no lesions anywhere, no absence of physiological reflexes (as there often is when there are organic diseases). And yet the individual has a sick personality. His behavior may be so badly disturbed or so involved that we call him insane (a purely social classification) and have to commit him temporarily or permanently.

No one has yet given us a sensible classification of the various types of behavior disturbance that are present in a social structure such as ours. We hear of manic depressive insanity, anxiety neuroses, paranoia, schizophrenia and many others. To me as a layman these divisions mean nothing. I know in general what is meant by appendicitis, cancer of the breast, gall stones, typhoid fever, tonsilitis, tuberculosis, paresis, brain tumor and even cardiac insufficiency. I know in general something about the organisms present when any are present, the kind of tissue attacked and the general course of the disease and I can understand the physician when he tells me more about them. Yet when the psychopathologist tries to tell me about a "schiz" or a "homicidal mania" or an "hysterical" attack, I have the feeling, which has grown stronger with the years, that he doesn't know what he is talking about. And I think the reason he doesn't know what he is talking about is that he has always approached his patients from the point of view of the *mind* rather than from that of the way the whole body behaves and the genetic reasons for that behavior. The past few years have unquestionably seen considerable progress in this direction.

To show the needlessness of introducing the "conception of mind" in so-called mental diseases, I offer you a fanciful picture of a psychopathological dog (I use the dog because I am not a physician and have no right to use a human illustration—I hope the veterinarians will pardon me!). Without taking any one into my counsel suppose I once trained a dog so that he would walk away from nicely-ground, fresh hamburg steak and would eat only decayed fish (true examples of this are now at hand). I trained him (by use of the electric shock) to avoid smelling the female dog in the usual canine way—he would circle around her but would come no closer than ten feet (J. J. B. Morgan has done something very close to this on the rat). Again, by letting him play only with male puppies and dogs and punishing him when he tried to mount a female, I made a homosexual of him (F. A. Moss has done something closely akin to this in rats). Instead of licking my hands and becoming lively and playful when I go to him in the morning, he hides or cowers, whines and shows his teeth. Instead of going after rats and other small animals in the way of hunting, he runs away from them and shows the most pronounced fears. He sleeps in the ash can—he fouls his own bed, he urinates every half hour and anywhere. Instead of smelling every tree trunk, he growls and fights and paws the earth but will not come within two feet of the tree. He sleeps only two hours per day and sleeps these two hours leaning up against a wall rather than lying down with head and rump touching. He is thin and emaciated because he will eat no fats. He salivates constantly (because I have conditioned him to salivate to hundreds of objects). This interferes with his digestion. Then I take him to the dog psychopathologist. His physiological reflexes are normal. No organic lesions are to be found anywhere. The dog, so the psychopathologist claims, is mentally sick, actually insane; his mental condition has led to the various organic difficulties such as lack of digestion; it has "caused" his poor physical condition. Everything that a dog should do—as compared with what dogs of his type usually do—he does not do. And everything that seems foreign for a dog to do he does. The psychopathologist says I must commit the dog to an institution for the care of insane dogs; that if he is not restrained he will jump from a ten-story building, or walk into a fire without hesitation.

I tell the dog psychopathologist that he doesn't know anything about my dog; that, from the standpoint of the environment in which the dog has been brought up (the way I have trained him) he is the most normal dog in the world; that the reason he calls the dog "insane" or mentally sick is because of his own absurd system of classification.

I then take the psychopathologist into my confidence. He becomes extremely angry. "Since you've brought this on, go cure him." I attempt then to correct my dog's behavior difficulties, at least up to the point where he can begin to associate with the nice dogs in the neighborhood. If he is very old or if things have gone too far, I just keep him confined; but if he is fairly young and he learns easily, I undertake to retrain him. I use behavioristic methods. I uncondition him and then condition him. Soon I get him to eating fresh meat by getting him hungry, closing up his nose and feeding him in the dark. This gives me a good start. I have something basal to use in my further work. I keep him hungry and feed him only when I open his cage in the morning; the whip is thrown away; soon he jumps for joy when he hears my step. In a few months' time I not only have cleared out the old but also have built in the new. The next time there is a dog show I proudly exhibit him, and his general behavior is such an asset to his sleek, perfect body that he walks off with the blue ribbon.

All this is an exaggeration—almost sacrilege! Surely there is no connection between this and the poor sick souls we see in the psychopathic wards in every hospital! Yes, I admit the exaggeration, but I am after elementals here. I am pleading for simplicity and ruggedness in the building stones of our science of behavior. I am trying to show by this homely illustration *that you can by conditioning not only build up the behavior complications, patterns and conflicts in diseased personalities, but also by the same process lay the foundations for the onset of actual organic changes which result finally in infections and lesions*—all without introducing the concepts of the mind-body relation ("influence of mind over the body") or even without leaving the realm of natural science. In other words, as behaviorists, even in "mental diseases" we deal with the same material and the same laws that the neurologists and physiologists deal with.

HOW TO CHANGE PERSONALITY

Changing the personality of the sick individual—the psychopath —is the work of the physician. However badly he handles his job at present, we have to go to him when a habit breakdown occurs. If I got to the point where I could not pick up my knife or fork, if one arm became paralyzed or if I couldn't visually react to my wife and children, and a physical examination showed no organic lesion of any kind, I should hasten to my psychoanalytic friends and say: "Please, in spite of all the mean things I've said about you, help me out of this mess."

Even we "normal ones," after having looked ourselves over and decided that we'd like to slough off a few of our worst carry-overs, find that making these changes in our personalities is no easy task. Can you learn chemistry over night? To be a finished musician or artist in a year's time? It would be difficult if you only had to learn these things, but it is doubly difficult when you have to unlearn a vast organized system of old habits before you can begin to put on the new. And yet this is what the individual faces who wants a new personality. No quack can do it for you, no correspondence school can safely guide you. Almost any event or happening might start a change; a flood might do it, a death in the family, an earthquake, a conversion to the church, a breakdown in health, a fist fight—anything that would break up your present habit patterns, throw you out of your routine and put you in such a position that you would have to learn to react to objects and situations different from those to which you have had to react in the past—such happenings might start the process of building a new personality for you. During the formation of new habit systems, the old begin to die through disuse—that is, there is loss in retention and hence the individual will be less and less dominated by the old habit systems.

What do we have to do to change the personality? There must be both *unlearning* the things we have already learned (and the unlearning may be an active *unconditioning* process or just *disuse*) and *learning* the new things, which is always an active process. Thus the only way thoroughly to change personality is to remake the individual by changing his environment in such a way that new habits have to form. The more completely they change, the more personality changes. Few individuals can do all this unaided. That is why we go on year in and year out with the same old personality. Some day we shall have hospitals devoted to helping us change our personality because we can change the personality as easily as we can change the shape of the nose, only it takes more time.

LANGUAGE ONE DIFFICULTY IN THE WAY OF CHANGING PERSONALITY

There is one difficulty in changing personality by changing environment, hitherto all too little thought of. It lies in the fact that when we attempt to change personality by changing the individual's external environment, we cannot prevent the individual from taking his old internal environment with him in the shape of words and word substitutes. You can take a man who has never worked in his life, who has always been the spoiled darling of his mother, who has been a constant attendant upon the ladies of the stage, a patron of the best restaurants of the city, of the fine haberdashery shops, send him to the Congo Free States and put him in a situation for making a frontier individual out of himself. But he takes with him his own language and other substitutes for the world he has left, and we saw in studying language that language, when fully developed, really gives us a manipulable replica of the world we live in. Hence, if his present world does not begin to take hold of him, as it may not, he may withdraw from his frontier world and live the rest of his life in the old substitute world of words. Such an individual may become a "shut-in" —a day dreamer.

But in spite of all the difficulties in the way, individuals can and do change their personalities. Friends, teachers, the theatres, the movies all help to make, to remake and to unmake our personalities. The man who never exposes himself to such stimuli will never change his personality for a better one.

BEHAVIORISM A FOUNDATION FOR ALL FUTURE EXPERIMENTAL ETHICS

Behaviorism ought to be a science that prepares men and women for understanding the principles of their own behavior. It ought to make men and women eager to rearrange their own lives, and especially eager to prepare themselves to bring up their own children in a healthy way. I wish I could picture for you what a rich and wonderful individual we should make of every healthy child if only we could let it shape itself properly and then provide for it a universe in which it could exercise that organization—a universe unshackled by legendary folk-lore of happenings thousands of years ago; unhampered by disgraceful political history; free of foolish customs and conventions which have no significance in themselves, yet which hem the individual in like taut steel bands. I am not asking here for revolution; I am not asking people to go out to some God-forsaken place, form a colony, go naked and live a communal life, nor am I asking for a change to a diet of roots and herbs. I am not asking for "free love." [1] I am trying to dangle a stimulus in front of you, a verbal stimulus which, if acted upon, will gradually change this universe. For the universe will change

[1] Note: I am not arguing here for free anything—least of all free speech. I have always been very much amused by the advocates of free speech. In this harum-scarum world of ours, brought up as we are, the only person who ought to be allowed free speech is the parrot, because the parrot's words are not tied up with his bodily acts and do not stand as substitutes for his bodily acts. All true speech does stand substitutive for bodily acts, hence organized society has just as little right to allow free speech as it has to allow free action, which nobody advocates. When the agitator raises the roof because he hasn't free speech, he does it because he knows that he will be restrained if he attempts free action. He wants by his free speech to get some one else to do free acting—to do something he himself is afraid to do. The behaviorist, on the other hand, would like to develop his world of people from birth on, so that their speech and their bodily behavior could equally well be exhibited freely everywhere without running afoul of group standards.

if you bring up your children, not in the freedom of the libertine, but in behavioristic freedom—a freedom which we cannot even picture in words, so little do we know of it. Will not these children in turn, with their better ways of living and thinking, replace us as society and in turn bring up their children in a still more scientific way, until the world finally becomes a place fit for human habitation?

Index

305